AWAY THE GAS

THE UTTERLY MARVELLOUS AWAY GAME MEMORIES OF BRISTOL ROVERS FANS

EDITED BY
MARTIN BULL

Book Donations

In March 2013 Nathanael Hornby, a 25 year old Gashead, sadly passed away after a battle with a brain tumour.

10% of any profits from this book will be donated in his honour to The Brain Tumour Charity (registered charity #1150054)

TOP - Stuart Neely and his father Bob.

BOTTOM - Jon Krencjasz (far right) and friends

This book is dedicated to all the Pirates and Gasheads who are no longer with us, including:

Harold Clark

Roy Clark

Albert Colley 1914 - 2005

Anthony Charles Cousins 1925 - 2014

Mark Feltham

Ken Goldsmith

Thomas Hodgson 1906 - 1993

Nathanael Hornby

Ann-Marie Irene 27/3/1992 - 13/3/2014

Dennis Kingston

Jon Krencjasz

Alan Lacock

Stephen Larkins

Bert Marsh 1891 - 1973

Jim Marsh 1924 - 2010

Peter J Missen

Stuart Neely

Gordon Pearce

Vinnie Randall

Colin Richmond

John Robson 12/6/1938 - 12/6/2014

Joan Webb

Roger John Wilton 16/10/1940 - 14/6/1990

Jon Wood

Plus all those deeply associated with the club, including Ron Craig, Denis Dunford, Roger Harding and Ray Kendall.

This book is also dedicated to my father, Vic Bull [1937-1992]. He was a Spurs fan, not a Gashead, but did take me to a couple of matches at Eastville, and I'd like to think he would be intrigued to see me producing a book made solely to celebrate Gas away matches.

A note on Credits / Acknowledgements -

At times it has proved hard to contact some of the kind people who wrote away memories on forums, in order to thank them and properly credit them. This wasn't helped when the Official Rovers Forum was unceremoniously and unilaterally shut down without any warning. If anyone has contributed but could not be properly credited, please feel free to make yourselves known to me.

Email = hello@awaythegas.org.uk

Away The Gas
Published in the Independent Peoples' Republic of Wiltshire by shellshock publishing
First Edition
Copyright © Martin Bull 2014

ISBN 978-0-9554712-6-1

Print Management by Sam @ TU Ink - www.tuink.co.uk
TU Ink are specialists in managing print projects for Trade Unions so I am very happy to use them for my print needs and feel I am doing my little bit to help them continue to support Trade Unions.

The authors assert their moral right to be identified as the authors of this work.

The editor and principle author has also had some nasty tropical diseases, slept in a hedge and fallen in a hole like an idiot, and probably doesn't wish to be identified for any of those.

The editor/publisher apparently should also add some standard guff in here about 'all rights reserved', whatever that means. Ok. Please don't nick stuff from this mint book like. Instead, please contact the editor and bribe him with proper cider (not dirty apples), and he'll probably do anything you ask.

This book was NOT printed in China, and hopefully none from shellshock publishing ever will be, despite tempting prices. This book was actually printed in lovely Aberystwyth, by Cambrian Printers, a nice old independent printer.

CONTENTS

"As a Gashead exiled in Manchester since 1986 I see more away games than home games. Rovers away fans are a special bunch – they have to be. Over the years I have seen the same familiar faces and their loyalty, passion, humour and commitment to supporting Rovers at away games has not wavered. Long may that continue."

Pat Stokes

"My first away game was on 29th April 2006; a three hour trek to Rochdale to witness Rovers succumb to a 2-0 defeat. From at least half an hour before kick-off I was part of a wall of noise. 'Goodnight Irene' rang out around Spotlands as various inflatable's came floating my way before being batted back into the vociferous Rovers contingent. The atmosphere I experienced was what convinced me Rovers were the club for me, the only club. The Chelsea apparel I had acquired found its way to the charity shop the next day."

Josh Searle

"Having moved up North nearly twenty five years ago ... I only have to enter the away end of a ground and hear the burrs and nuances of a West Country accent and dialogue to know that I am with my people and even though I am away, I am nevertheless home, regardless of wherever that ground might be."

Chris Bull

"...it always seems to me that BRFC supporters travel more in hope than expectation."

John Coles

"Life, as I age, I realise was merely a memory. The recollection of moments often prove richer than the moments themselves."

David Roberts

INTRODUCTION

I have a confession to make.

My name is Martin and I'm a Gashead. Yes, I know... Dr Frasier Crane would like to talk to me once the massive queue subsides.

Life as a Gashead isn't all grim though.

Away games are still special to me, and many others.

So I thought to myself, let's celebrate them. The highs, the lows, the loves, the arguments, the times we got lost, wet or hideously late, and also the times we lay on a terrace in the lovely Spring sun, made some great mates on the journey home, or found the finest beer available to humanity in a tiny little pub.

I asked fellow Pirates / Gasheads to send me their away memories, stories, and photos, and here they are. Simple as that. Why wait for the middle man when you can DIY - Do It Yourself.

Meanwhile, I wrote up my own copious memories, which was cathartic in itself as we had just been relegated to non-league and I urgently needed a distraction and a syringe loaded full of nostalgia.

I didn't give claustrophobic guidelines to contributors and generally didn't edit work much (or at all). The main guideline was that I won't glorify any sexism, racism, swearing, violence etc. This book shows Gasheads in a good light and is a positive book you will hopefully be proud to show your kids, grandkids, next door neighbour, Auntie Ethel etc. That doesn't mean it is dreary; it's a cracking laugh I think.

I hope the result is a good read for you.

Please send any feedback to me at - hello@awaythegas.org.uk - and please keep contributions coming in just in case there is a 2nd edition.

Martin Bull

www.awaythegas.org.uk

PRELUDE A

ON THE BALL IRENE

BY MIKE HUTCHINS

Editor's explanation [if needed by any readers] - Norwich City's nickname is the Canaries, and their iconic song, 'On The Ball City', has Victorian origins that even pre-date the 1902 club itself. It is often described as the oldest football song in the world still in use today.

My best friend (Martin; the editor of this book) is a Gashead and I'm a canary. We've now got 25 years of trials and tribulations following each others' clubs as well as our own. Of course just the one club can feel like one too many, and then look at what happened back in May 2014 – enough said of that *[Editor's Note - Norwich were also relegated in 2014]*.

At such times I always think of the better days. As fans of all clubs outside of the chosen few know, there's the fleeting moments where dreams and reality meet for truly better times ahead, by some miracle becoming the next Nottingham Forest in Europe, or Wimbledon in the F.A. Cup.

There is something unique going to my best friend's games. Such days are frozen in time, rarely feeling linked to the long-term story of the club. They're pilgrimages sitting in isolation, detached from the rest of life in a strangely wonderful but everyday sort of way. It's about the tour of Britain, seeking out all the overlooked places off the tourist trail. The planning, the parking, the midday beers, the neighbourhoods, the terraces. Of course being away they more often than not end up in deflation. And how many times has the disappointment set in just a few minutes after 3pm? A defensive lapse or a free header and the ball already nestled into an empty net. Sitting with a hoard of Gasheads looking at the half empty outnumbered home ends thinking what are Rovers doing here, what's it all for?!

Away games often mean long journeys home; coming back in January 1994 from the rain and rubble and corrugated iron of Blackpool's ground like drowned rats. Blackpool may be famous for 1953, but last season [2013/14] took us two to newer clubs still finding their way: Dagenham & Redbridge, leaving afterwards through the concrete and suburbia of the East End to be welcomed by a blast of Beethoven's Pastoral Symphony in the tube station; and then the brewers of Burton Albion with beer guts proudly immortalised on their badge, and what a decent well-oiled side they were, putting the "team" into pub team as well as the "pub". Apart from the preserved 19th century bar saloons of Burton, heritage is rarely found on these travels. Yet I've been to The Millennium Stadium and the new Wembley, and only with Bristol Rovers.

But that's nothing as I've also been to Leyton Orient ... and I've been four times ... and all to watch Rovers. Always seemingly in some transient stage of redevelopment there's something surreally haphazard about Brisbane Road. So much so that the second time having gone through an away turnstile and a warren of corridors at the back of the stand I managed to end up in a home section! At half-time I got back to the away end, stewards casually letting me through as if it happened all the time! Seeking further adventures and added kudos I've been back twice more since, the most recent being the F.A. Cup in November 2007. Then, the prospect of Brisbane Road still obviously hadn't dimmed despite my previous trip: a slow-moving and forgettable, even to diehard Gasheads, Auto Wind-screens Shield tie one freezing midweek evening in January 2005, when of course it inevitably dragged on to extra time (eventually ending happily in a 1-2 away win).

Going back to those dreams, looking back I'd pick out the Roberts/Cureton team of the late 1990's. This is the clearest memory I have of being there seeing your team in action and getting that feeling of potential. For once the long term picture was there in front of us: 4-1 away at Luton at Kenilworth Road, and a performance oozing class. Jason Roberts was a complete handful running onto through balls holding off the centre backs in the way that Romario did in those days for Brazil, finding time and space to slide it past a stranded keeper; and Jamie Cureton too, very gifted, picking out a finish from a tight angle. You had him at his best. The green dye of his premature Premier League days with the Canaries had long since run out of his hair (well actually just an hour on the pitch in the rain did for that!). How often can we say we had players at the peak of their careers?

Reminiscing about Jason Roberts brings to mind namesakes. Whilst you had Jason, we had Iwan Roberts (third highest scorer in our history). Then there's the Lamberts. Rickie, your first ex-Rovers England International since I guess Nigel Martyn? *[Editor's Note - it's genuinely easy to forget Bobby Zamora's two caps in 2010-2011; I suspect even he has].* Paul, the best manager in our history. Two pairs of namesakes coinciding, and both the big names of their clubs at those times.

What we haven't had though are coinciding seasons, only one since the mid-70's - 2009/2010, our first season in the Third Tier for 50 years. Warning, what follows is painful... What a watershed moment that day at Carrow Road in October 2009 proved to be. With the unique rarity of the occasion I was more than desperate for us to win that game and was a bit nervous. You, above us in the table and looking very promising and composed; all this despite losing Rickie. Us, picking ourselves up off the floor thanks to new manager Paul. In the end, like everyone else for the rest of that season, you found Grant Holt, Wes Hoolahan and Chris Martin far too good and it was over by half-time. Yet for you it might have just been a matter of the game coming 15 minutes too late, such are the small margins in life. After a mediocre early season we suddenly scored four in the last 15 minutes of our previous home game, against 10 man Leyton Orient (!), to turn a draw into a 4-0 win. And of course, of all people Jamie Cureton scored in both games, his only goals of the season.

After all this we didn't look back once until Paul left for Aston Villa. Well for you, find another Lambert and you can be like Norwich and get back-to-back promotions – you'll be in League One again by 2016-17...and I badly need a reason to go back to Leyton Orient. Seven years and counting is too long!

PRELUDE B

AWAY DAYS RULE OK
(& THE 92 CLUB)
BY MARTIN BULL

Fans who have seen a competitive home game at all current 92 League football clubs are called 92'ers, which is certainly not to be confused with the 82'ers club from over the river. That club is one of the least exclusive in the world, after becoming a parent.

But don't panic, this book is **NOT** about the 92 club.

This book is also **NOT** about 'collecting' away grounds like little tokens, or about 'ground hopping' and being neutrals. No-one really wants to be a neutral at a footy match, do they? Especially Accrington Stanley vs. Bristol Rovers on Tuesday 22nd October 2013 in front of precisely 1,101 people, probably the lowest League crowd at a Rovers match since 1927. Any neutral who went to that just to say they had 'been to' Accrington, and in the blink of an eye tick off another of the 92 from their list, deserves banging on the head with a comedy frying pan and cautioned to 'get a life'.

This book is about what away games mean to most hot-blooded fans, such as passion, adventure, adversity, and the quirky things that happen whilst on your travels, which is just about the antithesis of joining a club with no benefits or loyalty card except maybe being able to feel smugly superior to people who go to matches less mechanically than you, but are most probably having a better laugh. The old adage that 'it's better to travel than arrive' (a mutation of Robert Louis Stevenson's "To travel hopefully is a better thing than to arrive...") is so apt for proper away rovers.

Having said that I am enthused by the motivation that visiting new clubs imparts, and I'm the type to often jot down the date of the away matches I've been to. And whilst writing this specific piece, and editing this book in general, I have happily become more engrossed in any interesting stats linked to away games (some of which are sprinkled through the book), as well as the whole history of who we've played, and with what outcome.

I only know one 92'er, and that is mainly vicariously through my best friend, plus a brief meeting with him at Ninian Park the season they knocked it down. He is apparently rather serious at it and now makes sure he swiftly 'tops up' his membership by going to see any new clubs that get promoted into League Two, and any new stadiums if a club moves, even though the later is not a criteria for my idea of a fair 92 membership. He has a decent job, no children and is married to a widow.

I am sort of doing it, but it's just a long term goal and not something I treat that seriously. I'm also more relaxed about the stadia issue than some. I've been to Gay Meadow, Millmoor, the Goldstone Ground and others, but not to Greenhous Meadow, the New York Stadium or the Amex, but I still count those clubs towards my 92 at the moment. I don't see why I should be forced to re-visit those clubs as, in all good faith, I did watch a competitive game of footy (nearly always a League game) at the ground that was their home at that point in time. With 'only' 66 clubs visited since Reading FC vs. Bristol Rovers on 21st November 1989, and now with two young kids, no cash and many of the furthest Northern ones left, I know it'll probably take me another 10 years or so to finish this miniature aspiration. Patience young grasshopper…

Why do men do this?

Well why do people climb Everest? Because it is there.

Men are collectors. And not only collectors of physical things, but also collectors of trivia and pointless knowledge. Let's be honest with ourselves; lots of men are geeks! Most people enjoy music but on a foray into a Music & Video Exchange shop a woman will be metaphorically slobbered all over, such is the dearth of their delightful form in dank back rooms with clammy peeling walls. Even people in Wiltshire point at airplanes less often than men stare at a woman in a bargain basement full of haphazard, dusty books. And although cinema audiences are split pretty much 50/50 by sex, only men can relate all the films Bernardo Bertolucci has made to a impassive stranger at a dinner party, PLUS when and where he saw them.

Dagenham & Redbridge in September 2103 was my 63rd away club although it made me feel like I was embroiled in a sick game of 'Snakes & Ladders' as I had already accrued my 63th and 64th the previous season. But when Barnet & Aldershot were relegated in May 2013 I was on that crafty serpent and back down to 62. I now have a growing list of clubs (7 so far) who have slipped into non-league since I saw them at their ground.

Thankfully Luton Town and Cambridge United finally awoke in 2013/14. I was not only chuffed to have those two clubs on my list again, but also to be able to feel as though the half dozen matches I enjoyed there in the early 2000's were real again. The problem with the 92 Club is that when a club departs, it almost taints and snatches away the great memories you had at Hereford, Stockport County, Barnet, Aldershot and the like. The dangers of the ups and downs of the 92 Club hit me in mid-May 2014 when I suddenly realised that I had 'lost' one club who had been relegated out of the 92. Us! Bristol Rovers F.C. I think that was when our relegation really sank in; it was the day I couldn't even list my 100's of trips to my own club as one of the 92 League clubs I've visited. Grrrrr!

I 'only' have 48 of my 66 clubs by following the Gas. Most of the rest are with my best friend Mike who is a Norwich City fan [see the previous prelude]. This comradeship often helps me with the 'bigger' clubs and mercifully he never reminds me of the inequality of the football we get to watch when we go to each others matches. Nor does he carp about the god forsaken places I drag him to; Dagenham & Redbridge last season [2013/14] was another low-light in our 'Odd Couple' relationship, even if it did at least bestow on him a full house of London clubs (I still have Chelski to visit). I've tried a handful of games as a total neutral but compared to the unexpected mysteries of following the Gas to Hartlepool on a balmy Tuesday night and being offered my first ever deep fried Mars bar, they were tedious in the extreme. These have taught me that I can only really get enthused by a Gas match, or Norwich to a degree; the Canaries always try to play decent footy, they travel in vast swarms, and 'On The Ball City' is just as unique, anthemic and spine tingling as 'Goodnight Irene'. I've therefore decided to wait for my teams of choice rather than go as a neutral again, even though the later would surely shorten my wait to join the club.

There is no rush for me. Not even the most fervent Gashead (or more likely a 'Pirate') can ever have done the 92 just by following Rovers in the League. Arsenal remain an immoveable impediment as the solitary club we have never faced in a League match. Apparently we hope to play them in the 2016/7 season. In the League...

Some younger fans may be surprised to hear that we have met Chelsea in four League seasons, and although we haven't met Liverpool in the League since 1961, we did regularly play the Reds throughout the 1950's. Most middle aged Rovers fans will therefore only have managed to visit the famed Anfield at our one and only ever meeting in a Cup competition, that famous F.A. Cup Fourth Round replay on a bright February evening in 1992 when Billy Ocean temporarily dazed the packed Kop with that sizzling opening goal that sent thousands of Gasheads wild with delight.

Another illusive surprise to some would be Coventry City, as you'd have to be at least 50 years old to have seen them play us in the League (1963) and even then you would have been a babe in arms.

So what makes away games so special, and worthy of an entire book?

I still get a sense of adventure going to away games, especially to a ground I've never been to before. Part of the fun of away grounds is getting lost, wandering into an awful boozer, and seeking out the local ale and grub (oatcakes in the Potteries, oven bottom muffins around Oldham and Stockport, fresh pasties out of the back of a van at Plymouth, hot parkin on a cold night at Rochdale, etc.) although increasingly these days there is no food near a ground due to the industrial park wasteland localities that have infiltrated our proud quest.

When travelling away you know you'll be in the company of hard-core Gasheads and famished exiles, and most will want to sing and have a laugh. You don't go to away games for a guaranteed win so you might as well not treat the game too seriously and find something to distract you from the probable result. I usually end up looking at silly haircuts or funny signs. Enough said.

Away days rule ok, and may they continue to rule for a very long time!

LOST, BROKEN DOWN & LATE

To be honest this chapter heading is one of several 'Ronseal' titles.

There are no clever puns or word plays this time; it really is all about the times when us Gasheads have been lost, broken down or late for away matches.

After reading the stories that were sent to me I suspect the moral of this chapter is 'never use a train in the 1970's, particularly a football special!'

I ♥ EDGAR STREET
BY MARTIN BULL

I'm usually pretty good at getting places on time, but there are obviously the odd mishaps in life.

As I'm vaguely trying to visit all 92 League clubs (albeit very slowly) and can only do a handful of away trips per season I tend to have to ration my away days. A by product of this is that I don't often get to go to the same ground multiple times, unless it happens to be close and / or we're in the same division as them for a long time. It may take readers by surprise that my most visited away ground is actually Leyton Orient's Brisbane Road, a legacy of living in or near London for eight years and not having many others to visit in the area. My six visits there just top my five to Reading (where I went to Uni), although one of those was a Norwich match. Reading has a special place in my roving journey though as my first Gas away game was there, at their crumbling old Elm Park ground on 21st November 1989, an F.A. Cup First Round replay. I've therefore witnessed their transition from a cash strapped club with a traditional, run down stadium once made with half of Berkshire's entire quota of rusting iron and sub-standard concrete, to a millionaire backed ponce fest ingloriously plonked on the omnipresent industrial park backdrop.

Anyhow, the up shot of all of this is that it is rare that I know how to get to the ground, where to park, how long it will take etc. I am usually quite good, and increasingly a little anal, at what to expect though. I used to do most places by train, but as I've got older and more stadiums are moving out to the edge of towns, it's more likely to be car now. My 'helper' used to be the little football ground guidebook, but since the 'net took over, everything you need, and more, is available there for free. My favourite tools now are maps and aerial photos as you can get a good idea of what an area is like to park in. Even better is an OS map as it can show the public footpaths and short cuts which usually only the locals know. Be careful though, finding this amazing, but long and narrow, alleyway to get to Elland Road from the area where my brother lives, did create some anxiety in itself as two West Country voices tend to stand out amongst whippet pie eaters and get magnified by your own sense of not belonging around these parts.

The time I got everything hideously wrong was my first trip to Hereford, on a March evening in 2009. I swear I had gone on a route finder, looked at its advice on how long it would take, and made a mental calculation of when I should leave. Something somewhere went wrong; sinisterly wrong, as if Beelzebub himself didn't want me to get there. As I drove I knew I was cutting it fine, but what started to worry me is that no matter how much I started to put my foot down (usually I don't drive fast) the motorway just seemed to go on and on, and the time got later and later. I knew there was no 'easy way' to Hereford as it really is in the middle of nowhere, but as the motorway petered out I plumped for the A417 and A438.

Even though I was pretty sure I was on the right road and knew what route to expect to take, I had the satnav on as a belt and braces approach. Usually satnavs are good in the dark, or when on a new route, as they help you when your senses are dulled and confused. This time it really didn't help as it was telling me to turn around, go to the East (which seemed completely wrong to me), regularly changed its mind and re-booted the route it was suggesting, and several times it even claimed that I (the little car icon) was driving straight through lush green fields, which really spooked me out. And all this whilst it was getting later and later, and I was trying to drive faster and faster. I was in full panic mode by now and began to suspect I had driven into the 'Herefordshire Triangle' (twinned with Bermuda) or something. Or maybe it was the SAS and their communication scramblers I reasoned?

I stuck to my gut feeling and kept on the road I had planned, just to spite the bad advice from the drunken satnav. When I finally arrived I was well late of course and all the decent parking slots had gone. I drove around and around, until I somehow found the last space in a little car park pretty near the ground. For once in my ascetic life I was actually quite comfortable having to pay for the stupid privilege of parking at gone 8pm on a lifeless March evening in a small City whose Council will probably only waste my contribution on subsidising badger baiting, gurning competitions and prizes for the funniest shaped vegetables in the County.

I ran to the away end. The first turnstile door was shut. And the next. And the next. No stewards or Police to be seen. No way to get in. And I'd bought my ticket in advance! I was panicking by now. I'd never been in this position before. Like a new father faced with his first tiny caterwauling baby in his enormous apprehensive arms I frankly had no idea what to do now as it was a completely alien situation to me. From the back of my brain I summoned up all the things they taught me at school; I dreamt of my departed Dad and wondered if he would have a little gizmo at the bottom of his fatherly tool box that could bust the door open; I tried to visualise what that wise old Buddhist book contained that my friend pretended to read at Uni; I reasoned 'what would Nelson Mandela or Ghandi do?'; I dredged up my life experience of how to get back on your feet when faced with doors closing in your face; I cursed myself for never joining that transcendental meditation class (even if it was just to meet women), and after all of that … I… banged on the door and bawled "let me in..!" like a baby.

But wait.

I'm sure I heard a muffled voice from behind the door...

Like a scene from the 'War of the Worlds' I all of a sudden knew I wasn't alone. I knew that humanity had survived the Gas invasion. After a short but surreal conversation through a thick wooden door I was told to try the late entrance around the corner. This I did and ended up in the reception of the club, under the main stand. I was asked to stand near a tunnel until a steward could escort me to the away section.

Radios crackled and requests were made. After a minute or so a dayglo jacketed one came and I solemnly walked a pace or two behind him like a naughty schoolboy at a funeral. Once out of the tunnel I realised I was at the right end of the ground, but he had to walk me down the goal line and round to the gate at the other corner flag. As we walked towards the goal

I could see Rickie Lambert shaping up to take a free kick on the other flank and in a whoosh it was in the net and Gasheads were going mad. This was already the 26th minute! You can actually see me walking behind the goal on the special double header DVD that Screen Soccer released of this win, plus the 5-0 hammering we gave to Walsall a few days later.

But like a total pussy I didn't celebrate wildly, or run onto the pitch and kiss our wonderful goal scorer. I was still so stressed from the journey, and my unorthodox entrance into Edgar Street, that my mind was partly elsewhere and I was cagey at the prospect of getting thrown out of the ground before I'd even been able to set foot on the terrace.

Looking back, maybe I should have ran 'round like a man possessed and got myself instantly chucked out as THAT really would be an away story to tell the grand children!

We cruised to a 3-0 win, our first ever win there, with a hat trick for our kid Rickie, who was Captain for his first ever time. We really were a cracking team then and there is a tinge of sadness whenever I now see Rickie playing for England. Of course I'm happy for him but I feel we were as flawed as Esau; selling our birthright for just the solitary bowl of lentil stew.

Our bench that day included the wonderfully titled Danzelle St. Louis-Hamilton, an emergency loan keeper from Stoke City who never actually played a minute for the Gas, and has hardly ever played competitive footy in his entire career really. He must have the strongest backside in Britain.

The win was so easy that we had the luxury of taking Rickie off after only 69 mins, and I could now let my eyes wander around Edgar Street, the Bull's home for over 90 years now. It is one of the most wondrous grounds I've ever been to. The away end had a massive curve on it and the terrace was miles away from the pitch; a throwback to a century ago when it had an athletics track around the pitch. You could however decide to stand right up to the barrier which not only meant you were virtually on the pitch, but also meant you were about 20 metres in front of the rest of your fellow fans! (see photo on page 71)

A few months after our visit the away end failed a safety inspection and was closed as a terrace. A Twerton Park-style golf stand replaced it.

As geography dictates a dearth of local rivals, the away end wasn't really geared up for 1,000 Gasheads arriving mob handed. The refreshments hut was reminiscent of an old wartime Anderson shelter at the bottom of your garden, and it had chicken wire grills as if security is often a problem! The toilet had space for about three blokes plus someone desperate enough to want to sit down in that brick outhouse. I'm not sure if women even had a toilet. How dare they need one.

Quirky advertising hoardings dominated the perimeter. The best was 'Luk Clutches Say No To Drugs' (see photo on page 71) which sounds like it was inspired by a 1980's episode of Grange Hill, or a charity record featuring various Z-list celebs.

I was impressed that their fans made noise nearly all game despite getting a whupping, and I liked the look of the similarly sweeping crescent shaped terrace at the Meadow End where all the Hereford lads went.

The main stand is funny because it is rather small and all the hospitality facilities are beneath it, meaning the 'executive' boxes are at pitch level (see photo on page 70). It seems bizarre that the most expensive niche of the ground must have a dreadful, flat, and frequently obstructed, view where you might see the linesman's legs more often than the ball. The windows also seemed to have net curtains on them, making it look like you were peering inside someone's front window. If they added red light bulbs it could almost double for an Amsterdam back street. Probably … not that I have been to those places. Hole. Dig. Deeper.

The Edgar Street stand is actually the newest although it did make you wonder why they bothered. It holds less than 2,000 and is barely five rows of seats deep due to the tightness of the ground against the main road (A49) directly behind it. That in itself is yet another interesting idiosyncrasy of the ground, because the entrances to this stand are directly onto the pavement of this busy main road, as if the builders had no concept of motorised vehicles and had never been informed that Queen Victoria was no longer on the throne.

Like the peculiar West stands at both Brentford and Southend, this stand is terracing underneath (with a thousand very thick concrete pillars to spoil your view) and seats on top. The latter are so cramped and steeply sloped that most seats don't even let you see the pitch beneath you. The good news though is that the terrace is right up to the grass, and you can hear every word that is said and can smell the Deep Heat; a proper traditional football experience and one that also gives you the real feel of how fast and furious professional football is. The next time you accuse a player of being a lazy wimp, get yourself down to Edgar Street, Twerton Park or any other tight stadium, stand at the front, and remind yourself just how athletic and full blooded most footy is.

It's a shame we've never met Hereford in the F.A. Cup at Edgar Street because apparently one of their F.A. Cup traditions is for a group of supporters to dribble a swede before kick-off towards the Meadow End and score a goal for good luck. Forget pre-pubescent cheerleaders, or out of tune Samba bands full of middle-class whities feigning multi-cultural-ism, that is what you call good old fashioned pre-match entertainment!

I now have a soft spot for 'the Bulls', not only due to my surname and the beautifully quirky ground, but because it is such a lovely area (the charm-ing motto of Herefordshire is "This fair land is the gift of God"), and because you've got to have admiration for anyone who takes up the thankless task of trying to keep a historic football club viable in the middle of no-where.

[Editor's Note - My last sentence above was written before financial prob-lems resulted in Hereford being thrown out of the Conference leagues in June 2014, and just about sums up how hard it is to keep a footy club afloat in a small City, which is the hub of the fourth lowest populated County in England].

TRAINS, STONES AND WALKING HOME
BY MARK COUSINS

We went to **Southport** on a Friday night in April 1974. Like Tranmere they played Fridays because of Liverpool and Everton games. We lost and to make things worse the last side window and the back window of the coach were put through by the locals, so the poor guys sat in the back row had the freezing night air blasting straight at them all the way back to Bristol. They had scarves tied around their faces to try and keep warm, but they might as well have been sat outside on the roof!

After one evening game at **Watford**, we weren't many miles down the road before the coach driver started having a bit of a problem with the accelerator. A couple of lads started having a go at him. He stopped the coach abruptly, sat one of them in the drivers seat and told him to have a go if he thought he could do better. He then chucked them off the coach and left them over 100 miles from home.

Then there were the two aborted special trains to **Luton**. First time we got right into Luton station before they found out the game was post-poned. We then got shunted down to Kings Cross before finally leaving London but it lasted all day. I think we got home in the early evening.

On the second attempt we got as far as Acton in West London when the train was stopped and returned to Bristol after what seemed like ages.

The trains they gave us must have been the sickly ones as another broke down on the way to **Crystal Palace**. We finally got to Selhurst Park just in time for the start of the second half. It was 0-0, but then Steve White scored the only goal of the game so it was suddenly all worth it.

[Editor's Note - this was the last we played Southport, although just as this book went to print we did meet them again... in the Conference! Southport were voted out of the League in 1978 after three consecutive 23rd place finishes. They had a mere 31 points. Rochdale were 7 points worse off though, and had been rock bottom of the table since the 4th game of the season, but it was the Sandgrounders who failed to get re-elected, letting in Wigan Athletic from non-league. They were the last club to leave the League through the re-election process.]

AROUND THE BIG SMOKE IN 80 FAGS
BY SHANE LEONARD

It was Boxing Day 1978, when just me and another mate from Staple Hill, 15 years old and full of it, got the RATS train to go watch the Rovers at Crystal Palace. We broke down just outside Slough and were stuck there for hours. No food, no drink; nothing to do but smoke cigarettes. We were sharing the carriage with a couple of slightly older lads from Shire and between the four of us we must have got through about 80 fags in a couple of hours!

Anyhow, they eventually got a new engine out to us and we rolled into Norwood Junction at about 3:45pm. Feeling sick as dogs we got to Selhurst Park at about 4:05, just in time to see Steve White score the winning (and only) goal in front of over 21,000!

Then back to the train after the game where Palace had laid on a bit of a reception committee (armed with plenty of bricks, bottles and other ammunition) and a draughty train ride home 'cos all the windows had been put through!

[Editor's Note - As seen on the previous page, and on page 48, lots of Gasheads remember this sickly train! Before that match we hadn't beaten the Glaziers away since 1951. Sadly it was the last season we ever played Palace in the League. The good news is that we are currently unbeaten against them away for 36 years and counting!]

NOT ALL THOSE WHO WANDER ARE LOST

(BUT BE CAREFUL WHO YOU FOLLOW...)

BY DAVID COLLEY

On 29th November 1992 we travelled north on the M1 to Leicester City, just before they moved out of Filbert Street.

Rovers were well supported in those days and streams of cars were all trailing Rovers scarves and banners all the way up the M1. As we left the motorway at the Leicester signs there must have been six or seven other cars in front of us all of who were obviously Rovers fans on their day out. All of them went right round the first roundabout to the last exit while my son, Paul (Roadman) spotted a solitary Leicester scarf and said "Hey Dad follow that one in front, he's a Leicester fan and knows the way". So as he turned off at the first exit we merrily followed as the rest of the Gasheads went in the other direction.

There we were for the next 30 minutes or so following this guy right through the middle of Leicester, past De Montfort Uni, past Leicester's rugby ground at Welford Road, down little back streets, across housing estates; on and on we went. So much so my brother Pete and Norman Maslin in the back seat were both beginning to say that this can't be right.

Eventually this guy in front pulls into a very nice tree lined suburban avenue at the far end of Leicester, and parks alongside a very respectable dwelling. My brother Pete wound the window down and called out to the young Foxes fan, "Hey mate where's the ground?". He says "Oh the ground? It's on the other side of town mate. I'm just going into me Mum's first to have a bit of lunch before the match".

We laughed it off and in the light of day it was a worthwhile detour, as I sent the story to the Readers Digest. They published it in the "Life's like that" section and paid me the princely sum of 70 quid! The game was quite good; a solitary goal won it for us 1-0. This was the first of a four match winning streak that sparked a mini revival under Malcolm Allison.

Great memories, great result, I made £70, and it got me into publishing!

BUZZING FROM THE PARK TO THE COTTAGE
BY RICK WESTON

One of my first away trips with the Gas was in December 1988 away to Fulham.

My brother Shaun and I travelled on the Young Pirates coach, which was organised by Bernie Green. During the morning we had a tour of Wembley Stadium, and at about 1.30pm, we boarded the coach to take us to Craven Cottage. Or so we thought. The coach driver thought Rovers were playing Brentford and next thing we knew we were outside Griffin Park.

After turning around and battling through the London gridlock, the driver announced there was no way he could get the bus down any of the side streets off Fulham Palace Road. This was at 2.58pm. So we were forced into making a dash for it for the last 200 yards or so.

As my brother and I got through the turnstiles at 3.03pm we heard an almighty roar and my first thought was "typical, we've had a nightmare getting here, now we're 1-0 down", but as I reached the top of the stairs into the stand, my anguish turned to joy as I realised David Mehew had put Rovers ahead.

In the second half, Gary Penrice scored one of the best Rovers goals I've ever seen, a scorching volley from a deep Devon White cross. Rovers held out to win 2-0. An autograph from Christian McClean after the match, followed by a bag of greasy chips, ensured it was a great journey home.

GAS GIRLS ON TOUR!
BY TILLY'S THIGHS

A pre-season friendly at Mangotsfield United probably isn't the first fixture that would spring to mind if you were thinking about away days that stick in the memory due to travel problems. The majority of you readers are probably not females though and more than likely you don't have the misfortune to have your 'sense of direction' permanently switched off!

Still, never ones to let the finer details of life deter us, after looking at the AA map (we are talking pre-Sat Nav days here!), myself and my co-pilot decided that it shouldn't be too difficult to find our way to the ground, even though, being born and bred in Bath, the depths of South Glos were like visiting a foreign land to us. As always, there had been the usual build-up of pre-season expectation (as was the norm back in the day), and we were eager to get our Rovers fixes wherever we could, even if that meant visiting uncharted waters.

All was going well, it was a perfect summer evening, just what you want to ease yourself into the season – plenty of time for frostbite further down the line. We navigated our way to Warmley, then Mangotsfield, where we stopped and asked for directions. Unfortunately, either we were sold a bum steer, or, more likely, we got a bit confused with our left and right and ended up back in virtually the same spot that we had started from. I pulled over, so that we could consult the map again, realising that an actual road map of the area would have been useful, when my co-pilot recognised some people who had just driven past. Apparently the car contained a family that she had "seen at loads of Rovers matches", so they were sure to be en route to the game.

Just like an episode of The Bill, I slotted into the traffic, just one car between us and them, and we kept on their tail along the main road. They eventually turned off, although the car in front didn't, so we hung back slightly, to give us an opportunity to see their indicators in plenty of time.

This was an excellent strategy (I was sensing that I had missed my vocation as a Private Investigator), we tracked them through a few turn offs on a modern estate. They obviously knew a shortcut to the ground – happy days! Couldn't be too far now I thought, as we followed them round a bend, they were indicating left. I did the same and rounded the bend as they took another immediate left. As I turned the steering wheel to follow, I realised – too late - that they had pulled up on the driveway of a house.

I performed an excellent emergency stop as the parents got out of the car, looking somewhat perplexed. The sensible thing to do would have been to stick my head out of the window, and explain what had happened – I'm sure they would have had a good laugh at our expense. However, panic set in, I stuck the car into reverse and headed back in the direction that we had come, catching a final glance of their bewildered faces in the mirror.

Somehow, we did eventually find the ground, but I can't remember a thing about the match – it's not always what happens on the pitch that leaves the lasting impression of the day.

THE FULHAM MYSTERY TOUR
BY PAUL BRADBURY

Mainly we went away by car, but every now and again we used to go on supporters coaches. I particularly remember one Saturday afternoon game at Craven Cottage. After the game we left in the coaches and the lead coach took the wrong direction and turned right towards London instead of left towards the M4. All the other coaches blindly followed him and we ended up going almost into the centre of London before they found their way back out again, I think it was near Christmas so the traffic was terrible and we were delayed about 3 hours in London before we got back on to the M4.

THE LOST GASHEADS OF HERTFORDSHIRE
BY MARTIN BULL

Throughout most of 1995 and 1996 I worked / volunteered in Ethiopia. Amongst other things it provided me with a good, and vaguely true, riddle about how it was possible for me to have visited Ethiopia, Britain and Japan all in one day, without air travel.

It was the day I visited the British and the Japanese Embassies in the Ethiopian capital, Addis Ababa, because, although I've recently learnt it is a misnomer to call embassy land 'sovereign territory', most people think it is, so it was like steeping onto the good old soil of Blighty that day when I went through the gates of the British Embassy. The great explorer, Wilfred Thesiger, was born within those very walls in 1910. His father had been a diplomat there, and Thesiger himself later became a favourite of Ras Tafari Mekonnen, and even kept his hand written invitation to his coronation until his dying days. That coronation, in 1930, saw 'King' Tafari magically transformed into a much more familiar name; Emperor Haile Selassie I. His original name may also sound familiar to many readers, as it is how Rastafarianism got its name.

Thesiger met another famous explorer and writer, Laurens van der Post, in 1941 during their labours within the Gideon Force which helped liberate Abyssinia [Ethiopia] from the temporary rule of fascist Italy. The day I went to see the Gas play **Watford** in November 1990 I felt like one of Nambia's San bushmen in van der Post's influential book, 'The Lost World of the Kalahari'; roving in a barren wilderness, foraging on wild flowers, and hunting for waterholes to satiate my thirst.

This was Rovers' first visit to **Vicarage Road** since 1981, and rather like waiting hours for a bus and then several coming along all at once, an uncanny twist of timing meant we played there for a second time only three days later in the Zenith Data Systems Cup, when we recorded our first victory there since 1962.

As usual I don't remember the game I seemingly paid to watch, but I do remember the enormous walk around some allotments and a stinking power station in order to get into the away end. Apparently it was famous in the away fan world, almost a rite of passage that you had to go through in order to call yourself a true away day traveller. It felt like I had metaphorically gone 'walkabout' in my effort to get into the ground, like a young Aboriginal male. I'm sure I recollect the excellent '2nd of May' fanzine comparing it to a journey to the moon on their next front cover.

By my next trip back there in 2001, with my Norwich City supporting best friend, away fans were now housed in a much more benevolent position, near the main road, but it mattered little as we had already suffered hideous tube trouble getting there and didn't reach the ground until just before half-time! They still made us pay full price and didn't let on that the Canaries were looking shaky. They went on to lose 4-1. Not even the wonderfully entitled Jean-Yves de Blasiis coming on as sub could raise our spirits. Try making up a chant about him!

The time problem we had was partly self-inflicted. A tip to the prudent; don't sit eating and drinking above Baker Street tube station in the plushest Wetherspoons this side of Monaco when there is the chance you could be hit later by a journey straight out of Dante's Fifth circle of hell.

Aldershot has a similarly out of the ordinary away entrance. Whilst home fans get the privilege of stumbling out of a pub on the main road and straight through a rusty turnstile like a drunk whale, away fans have a military style yomp to what seems like a neighbouring county. Given Aldershot's rough, squaddie reputation, I guess it is a deliberate manoeuvre to keep fans separate and away fans disorientated, as once in the stadium you regain your bearings and swiftly realise you are standing merely a coins throw away from a Shots fan you might have been having a chat with just 10 minutes ago, before you embarked on your oxygen fuelled walk around the entire ground, up through a park, and then back down a hill to get to their curious away entrance.

When I made a trip to the Recreation Ground in 2001 for a drab 0-0 F.A. Cup First Round tie (the Shots were in non-league at that point), the away access seemed to be very old and small for such a large terrace. A mere brace of turnstiles greeted the footsore fans, and once that queue had been negotiated refreshments could finally be found being sold on long fold up tables more akin to wallpaper paste than greasy burgers. A short row of Portaloos completed the spartan experience.

The dark away terrace was a throwback to the boot boy era of the 70's and 80's, with huge fences separating the fans, plus coin catching nets above, all under a vast barrel shaped roof the Industrial Revolution pioneers would have been proud of. The last away section I had seen like this was on my sole excursion to Birmingham City in 1990.

The last time we had met the Shots before this was the season they lost their Third Tier status (1988/89). Two desolate seasons later and they were in non-league and about to go bust. That January 1989 match was before I started going to away games but I do remember the Uni friend who got me into Rovers, Mark Drew, going to the match and coming back elated at a 3-1 win. It shouldn't have been a surprise though as we had the second best away record in the Third Tier that season. These were happy days as I slowly got deeper and deeper into the greatest footy team in the world, prodded along by Mark.

To complete this triumvirate of interesting away entrances, I offer you not for once a protracted voyage of discovery to get into a ground, but the quaintness of parking at **Nene Park**, the home of the now defunct **Rushden & Diamonds F.C.**. Their rapid rise was bankrolled by Max Griggs, the then owner of Dr. Martens, the bovver boots of choice for 70's skins and punks, and their spotless ground was a £30m refurb of the Irthlingborough Diamonds stadium, located next to one of their shoe factories.

I went to our first ever meeting with them, in December 2001, and as we drove into the car park it seemed full but a steward directed us around to the factory area where they parked cars for free next to the loading bays that during the working week would be bashing out boxes of famous 14 hole yellow stitched Oxblood boots. That magnanimous parking arrangement was a lovely touch, but it was about as good as the day got for us away fans.

The early fervour of Gerry Francis's second spell at Rovers was already beginning to wear thin. There was no way of covering up that we had a poor squad and a lot of psychological baggage from the relegation in May 2001, and not even King Gerry could do much to annul that. I always got the feeling that he had been dragged back to Rovers and that he didn't really want to bear the position he had been predestined for, namely the infallible white knight on horseback who would instantaneously restore us to position of the elect, a.k.a. the Third Tier. We lost 3-1, and we were truly grateful for that lone goal, even if it was a penalty, as we hadn't scored at all in the previous five games.

Rushden & Diamonds were a decent team and also tonked us 3-0 in the reverse fixture. They were one of the first in a long line of ex-non league clubs who came up from the malodorous guts of the earth and yet rapidly, and deservedly, left us trailing in their wake. Think Wycombe Wanderers, Yeovil Town, Crawley Town, Stevenage Borough, Dagenham & Redbridge, Fleetwood Town, Morecambe, and Burton Albion. Even the recurring monikers 'Town' and 'Borough' stick in the throat as they merely emphasise how small these places are and how much we underachieve in our massive catchment area.

Rushden & Diamonds were getting quite impressive average crowds of almost 4,500 when we played them, and gained promotion in 2003, but after a solitary season in the Third Tier crowds haemorrhaged and it was pretty much all down hill for them after.

The ground now stands empty as a white elephant. Not even Coventry City decided to use it as they forsook the Ricoh Arena and searched for their own Twerton Park to play in.

Now that really is a sign of being Billy No-mates.

FLAT TYRE, FLAT PERFORMANCE
BY PAT STOKES

We decided in 2003 that a Christmas holiday road trip to watch Rovers at Kidderminster Harriers was a good idea. It was the Graydon years so no need to tell you the result. We set off in my sister's Fiesta which had seen better years. Half way up the M5 disaster struck with a flat tyre. We debated the merits of going ahead or turning back as we waited for the AA to come to our rescue. I, being the eternal optimist, convinced the rest that we should press on; "We'll only miss the first ten minutes".

This was a ground I had never been to so was keen to press on regardless. Kidderminster is further than you think. We got there at half-time. The gates were locked; I think that was to stop the crowd leaving early. The stewards weren't going to let us in! We pleaded and pleaded. They eventually took pity and let us in (for free) to watch an awful second half display by Rovers. Our timing was perfect. We settled down just in time to see Kidderminster score at the start of the second half.

Somehow it all still seemed worth it though.

QUITE INTERESTING AWAY STATS

Rovers' goalkeeper Kossuth Seed Barnes was named after Lajos Kossuth the 19th Century Hungarian revolutionary leader. The first of his 17 matches came at an away game to Brighton & Hove Albion on 27th December 1921. He played most of the second half of the 1921/22 season, although he fortunately missed the 8-1 drubbing at Swansea Town in April 1922. Rovers played 10 games in April alone!

Kossuth's debut game was also the debut of a certain Wally Hammond, later to be far more famous for captaining the England cricket team for 20 test matches and leading the first class batting averages in seven separate seasons. He played 19 times for Rovers.

SPECIAL FEATURE

I CAME FROM GERMANY AND NEVER EVEN GOT TO SEE A GAME!

Not long after starting to receive submissions for this book I noticed I'd had quite a few stories of postponed matches, broken down trains, complete disasters, getting lost, turning up at the wrong ground, etc.

I started to wonder who on the forum I used at the time (the official club forum) had travelled the furthest yet never even got to see a game, so I started a thread to ask that very question.

Fortunately I copied the answers off the thread as a few weeks later BRFC unceremoniously and unilaterally shut the forum down without any warning and everyone lost all the info they had on it.

I've presented below what I managed to save, although I now have no way of getting in contact with some of the kind people who contributed, in order to thank them and properly credit them. If anyone wishes to make themselves known to me, please email me at - hello@awaythegas.org.uk

MY OWN EXPLOITS in this area are not very impressive.

I've been seriously late for a few matches, but never totally missed one or had one called off as I got towards the ground.

The following doesn't technically count but I used to live in Staines [since rather pompously renamed Staines-Upon-Thames] and was driving to the Mem one Saturday when the old car started giving me grief. I turned into Membury services and called Green Flag. They came out quite swiftly, told me what it was and added that I might get to Bristol, but might not. As a bit of peabrain when it comes to cars I didn't want to take the risk so I sacked it off and turned to go home. I didn't fancy going all the way to the next junction to turn around, and as most drivers will know lots of the older Motorway services will have a hidden, and forbidden, service road that will take you over the other side of the motorway. I went to use it and there is a jam jar waiting near the turning. I could have driven on but I decided to politely pull up by the copper and explain why I'm using the service / locals bridge. I explain and he's fine, but he starts looking at my tired old 'E' reg Nissan Coupe. The Officer gets out and starts checking the tread on my tyres with a tyre gauge! He tells me they are very bad and I really should have them changed ASAP. He checks my license, insurance, MOT, tax etc. Thankfully I have everything with me and it's all ship shape and Bristol fashion. He asks me where I'm going, and after I say Staines (only 60 miles away) he lets me go as long as I swear to drive straight home and then get new tyres.

So... 120 miles (round trip) without seeing anything is the best I can do, but that was for a home match anyway...

'MIAGSYGAS'

Believe it or not, I've been to an away game on the wrong day. I went to the away game to Fulham on Saturday when it was a Sunday. I still don't quite know how I got that one wrong, but have a feeling it was due a night of drinking on the Friday.

I even got relatively close to Craven Cottage, then realised when I thought to myself, "hmm, not many Rovers or Fulham fans about... Quite a few Chelsea though."

'GERMAN PIRATE'

Home game against Millwall in, I believe, 1998 or 1999, which was called off due to black ice. I was coming all the way from Hannover/Germany by coach (Transline service, took about 15 hours each way) just for that match. Due to the weather the coach was running late and I had to catch a taxi up to the Mem only to learn, the game was off. I stood a night in the hotel then and went back to Germany next day.

'FRANCE GAS'

A few years ago I arranged my annual trip back to the UK for a yearly appointment to coincide with a home match (against Huddersfield Town I think) only for the match to be postponed due to snow. So I claim a return distance of 1500 miles not to see a match!

2nd April 1996. Travelled down from London to Twerton for an evening match against Bradford City. I exited the M4 at Bath but after about two miles the clutch arm snapped on the car. Much to the amusement of the passing Bradford fans I was stranded by the side of the road waiting for the AA to arrive. The car couldn't get fixed so I had to wait for relay to arrive to take me back home to Surrey. The coach of Bradford fans passed on the way back, after the game, still taking the mickey out of me even though they lost. To rub salt in the wound I found out later that when the wife renewed the AA membership she cancelled relay and only kept roadside assistance, so not only did I miss the match but it also cost me in excess of £200 to relay the car back home. Needless to say she is now the ex-wife.

I also travelled down from London for an evening match at the Mem against Wycombe. When I was about 10 miles from Bristol the heavens opened. I arrived for a swift pint at the Vic only to be told the match had been postponed about 20 minutes earlier.

'MJHGAS'

Wigan - game called off 10 minutes before kick off! Gerry Francis did a sterling job of calming a none to happy away following. Good day out though!

'BISHOPSTONBRFC'

Gillingham in the FA Cup. I got to the ground after a four hour coach drive to be told by a copper the game was off. It was about a nine hour trip in the end. Haven't been since.

'QUARTERMASTER'

I've been inside Brisbane Road when the game has been called off before KO (frozen pitch I think). I've also arrived in the car park at Plymouth Argyle to find the game was off.

However the longest distance must be to Bradford City. It rained all the way, Police still escorted the coaches off the motorway and when we pulled up outside Valley Parade the locals took great delight in telling us the pitch was waterlogged! It was a long journey home.

I don't think I've ever missed a match but I remember driving some mates to Shrewsbury for the Area Final of the LDV one evening in March 1996. I was probably only about 20 but I'd driven there before and remembered the ground was in the town. Well we drove into the town and back out at least a couple of times but no sign of the ground (pre sat nav days!). Eventually we spotted a set of really bright flood lights so we navigated our way towards them. I had a niggly feeling this wasn't right though as we were in the middle of nowhere, certainly not in town. My fears were confirmed when we found the floodlights...which were illuminating an outdoor hockey pitch!

No idea how we still made it for the kick off!

'HUNG DRAWN AND QUARTERED'

Gillingham F.A. Cup, about 10 years ago. Called off whilst in a pub 1/2 mile away.

'LPGAS'

Many years ago, I think it was a Boxing Day match at Plymouth, I drove from Brentford only to get there and find it had been postponed due to a water logged pitch.

'GREGSGAS'

I remember going to Orient away for a LDV match that got called off late on because the pitch was frozen... the thing was that the pitch had been frozen all day... shambles....

'WRECKLESS'

My best effort was actually being a part of preventing some supporters from getting to a match.

I was living "up north", and travelling one evening from Chester to Liverpool. I was in a carriage with a load of ordinary commuters, politely minding our own business. On get a group of football 'fans', carrying booze, shouting and swearing, making lewd comments about the women - total idiots.

They are away fans going to Tranmere, and cutting it fine for the kick off. It's dark. We get to Bebington station and the fans see the floodlights of the Oval Sports Centre.

"That's the ground" says one - we keep silent and hold our breath, not daring to exchange glances. They all pile out, abusing us as they go. The train moves off and we all collapse in polite but hysterical laughter. They should have gone on to Rock Ferry; it's probably half an hour to the next train and there is no way that they are getting to the match on time.

Happy Days.

'BRFC 1883'

I remember a night game (must of been a Tuesday) against Shrewsbury. It took hours to get there and then as we got into the ground we were told that the referee had called the game off. It must of been only 30 mins from kick off.

AWAY THE GAS Q&A

Imagine you are at an Alcoholics Anonymous meeting. Please stand up and say...

My name is **Mike Jay** and I have supported Bristol Rovers for 47 years

We were in Division Three when I started supporting Rovers / ~~the Pirates~~ / ~~the Gas~~

My first ever away match was on 19 August 1967 at Dean Court Bournemouth (lost 3-1).

I have been to approx 220 away matches at 127 different grounds

---

My favourite away grounds are ...(and why)

Fulham FC Craven Cottage - *lovely old fashioned ground by the River Thames. Happy trips there including Rovers winning 4-0 in the Play Off Semi Final in 1988. An all ticket match; I lost our tickets on the way to London on the coach. I went to see Rovers Secretary Bob Twyford and he got us two tickets for the Director's Box.* **Everton -** *Rovers in FA Cup in 1969 lost 1-0, in front of 55,000 fans.* **Liverpool** *- FA Cup tie in 1992; Carl Saunders put Rovers one nil up. Finally,* **Arsenal's Highbury -** *Sept 1984, Rovers beaten 4-0 in Milk Cup.*

I remember my worst ever away journey ...

Always Ashton Gate - so many of their fans hate the Gas... probably worst memory was the 6-1 defeat in Anglo Scottish Cup... but Gary Smart's winner on New Years Day 1987 made up for it... and the 3-1 win in FA Cup when Paul Randall (2) & Mark O'Connor scored in 1983

The furthest I've travelled away is ...

Darlington or Carlisle... came home from Corfu at 4am on Saturday 12th August 1995. My friend Colin picked me up at 7am to drive to Carlisle United for the first game of the season. We won 2-1; Billy Clark and Marcus Stewart. My wife was not amused at me going!

The earliest / latest I ever got to a match was ...

Earliest = Wembley Stadium for Play Off Final v Huddersfield we got there 3 hours before kick off. Latest = Port Vale for Play Off Final on 3 June 1989. Major traffic jams - got there just as the game started.

Best / worst grub - Best = Meat pies at the KC Stadium, Hull City.

Worst = Boston United. Very poor choice and awful tea and pies. Most expensive and poor was Play off Final at Wembley, May 2007.

Best / worst boozer =
The one right by the Kassam Stadium, Oxford United.

Best / worst half-time 'entertainment' =
Fans races at Gillingham FC. Live band - think it was at Morecambe.

My favourite home fans are ...(and why)
Sheffield Wednesday and Stoke City - so loud!

The best [clean] chant to home fans has been ...
"Does your ferret know you're here?"

The best away goal I've seen was ...
Carl Saunders' cracker at Anfield v Liverpool in the FA Cup 1992.

I really, really wish I had gone to these away games ...
Man Utd - the 2-1 league cup win at Old Trafford in 1972.
The 8-2 win at Brighton in 1973, when Brian Clough was manager.
I had been there the previous season but missed this one.

I regret ...
Rovers failing to stay in the Football League. Just a draw was required at home to Mansfield in May 2014. Still upsetting now.

Have you ever smuggled Weetabix into Shrewsbury?   NO

Have you ever worn fancy dress?   NO

Have you travelled away on a supporters train?   YES

Our worst shirt sponsor was - Snack Box / ~~Peter Carol~~ / ~~Elite Hampers~~

A PIE & A PINT

Another 'Ronseal' heading.

Food and drink.
From the landlord who happily let Gasheads drink until kick-off near the wrong ground, to the smallest sugar sachet in the world and the inability to make a black coffee.

HAPPY OXFORD LANDLORD

BY PAUL BRADBURY

I remember my first away game at the old Manor Ground. In those days we went away with my wife and young daughter, a friend and his son. I had a company car so always drove. Being families we liked to get to grounds early and park up somewhere we thought was safe, usually in a pub car park as near to the ground as we can.

On this occasion we arrived, parked up at the pub car park, and disembarked into the pub, which was quiet, with only about 20 other Gasheads in there. We had a few drinks and something to eat and at about 2.40pm left the pub to head to the ground. Strangely we didn't see anyone else outside the pub, and after walking a few hundred yards to the ground we found nobody about at all and the ground locked up .

We rapidly realised we had parked outside Oxford City's ground, who were playing away in the Conference or some other non league game at that time, and found that the Manor Ground was about five miles away. We went back to the pub and told the rest of the Gasheads in there, who all made a quick exit, much to the amusement of the landlord. We eventually got to the Manor Ground and parked in the hospital car park next to it and got in the ground about 3.10pm.

Since then we have obviously checked the pubs and grounds to ensure we have the right place!

QUITE INTERESTING AWAY STATS

We had never won at Southport until literally two days before this book went to the printers! Until then we had only played them 4 times, losing 3 and drawing 1. Then we won 1-0 on 27th September 2014 and ruined my clever away stat. Ray Mabbutt was previously our only goal scorer at the Sandgrounders and that was in the first encounter ever between us in 1968.

We've never beaten Chelsea away and had the same record as at Southport (i.e. lost 3 and drew 1). No Pirate has ever even scored at Stamford Bridge.

THE CURIOUS INCIDENT OF THE DEEP FRIED MARS BAR
BY MARTIN BULL

The visit to Scunthorpe United on Valentine's Day 2009 was unremarkable overall. It was rather like the opening gag in one of Lee Evans's old comedy routines as he enters the stage already stressed and dripping with sweat and states; 'oh the trouble I had getting here, the trouble I had getting here... nothing, straight through'. Apart from the splendid 2-0 win against a team that was flying, the only other memory was of the local McDonalds taking ages with my food and messing it up several times. It meant we only had five minutes or so to get through the turnstiles, but the steward said I wasn't allowed to bring hot food in the stadium.

Thankfully for my short fuse I found this went over the edge of annoying and into the realms of absurd and funny, and we cracked jokes with the steward who knew that the rule she had to enforce was blatantly ungracious and supercilious, especially to a vegetarian (almost vegan) who was confident there would be nothing in the stadium he could eat except a stale bag of Ready Salted crisps that had probably been in the bottom of the super mega size catering box since the previous season.

Ironically the delay I had in getting my food meant it was piping hot. I huffed and puffed on the food to cool it down whilst also stuffing my face, egged on by my brother and best mate. I was loathe to lob it, but did have to leave some outside. The steward said I could collect it later if I wished. That was an offer I could refuse.

I like going to new grounds and whilst recently spending 2½ years living near Manchester I took the opportunity to visit some Northern clubs I would have little chance getting to if I was back down South. The dawn of the 2009/10 season started on a huge high for Rovers. At our first away game of the season we were two up at Stockport County within a few minutes, so coasted the rest of the game. It was embarrassingly easy, and made even more enjoyable by the clement summer sunshine. It's sometimes easy to forget how watching footy in the sun can be so special.

A few days later (18th August) we travelled to Hartlepool and won 2-1. It was still only August but we felt invincible. Little did we know that Pools would eventually escape the drop that season only on goal difference and that Stocky would be effortlessly relegated at the bottom of the League with a frankly pathetic 25 points, and even worse would be in the Sixth Tier of footy within three more terrifying seasons. We did the double over both teams, bettered only by a 7-0 aggregate double over the eventual play-off finalists Swinedon. Oh how that bobble on the Wembley pitch in May 2010 made so many Gasheads laugh though!

I was going through a lot of anxiety at the time so having to negotiate rush hour traffic, pick my brother up in Leeds (with his new girlfriend who I'd never met before), time it just right to Hartlepool, AND get home before a football hating partner tutted a thousand times, filled me with dread. As usual I was the 'responsible' one who had to drive, sort out timings, make witty small talk, find out where the ground was and where to park. There was no way I was going to give up smoking at this rate.

But something clicked that day and it ranks as the most perfect away trip in my 25 years following the Gas. The journey was a wonder to behold as we talked all kinds of complete rubbish and had each other in stitches, whilst the road at times seemed to be our own personal highway to Monkey Hanger land. We got there in perfect time, ready to get some greasy grub before a fag and the game, all on a balmy August evening. Indeed it was the first time in many years I was able to wear just a T-shirt for an entire evening game, and this was all on a latitude shared with Denmark and Sweden.

As we drove to the area the map suggested we might find some free parking and a back entrance into the ground we passed a chippy (see photo of hideously punctuated shop sign on the opposite page), so after pinpointing the ground I doubled back. As I ordered my chips I spotted chocolate bars for sale, and having a sweet tooth to satisfy after a long journey I asked for a Mars. It hadn't yet dawned on me why a hot and steamy chip shop would sell chocolate, and only two different versions at that; Mars and Marathon (I refuse to call it that stupid 'S' name).

The serving lady hesitantly, and almost apologetically, asked me in a very local accent, "Do you want that... um... deep fried?". "Good God no!", I instantaneously responded without realising I was setting North - South cultural relations back about 30 years.

At the age of 39 I had just been offered my first ever deep fried Mars bar, and it felt more like I'd been propositioned by a tramp hoping to cadge a bottle of White Lightning in return for certain... cough... favours rendered.

I immediately felt queasy and had an unnerving desire for a shower and an industrial sized barrel of Swarfega to purge me.

As a vegetarian most of my adult life I don't eat much at away grounds, and as I often used to be on my lonesome I usually don't even take any notice of the catering facilities. For some reason though I will always remember Colchester's old ground (Layer Road) on my sole visit there in January 2000. This was the infamous 5-4 match, and proved to be one of only two losses sandwiched between 10 wins under Ian Holloway.

The away end was a mess of fences, narrow entrances and shallow terracing. In the far top corner there was a tiny wooden food hut that looked more like an outdoor toilet. A lone 12 year old manned it, presumably on day release from climbing up Victorian chimneys. The queue of hungry Gasheads got longer and longer, although strangely I overheard several people saying the result was really tasty.

Normally if you score four goals away from home you would expect to win, but oh no, this is Rovers we are supporting you know! Our list of goal scorers was like a who's who in Gas folklore. Two from super Jason Roberts, a penalty for Jamie Jamie Jamie Jamie Cureton and the final goal by Nathan 'The Duke' Ellington, on as a sub and pocketing only his second ever Gas goal.

The game never stopped for 90 minutes. Bang bang bang. End to end. Like two giant heavyweights slugging it out with their left feet tied together. Jamie managed to miss a second penalty; well I think he hit the bar actually. A young Titus Bramble (a.k.a. Bambi on Ice) was on loan at the U's from Ipswich Town and with a trademark ill-timed tackle ended David Pritchard's season. I don't remember him even getting a yellow for it. It helped ruin Pritch's career, and spoilt this vital match as well. In fact I would say that this injury, and Ronnie Mauge's leg break in February 2000 playing for Trinidad & Tobago at the CONCACAF Gold Cup in San Diego, played a huge part in us not even reaching the play-offs after being in the top three for most of the season.

Both players were forced to retire in 2002.

I digress.

Although we had the most potent strike force in the country at one end, we had some rookies at the other that day. The two indomitable Andy's (Thomson and Tillson) were both missing, one of only three League games each of them missed that season. It was only poor Mike Trought's third ever League appearance, and it turned out to be his third time on a losing side. Tom White played only his second game of the season (out of just three) and Layer Road also saw Shaun Byrne's solitary start for us, on an emergency loan from West Ham United.

A certain young lad came on as their sub and terrorised us into defeat. His name was Tresor Lomana Lua Lua, and he turned out to be a player that no-one would easily forget in a hurry.

As previously professed, being a veggie I don't eat much at footy grounds. In fact, I was vegan (no animal products at all) for a good chunk of the 2000's, so I really didn't have any choice of drink, let alone food. The best attempt at a vegan drink came at Southend. It was an Auto-Windscreens Shield tie in late January 2001, in front of only 2,192 hardy souls.

I had inexplicably decided to take a day off work and 'make a day of it', even though I was on my tod and it was the depths of winter. As the train trundled along the quiet route to Southend we passed the laughably entitled London Southend Airport, before coming into the main station after lunch time.

I instantly knew I had made a glaring mistake.

Maybe I thought Southend would be fun because I have fond memories of the seaside as a lad, and as a teenager remember voluntarily enduring the slowest, most dreary bus journey in the universe just to get to Weston-Super-Mud (from Bath). When I think of the seaside I think of amusement arcades, sweets pumped full of entirely unnatural dayglo colours, the natural sea pool at Bude, winning best baby at Butlins in Minehead (true!), various B&B based family holidays at Weymouth, feeble wind breaks falling over, and even a trip to Belgium with the school, where women sunbathed topless and shopkeepers would happily sell you small cans of Stella even though you were far under age. Ah, the laissez faire attitude of those happy-go-lucky Europeans is so liberating for a teenage boy from boring Bath. Shame they put mayonnaise on your chips though. Deviants!

Pretty much nothing was open, including the famous mile long pier, and it was brassic. I spontaneously decided that the cinema was my best bet to stay warm and while away the time. After watching some film I can't even remember the title of, I felt a bit like a dirty hobbo trying to keep warm by standing over a Baker's hot air vent, so I had to face reality and go back a few stops on the train to the ground, even though I still had more time to waste. A slow bag of chips later and I reluctantly went in to Roots Hall early. As I was properly vegan at the time I assumed that a black coffee would warm me up.

You can't exactly get a black coffee wrong.

Can you?

The away end refreshments were under the corner of the stadium buried beneath concrete, with cheap plastic communal seats which made it look more like a Siberian death camp canteen than a hip and desirable coffee spot. As I asked the obligatory underpaid spotty teenager for a black coffee, I got a confusing reply that they couldn't make one. 'Uh?' I asked; that was the best I could do with a sub-zero temperature brain.

Clearasil boy just managed to put enough monosyllabic murmurs together to explain that all the drinks come pre-packed, and all coffees come with powdered milk in the bottom of the cup. I explained that I didn't eat any animal products, such as milk, and that it was so cold out there that I'd just seen a gang of snowmen ripping up wooden fences and huddling around a fiery brazier. Was there anything hot I could drink I pleaded?

"How about a hot chocolate?" came his pitiable reply.

I can't remember anything about the match except losing 1-0 and sitting on a small plastic chair with my hands under my bum for 90 minutes.

With no atmosphere, no away goals, nothing to get up and dance about, and icicles metaphorically hanging off my nose, it was one of the coldest matches I've ever been to. Fortunately I think I got in for only £5 with my student card which was very generous of them (adult ed evening class at a proper college; always worth signing up for and a little trick of the trade - you'll get your fees back in cheap footy entrance alone!). It was actually the first goal we had let in in the competition, following a 2-0 win at Torquay and a 3-0 home thrashing of Plymouth.

If anyone tells you Southend on a winters night might be fun, or a six hour ferry from Harwich to the Hoek of Holland will be better than the fast ones over the shortest bit of the English Channel [misguided trip to friend at University in Dusseldorf], you have my express permission to tell them to jump off a mile long pier... in winter... as naked as the day they were born!

WE WANT THE FINEST WINES AVAILABLE TO HUMANITY... AND WE WANT THEM NOW!
BY CHEWBACCA

Wycombe away in the Johnstone's Paint Trophy - October 2006

We got to Wycombe about one or two in the afternoon and drank practically every drop of booze in the town. Rovers won 2-0 with Jemal Easter getting the first and Sammy Igoe scoring practically with the last kick of the game. We spent the whole first half giving dogs abuse to the Wycombe goalkeeper as apparently our Grandmothers' thought he was an "utter sod". He repeatedly flicked the V's at us, much to our delight. It was all topped off with kissing Sammy Igoe.

I think we only took around 60 supporters. Six months later 40,000 would travel to Cardiff for the final, but it all started here.

Stockport away in the League - August 2009

I was staying in Manchester as my girlfriend at the time was living there. I met a couple of Gasheads in Manchester at about 11am and started drinking. We were in a pub and got talking to a couple of Norwegians who were off to the United game the next day. Next thing we know we're drinking with them and on the train to Stockport. One of them was sick outside Stockport station, so we of course continued drinking and then went to the ground.

Rovers took an early two goal lead and I can remember nothing of the game apart from Gasheads singing "There's only one Fraser Foreskin" and the Norwegians mooing and making milking gestures at the Stockport supporters!

[Editor's Note - I was also at that game. I was stone-cold sober but I also can't remember much about the game after taking a very early two goal lead. I suspect there there was not much to remember about it, whether sober or sozzled.]

THE SMALLEST SUGAR SACHET IN THE WORLD

BY MARTIN BULL

To me Swindon is still a good derby match, although I probably haven't been to as many as I should have.

My first ones were in September 1991, and then the next season, a year later. This was when we were packed on the Stratton Bank, a traditional old open terrace. At the first of these matches myself and a couple of mates wore Pirate moustaches and eye patches, amongst a bumper 11,000 crowd. 50p from a joke shop. We were surprised that we were the only ones who had bothered. We somehow expected people to make more of an effort for a local derby in what is now called the Championship. Several people said we looked good even though it only took us 10 seconds. I've never been one for dressing up, and this was about as far as I've ever bothered.

I'm sure I didn't go again until October 2010.

We were in the corner of the Arkells Stand now, and as the evening match was on Sky the atmosphere wasn't as good as usual for the Gas. The stand is very high and steep, and suffers not only from a tiny refreshments area, but also from huge solid doors back into the stand that are either impossible to move with your hands full, and/or guaranteed to swing open at the wrong time and end up in a type of comic 'spilt tea and burger all over the floor' farce not seen since a Buster Keaton silent film.

My abiding memories of the night are of denying Eliot Richards the second time (see page 81 for that story), and being given the smallest sugar sachet known to humanity. Well, to be exact there was nothing wrong with the size of the sachet; the problem was that you could count the grains in a sachet on two hands (or one webbed foot for home fans).

I'm not a particularly sugary tea person at all (½ a spoon if the tea is ok, a bit more if it's 'orrible) but it took five or six sachets even for me. I vowed to take one home as proof that I wasn't exaggerating. I offer up the evidence to the right. This of course was a false economy for them as I needed a fistful of them in my tea, and the little blue sachets lay strewn far and wide like discarded shell casings in a war zone, and I imagine one disgruntled member of staff would have to be allocated the chore of tidying them up as a full-time responsibility.

THE ALDERSHOT ROOF REPAIR FUND
BY PAUL BRADBURY

Back in the good old days Aldershot was a worthwhile away day, with the walk through the park to the portable turnstiles and then on through the park again. I remember being there on a cold wet day with the wife and daughter. Our friends went to get some coffees and as they were walking back through the crowd Gary Penrice scored. Needless to say the away end went wild and the coffees went everywhere up in the air and all over people. These were the days when you could stand and run up and down the terraces much like the Blackthorn End is at the Mem now.

The other memorable point about this visit was that the away end had a corrugated steel roof which was leaking all over the place. Some bright spark borrowed a bucket from the St. John Ambulance people sitting near the touchline and went around asking people for donations towards repairing the roof. I'm not sure how much he got, if anything, but it was fun to see, and maybe he got a few beers out of it on the way home. I do wonder if the St. John people got their bucket back though!

Thinking about food and drink, why did the Weetabix craze start at Shrewsbury? Gay Meadow was always one away game to look forward to and I remember once seeing the Police stopping and searching all the Gasheads, resulting in mountains of confiscated Weetabix stored up outside the turnstiles!

AWAY THE GAS Q&A

Imagine you are at an Alcoholics Anonymous meeting. Please stand up and say...

My name is **David Roberts** & I have supported Bristol Rovers for 65 years

We were in Division Three (South) when I starting supporting Rovers / the Pirates / the Gas

My first ever away match was 18th May 1963 at Halifax Town (won 3-2)

I have been to... too many away matches, at most grounds we've played at.

My favourite away grounds are ...(and why)

- Millwall, old & new Dens; dispelled the myths about the fans
- City, because of the sheer anticipation.
- Burnley & Preston because their grounds encapsulate the tradition of football and the atmosphere is electric.

I remember my worst ever away journey ...

Derby (1st time). My windscreen wipers broke from Darlington to Derby in heavy snow, then Derby to Bristol in driving rain. I had a huge headache by the time I got to Bristol, & my eyes were crossed for a week, but the 3 lads in the car were relieved to be alive.

The furthest I've travelled away is ...

Carlisle from Bristol, and Exeter from Darlington. I used to do the Mem' both ways (600 miles round trip) for a while when I moved up North ... so every game was an away game, of sorts.

Best / worst grub -

Best = Kiddie.

Worst = Halifax October 2001, and it was a soulless 0-0.

Best / worst half-time 'entertainment' =
No idea. I'm always in the bar!

Best / worst boozer =

Best = The Bloomfield (Blackpool)

Worst = Too many to mention, though the one at Bournemouth ?? (near the park) was rubbish. It was quicker to go to the off-licence just down the road, than to wait to be served in the pub.

My favourite home fans are ...(and why)

I was always impressed with the Blackpool fans. We used to drink in The Bloomfield. The Blackpool lads always made us very welcome.

The best[clean] chant to home fans has been ...

Anything at Ashton Gate; take your pick.

The best away goal I've seen was ...

Rickie Lambert at Hartlepool in May 2007, to secure a play-off spot.

I really, really wish I had gone to these away games ...

- Liverpool in the FA Cup 1992 - I was moving house!
- Play-off Final at Wembley 2007 - I was on holiday, which was booked when we looked a million to 1 against to get in the play-offs ... I was able to see it on TV though, and at least I was at the Hartlepool game which was very exciting.

I regret ...

Not having taken a camera (pre-mobile days) to games, to make an effort to record some happy and, most times, funny days out with my 'football mates'.

Have you ever smuggled Weetabix into Shrewsbury?   NO

Have you ever worn fancy dress?   NO

Have you travelled away on a supporters train?   YES

Our worst shirt sponsor was - Snack Box / Peter Carol/ Elite Hampers

GAMES FROM HELL

No matter how you dress it up there are often some pretty batty moments being a football fan.

It could be a local derby, a meeting with a team far superior to you, a crunch match that is super important to a League position or cup progress, a day where everything just goes wrong, or it was simply the 1970's when it seems like lots of matches were full of mad 'uns!

I'm too young for the 70s and quite glad of it.

I always planned to make sure this book doesn't glorify violence and it's been really interesting to see that I've hardly had to edit contributions at all even though lots of them are recalling memories of being subjected to very hostile and confrontational situations. Many of these 'games from hell' are not progressive examples of healthy entertainment but they are real life and it was never my intention to shy away from reporting the reality of being a footy fan at certain times and places.

The old adage is that if you look for hands-on trouble you'll probably find it. And let us not forget there are also many kind people out there who may be the ones that end up helping us in a time of need.

IT'S OK, IT'S JUST A FLESH WOUND
BY ANDY HOLMES

Lincoln City - 17th May 2007

After beating the Imps 2-1 at home in the League Two Play-Off Semi Final First Leg, a mate of mine said they had two spare tickets for the away leg and a mini-bus sorted, so asked if I was interested. I agreed and also brought my old man along for the ride.

I didn't quite appreciate the distance from Bristol to Lincoln, but brought a couple of crates of lager on the mini bus for the journey, and managed to drink a crate on the way. Much of what follows is therefore very hazy for me, but when we arrived in Lincoln we parked up and went to a seemingly away-fan friendly boozer and then on to the game.

My foggy memories include trying to take pictures and videos of the game (including the Sammy Igoe goal). Apparently I had been sleeping through most of the action, so I had no idea what the score was at this point really, but the atmosphere was telling me we were ahead. In fact when Lincoln got a consolation goal near the end, I was briefly dejected until my Dad let me know that we were still winning 5-3 on the night and 7-4 on aggregate.

The atmosphere in the away end was great. I think I had my shirt off for some bizarre reason, and we were going to Wembley!

There was a Lincoln pitch invasion after the game, but it didn't really register to me or my Dad that there was anything to be concerned about and after the game we left with the other fans.

Unfortunately me and my Dad were quite drunk and we had no idea where the other people from the minibus were. We had some vague idea that the plan was to meet in a pub, so we set off to find it. Each pub we tried to go in were now refusing away fans until we eventually found one that let us in and we sat and had a beer.

Gradually the pub filled up with Imps fans and we got chatting to them. They told us that it was all kicking off outside; running battles with the Police, bricks being thrown, etc. and that we probably shouldn't be wandering around in our Rovers shirts! My old man somehow remembered where the minibus was parked and a few of the Lincoln fans offered to walk us there to protect us.

Thankfully it wasn't a trap. They surrounded us and walked us through the carnage back to our minibus, where we discovered that one of our fellow passengers had been stabbed in the leg! He said he was 'OK' though and would go to hospital in Bristol when we got back, so we piled on the minibus and finished my second crate of lager.

Cheers to those Lincoln fans! They probably saved us from a hiding.

[Editor's Note - This was amazingly Lincoln's fifth play-off disappointment in a row, so I imagine the natives were getting pretty restless by now!]

Wonky scoreboard after stuffing Brentford 3-1 on 19th September 2009. I'm not sure what language that is, but it's not Wiltshireez.

Photo by Martin Bull

YOU'RE BLUE AND WHITE AND CALLED ROVERS SO YOU'LL BE FINE...

BY SOUTHMEAD GAS

I remember going to Blackburn Rovers on the coach (only two coaches went) with my mate Martin in the early Seventies.

All started well and we were told that after the game we would go on to Blackpool to see the lights.

We had been travelling for about an hour when the coach broke down and we had to wait for another one to come from Bristol. I am glad to say it still got us to the game, just.

We thought we would go in the enclosure, but it didn't take long for their mob to see us. They couldn't get at us because of a fence separating the enclosure from their end, but when we scored they went nuts trying to get at us, and the Blackburn fans around us told us that they will kill you when they get you!

Half-time came and we thought we would be better off going up the other end behind the goal. Little did we know that their fans could get close to us there as well. Thankfully the Old Bill kept them at bay.

We went on to win 2-1 but at the final whistle we had to find our coach, so I asked the coppers, "do you know where our coach is parked?". He replied, "there is one at each end of the ground". I asked if they could escort us, but he said, "no, you're blue and white and called Rovers so you'll be fine".

As we got outside there were hundreds of them waiting for us. We somehow got to the coach but it was the wrong one. We asked the driver if he could take us down to the other coach, but he said no way. So now about six of us had to get to the other coach, with their mob waiting. Again I asked a copper, this time one with a big dog, if he would walk with us, and this one said he would, so off we went.

As soon as they saw us they came at us and surrounded us. The dog stopped the ones in front of us, who backed off, but the ones behind came at us, so the copper then had to see them off with the dog. But as he turned we had to stay with him, so we were walking back the wrong way! We were going backwards and forwards, following that lovely dog, but getting absolutely nowhere.

Eventually, after what seemed like an age, we were edging forward and could see our coach, so as soon as the dog saw off the ones in the direction we wanted to go, we just legged it to the coach. I've never been so happy in my life to park my bum on a coach seat.

As we pulled away, singing and finally enjoying the win, I remembered that we were going to Blackpool. When we arrived we went for a walk to the beach where we wrote a huge 'BRFC' in the sand. Then it was back on the coach to drive the Golden Mile.

That's when our replacement coach broke down, and yet again we had to wait for another coach to come from home to pick us up.

I can't recall when we got home, but that was some trip.

It was all worth it though. We won!

[Editor's Note - this match must have been the 6th March 1976 meeting. It was the third 2-1 win up there in the space of four years, so it was no wonder the locals were disgruntled! We won 2-1 there in the League on 27th March 1972 and again in the Third Round of the F.A. Cup on 4th January 1975.]

IN SEARCH OF THE 'RIGHT' SCORE

BY JOHN COLES

I went on the Supporters Club coaches to Millwall in the mid-70s (most probably the final match of the season in April 1975). Everything went well until we reached the New Kent Road, when lots of people who were drinking on the side of the road would smash their beer glasses and show us the jagged edges as we passed by. I was definitely a little on edge.

When we were dropped off we made our way down Cold Blow Lane towards the stadium, and people were coming out of houses to confront the Rovers supporters. I particularly remember an elderly man kicking a Rovers supporter when still wearing his slippers.

We eventually made it to the ground and took our seat in the stands. Opposite us was a ship sailing up what must have been a canal; it really was a surreal sight. The Lions fans made a hell of a fuss throughout the game ('Knees Up Mother Brown', 'Maybe It's Because I'm A Londoner' and all the other London songs) until the Rovers scored.

0-1 was not the 'right' score, and foolishly we all celebrated the goal. Bad error on our part, and the Millwall fans let us all know all about it. The stand that we were sitting in was a wooden stand similar to the South Stand at Eastville, and very soon small fires started appearing and fans were trying to climb from the terraces into the stand. The Police were doing their best, but I really was getting concerned. Thank goodness Millwall eventually scored, and in time the game ended. The game passed by in a haze, and I was relieved when it was all over.

Millwall had already been relegated the previous weekend and outside the ground some of their supporters were physically trying to 'tip' a Police horse over, and very nearly succeeded as well, by using brute force and marbles. The whole day was an absolute nightmare from start to finish, and it's the only game that I have ever attended that I have been relieved to get out alive.

It wouldn't be an exaggeration to compare some scenes to a war zone. I've been to all the 'big' grounds, but I've never witnessed scenes like I did that day. I heard later that some Millwall fans had followed some Rovers supporters as far as Paddington Station, with obvious results.

I also remember going to an F.A. Cup Third Round game versus Leeds United at Elland Road in January 1972. My brother and I travelled to the game on the Supporters Club train, and on arrival in the area around Elland Road I was surprised by how run-down the locality was. We went to go into a pub, but after sticking our heads around the door decided against it. We had stand seats for the game, and it's fair to say that Rovers just didn't turn up for the game. Leeds were a very good team at that time so we had few expectations, and I believe that they had fielded a strong team on the day, as evidenced by the 33,000 strong crowd. We lost 4-1, after trailing 4-0 at one point. The Leeds fans followed Rovers supporters all the way back to the railway station, and there were fights on the platform. I was glad when the train finally pulled away, as it was the worst atmosphere apart from our trip to Millwall.

[Editor's geeky note - Leeds went on to win the F.A. Cup that season. This has happened six times to Rovers; Spurs in 1921, Arsenal 1936, Newcastle United 1951, Ipswich Town 1978 and Liverpool 1992]

QUITE INTERESTING AWAY STATS

We've never won at HOME to West Ham United in 13 League and Cup fixtures (unless you really want to add in the 1973 Watney Cup First Round 'win' on penalties), but we have won once AWAY in 13 League and Cup visits; a 2-1 win in March 1957.

We've also never won at home to Macclesfield Town in eight attempts, but have won twice at Moss Rose (1999 and 2007), with five consecutive 2-1 defeats sandwiched in between the prosperous trips.

MAYBE IT'S BECAUSE I'M A LONDONER...
BY PETE WEBB

Crystal Palace away on Boxing Day 1978 was a Christmas present never to forget. The Supporters Club train broke down and we didn't get there until half-time. We were bottom or close to it and they were top. As we got there late they let us in for free. Steve White got a goal and we won 1-0. After the game there was a Police escort back to the train station, but it didn't stop the Palace thugs trying a couple of ambushes on the way. I seem to remember standing behind a row of Police as bottles were being chucked at us.

I found out the hard way that **West Ham** away was never for the uninitiated. It would have been December 1979 I think. I was only eighteen and my mate Myles was sixteen. We went on one of the two supporters coaches. We went in the away end, which despite us taking approximately 100 on the two coaches had very few Rovers supporters in it. It did however contain a tremendous amount of West Ham fans (I use the term fans loosely). All game we were surrounded by them, offering to show us the way to the toilet and opening their Harrington jackets to show off blades. I was convinced I was going to die. I ended the game with the back of my head covered in cigarette burns.

We asked the Police for an escort back to the coaches, but they said if they protected us the West Ham fans would knock seven bells out of them! At the end of the game we just ran back to the coach. Thinking about it now the West Ham fans must have let us off, knowing we were young and utterly petrified. They could easily have beaten us up.

We also lost to West Ham 2-0 at Eastville on the last game of that season. I was lucky enough to get a couple of tickets for the F.A. Cup Final that year when the Hammers were rank underdogs against Arsenal. So one week I was hoping they'd lose and the next week I was at Wembley hoping they'd win. A couple of doors down from where I lived was a family from East London; Irons fans. So I took their young lad with me.

The following season I was down my local the night before we played **West Ham** away (April 1981). Some of my other mates wanted to go, but I wasn't up for it. I tried to tell them how bad it was the year before but they wouldn't have it. As the night wore on, and the more Hofmeister I drank (remember that dire lager?), the more it seemed like it would be a good idea to go. Suddenly I was even offering to drive.

Saturday morning came. I checked the oil level on the trusty Austin 1300. That car took us all over the country watching the Rovers in those days. The trouble was it used nearly as much engine oil as it did petrol. After checking the car was vaguely OK, I then nipped down the road to visit the young lad who was a West Ham supporter! I borrowed his West Ham scarf in exchange for agreeing to buy him a programme.

So off I set stopping to pick up the other three, who were not exactly amused about the West Ham scarf in the car. Up the M4 we went. Of course without the aid of GPS it was a bit harder to find a ground in those days. We went straight through London and eventually got to where we thought we were going, West Ham. We drove around and around but couldn't see any floodlights. We had to stop and ask someone for directions only to find out we needed to go to the East Ham area. After finally parking up the four of us walked to the ground. I was pretty apprehensive after my visit there the year before, but the other three were laughing and joking and generally taking the mickey out of me.

When we got to the Boleyn Ground I insisted on going in the home stand and wearing my borrowed Hammers scarf. We also split up into pairs, although I don't remember why. I used to go to a lot of Rovers away games in those days and I knew a lot of our fans to speak to, and a fair number just to say hello to. It was quite bizarre walking around the home stand seeing all the Gasheads in there. But no one spoke a word. Everyone just nodded to each other, as a covert acknowledgment of our little secret.

In front of us was this big fat West Ham supporter and his missus. He kept pointing at the half dozen or so Rovers fans in the away end, telling his missus that was all we brought because we were scared. I just hoped that they were fairing a bit better than I did the previous year. There was a Rovers fan sat behind me who kept nudging me in the back and laughing every time the bloke slagged us off. We lost 2-0 that day. I can't say I remember a whole lot about the match but Tom McAlister (who went on to play for the Hammers) was in goal, and I remember standing and clapping when West Ham scored, just to keep up the charade.

THE WORST VIEW IN THE WORLD
BY MARTIN BULL

[Note - this isn't really a 'game from hell', but it was hard to fit it into any other section...]

Away fans traditionally get the worst view of course, and the scabby little electronic scoreboard that most lower League grounds have is ALWAYS behind us, but of all the bad views I've had Exeter City's dreadful away terrace has to knock the others into a cocked hat.

In fact I'm not sure it can be called 'a view' as during the match there in September 2012 I don't think I saw any of the game beyond the 18 yard box at our own end. Thankfully not seeing the match didn't particularly bother me as we won, and I cared more about the atmosphere and the result than the on the pitch action.

The terrace only has a very shallow slope on it, and once full it also felt rather dangerous. It was certainly a throwback to the precarious days of old crumbling terraces where you could hardly move, and when you did move it was to be hurled around like a rag doll after a wild goal celebration. But this one was worse because at least the old terraces had crush barriers on them.

Funnily enough a QI fact is that the terrace at the other end of the ground, the 'Big Bank', is the largest terrace left in League football, although no-one seems to know EXACTLY what the capacity is, with even

Exeter's official web site enigmatically listing it as "just under 4,000". The second largest was our own North Terrace (call it Blackthorn, Bass, or whatever you prefer) with space for 3,710 ~~mugs~~ Gasheads.

Thankfully I managed to go the whole match without wanting the toilet as I doubt I could have got there even if I'd wanted to. I also heard through the 'man's grapevine' (a phenomenon rather peculiar to men at events like footy matches and music concerts) that the toilet was barely a trough to pee in, and as a bonus you could then watch your own urine flow out through the side of the lean-to as if you'd won a free trip to an Indian sewer.

If this is what you get when a Supporters' Trust run a club, and Danny Coles is adjudged to be a fit and proper person to captain the team, I can understand why fans sometimes prefer to tolerate the local milk round owner, or string factory proprietor, running their club instead.

The Trust must know that people can hardly move on it as they even had a lad with a hot water urn on his back, with a very important looking hose and nozzle contraption, who walks along the barrier at the front selling hot drinks. What they don't tell you is that the groundsman doubtless uses it during the week for spraying his weed killer. I presume 'elf and safety turn a blind eye to him though, as encouraging hot drinks in that crush seems akin to asking a toddler to hold a carving knife for you for a few minutes. By the by, I'm still waiting for someone to invent a portable urinal for use on packed terraces. Maybe this lad's back mounted urn and hose could be adapted for the cause?

The terrace crawls around the corner towards a block of seats for away fans. At this juncture there is a yellow painted gangway. Not surprisingly it was difficult to keep that empty in the sell-out conditions and it led to a running battle of wits between Police / Stewards and Rovers fans on the wind-up. Numerous songs accompanied this Mexican stand off, about being 'on the yellow line' and then not being on the yellow line. It was all very good natured but I suspect the worn out stewards and plod rather preferred the sedate visits of Accrington Stanley and Cheltenham Town that season.

WHEN THE ENTIRE FOOTBALL NATION WITNESSES YOUR HUMILIATION

BY MIKE FRY

'Spurs 9 Rovers 0 - 22nd October 1977

One I will never forget! Having been a regular away traveller since the mid Seventies and inspired by the 4-1 victory over Blackburn Rovers the previous weekend (including a Bobby Gould hat-trick), this was one away game I could not miss.

So together with my then girlfriend and best mate, I arrived at Eastville ready to board one of the Supporters Club coaches full of optimism. I can't really remember anything significant about the coach trip but soon realised on arrival in North London that White Hart Lane was nothing like the Shay at Halifax or York's Bootham Crescent.

The crowd was a little larger too, at 26,311. The loyal band of Gasheads sang a rendition of 'Goodnight Irene' but in truth the Spurs fans drowned us out. After almost 20 minutes it was still 0-0 and my optimism was growing; I should have left then! What followed was some awful defending and complete capitulation. With Hoddle out on the right and Peter Taylor on the other wing, they created chance after chance and Colin Lee did most of the damage, bagging four of the nine goals to hit our net.

The journey home is a blur but by the time I got home I'd just about managed to come to terms with the reality. Oh, how I wished Match of The Day's total fascination with top flight football had begun much earlier in history though, for there we were, the feature match, and I went through the whole disaster all over again knowing the football nation was witnessing our humiliation. Thank god me and the cameras were not around at our other famous away day thrashing, 12-0 at Luton in 1936; nine was more than enough for me to take!

Oh well, the more recent 6-0 win witnessed at Reading makes all the defeats and the nil-nils worth it, plus all those thousands of miles travelled over more than 40 years!

HAPPY TO LOSE AND GET OUT ALIVE
BY MARTIN BULL

Have you ever been to an away match and actually been relatively happy to lose as it means you'll get out alive?

Mine was Elland Road in 2010. The very last game of the season.

I'd been to Leeds in the 2007/8 and 2008/9 seasons, during a sojourn living up North, and I really didn't like the atmosphere. The siege mentality brought out the worst in some Gasheads, and in the December 2007 game it was particularly bad as it was the first time we'd played there in the League since 1962, and the one and only time we'd ever met in a Cup was also way back in time, in 1972.

I think we had around 2,000 Gas there, at precisely the time when Leeds were probably at their lowest ebb. They were 'only' fifth in the table at the time and the pressure was destined to be heaped on them until the end of time, or promotion; whichever came first. They were after all a club who'd been in the Premier League as recently as 2003/04, and got to the Third Round of the UEFA Cup in 2002/03. The mood was a heady mix of disgruntled locals, mouthy Gasheads, and a larger than average proportion of young impressionable Gas who probably couldn't believe we were playing there and were grabbing this chance whilst they could.

Given this vibe I had already said to myself that if Rovers needed anything from the 2010 match I wouldn't go, but as our play-off bus had crashed and burnt during April, I decided I would go to my last match up North before moving back to the Somerset / Wiltshire hinterlands, and I reasoned that even if Leeds fans did get anxious / snippy, us Gas could at least sit back and relax and be pretty non-committal about the result.

Leeds had lost six of their 10 previous games, and five of those had been crunch games against their promotion rivals (Southampton, Norwich, Charlton, Swindon and Millwall). This was their third season stuck in the Third Tier, and their mental strength was being severely doubted.

However this season they at least had the bonus of going into the final day holding their destiny in their own hands, as no-one could overtake them for the second automatic promotion spot if they won that day.

Most neutrals had already written us off, as we could no longer grab a play off slot and would apparently be 'on holiday' in front of a sell out home crowd. The situation reminded me of the old W.G.Grace story, when he refused to walk although he was given out; 'Play on' he is reputed to have said, 'they've come here to see me bat, not you umpire' (or bowl; versions vary). But what they all forgot was that we could put in a decent performance on our day, and more importantly we might need some points in order to finish in the top half of the table, which was not only a matter of pride, but also would give us a chance to improve on last seasons' 11th place finish.

The Peacocks (one of their older, and far more interesting, nicknames) were shaken when Max Gradel, hereafter to be referred to as Mad Max, was sent off after only a third of the match for an infantile stamp on Daniel Jones. No worries Mad Max, it was only their most important game for years you spanner! At first he refused to leave the pitch, then he shoved and jostled his own Captain (Jermaine Beckford of all people) who surprisingly was acting as peacemaker, and finally he had to be escorted off the pitch in his dirty nappy by two security guards. A village in the Ivory Coast truly was missing its idiot that day.

A lot of Leeds fans either didn't see the stamp, or didn't wish to see it, and booed Daniel Jones every time he got the ball. The hard-headed and slightly conceited Jones seemed to be quite at ease with that.

The home crowd were subsequently stunned after half-time when what seemed like an over hit cross from guess who... yes, DJ again... was cleverly kept in play by Jo Kuffour, and Darryl Duffy swivelled and shot into the onion bag. Gasheads were half elated and half mystified. Had Jo Kuffour and Darryl Duffy, one of our weakest ever League One pairings, really just made a lovely goal out of nothing? And even stranger, had they really just done it in a huge game in front of 38,000 people *, without the help of Rickie Lambert?

This lead didn't last long though, as you would never have known we were a man up on the pitch. In a purple patch Leeds took the lead 2-1, and in the tense final minutes, as the Leeds lads massed for the inevitable pitch invasion, our players were more interested in staying near the tunnel than giving Leeds a game of football. To see 10 players bunched up on one touchline was like watching my school mates playing for Weston All Saint's Under 9's on Newbridge Junior School's notoriously hellish pitch positioned on a hill last conquered by Edmund Hillary.

It was a shame that we ended up 11th in the League, although at least we got out of Leeds alive. As it turned out even a draw would have kept us in the ninth place we had rather surprisingly occupied all the time since early April, even though we'd lost four of the previous five games, two of them horrifically, getting stuffed 5-1 by Southampton and then 3-0 by a Norwich City team who played in flip-flops and budgie smugglers. I made that last bit up, but you get the point I'm sure. Both were our home matches as well. This end of season collapse was, for me, the start of our decline and ultimately relegation the following season.

We've never won at Leeds in nine attempts now, and going on recent history we sadly may not be visiting Elland Road again for a very long time.

Footnote

* - Although this crowd was impressive it's still no where near the record attendance we have faced in a regular season League away game. That honour does still lie with Leeds though, when 49,274 watched us at Elland Road in April 1956. Seven cup games or play-off finals top that figure, but no ordinary League matches do.

BLACK FRIDAY 2001

BY JON HUNT

The 2001/2002 season saw Rovers spend their first ever season in the bottom flight of the English football pyramid. With the exception of Nathan Ellington's goals and one cracking day out at Derby County in the F.A. Cup, being a Rovers fan that season was about as much fun as being trapped in a lift with an extended family of City fans.

After a disastrous campaign resulting in relegation the preceding season there were strong expectations amongst the fans that we'd bounce straight back up. There was even a widely touted urban myth that a Rovers Director had turned up late to the first of the Division Four Chairman's Meetings uttering the immortal line 'Sorry we're late but we don't intend on staying here for very long.'

He was almost right as eight months later we found ourselves second bottom of the entire Football League. Even then we could consider ourselves lucky as it was the last season when just a single club was relegated to the Conference. We would have been dead and buried if it weren't for Halifax Town who for reasons known only to themselves had obligingly decided to field the equivalent of a pub team that season.

By late December 2001 we were already looking at the wrong end of the table, in 22nd place. But buoyed by an exciting (and highly unexpected) 3-2 win over Plymouth in a mid-week F.A. Cup replay, my mate and I decided we should hit up Swansea for the away game a few days later. What could be more fun than Swansea City away on the last Friday night before Christmas? Probably quite a few things actually, but I can only surmise that we must have gone a bit heavy on the turps at our work Christmas party prior to making that particular decision.

We got the train from Temple Meads straight after work. It was freezing that night and we ducked into the station bar for a couple of looseners before setting sail for the badlands of South Wales. A bloke got on at

Bridgend and sat opposite us. Having engaged us in conversation and worked out we were Gas he starting cracking on ad infinitum about what a great player Kevin 'Roadrunner' Gall was.

Naturally we both assumed he was either clinically insane or he was talking about a different Kevin Gall to the one we'd seen play numerous times. Great bloke, sure. Great player, not likely. Anyway it transpired that this bloke reckoned he lived in the same street as Kevin Gall's family in Merthyr Tydfil, and reckoned he was best mates and drinking buddies with the Roadrunner's dad. It sounded like a bit of a tall story to me and my mate, but we thought it best to let him just get on with it, although we couldn't resist dropping the occasional 'meep meep' into the conversation when we thought we could get away with it.

After 45 more mind-numbing minutes of this the train mercifully pulled into Swansea station. Arriving in Swansea for the football can be a chastening experience at the best of times, but particularly so when an evening game coincides with Black Friday and you're the only Rovers fans getting off that particular train. Even though we'd hidden our scarves away before we got off the train we both got the clear feeling that all of the Swansea boys dotted around the station knew we were Gas.

We were genuinely the last people who'd be looking for any trouble, but when your mate is six foot four and decides to sport the grade one clipper look all over then you have a tendency to attract a bit of unwanted attention. We both took a bit of a nervous gulp and headed for the barriers, only to be approached by Kevin's dad's mate again. At this point I was starting to regret how we'd mocked him with the Roadrunner impressions, but despite now having the backup of about thirty of Swansea's finest he didn't seem too upset about it.

"You boys want to come to the ground with me?" he said in his Valley's accent, at which point we both just nodded in the hope that silence might provide a better outcome in our current situation than firing off an audible reply in Bristolian. It was clearly a good result as our new mate skillfully chaperoned us past the waiting crew.

We'd been to Swansea a few times before, but always in the daytime and never on Black Friday. It was only about half past six but it was complete pandemonium in town. You've got to hand it to the Welsh, they're mad for a few ales and a big night out. That night they also seemed pretty mad for emptying the contents of their stomachs onto the pavement and having peeing competitions in the middle of the main road. Don't get me wrong, I've been there and done that a few times, but I'd normally save it until after midnight when the traffic's dropped off a bit.

Soon we were into the darker residential streets heading towards the Vetch. Kev's dad's mate was helpfully pointing out all of the pubs not to go in if we wanted to stay alive - which so far seemed to be all of them. I was starting to get the feeling that he was leading us into an ambush. It was seriously cold, December dark, we had no idea where we were, and we'd put our trust in a stranger. To his credit though he ended up showing us to a pub with away fans in it, and then told us how to get to the ground when we were done. We thanked him profusely.

It had become patently clear in the boozer that the few Rovers fans who'd made the trip to South Wales were of the more hardcore variety. By that I mean the type that go to every game no matter how far, how cold, how dangerous and how unlikely the prospect of getting a result. There was a high degree of boasting going on by this stage and one young lad decided he wanted to show us his Gas themed tattoo to prove the depth of his allegiance to the cause. Lifting his shirt up over his back he proudly showed off his newly inked torso. It wasn't immediately clear what the tattoo was meant to be, but I do remember him catching me cocking my head to one side to try and see if his ink made more sense in landscape rather than portrait. He didn't seem that amused.

It turned out it was meant to be a tattoo of the outline of the Pirate from the club logo - stretching from the nape of his neck all of the way down to the top of his arse-beard. Sadly though, he'd run out of money before the tattooist could finish the job and the Pirate was incomplete. Take it from me, our own club logo is not that easy to identify if you remove several limbs and the cutlass from the Pirate and then freehand the result on someone's back in the equivalent of a thick black texter. For his sake I hope he's got the job finished by now, but even then it's going to be more than a bit annoying if the Board decide they've gone right off Pirates and the club changes the logo to something a bit more jazzy.

As we got to the ground the team bus was only just arriving. As it was barely forty minutes to kick-off, we assumed this was not a deliberate preparation for a bottom of the table crunch game. The players duly started trooping off the bus and true to form Kev's dad's mate popped up out of nowhere again and went on to accost the Roadrunner himself as he alighted from the bus. I swear I saw a look of pure fear in Kevin's eyes as he turned to look at his erstwhile stalker. But in fairness to the bloke Kev stepped out of line and had a chat with him so maybe there was some truth to it after all.

I'd like to say that the Vetch was a good place to visit but the truth is that by 2001 the place was a complete dump and quite literally on its last legs. If there had been a prize for the ugliest stadium in Europe it would have comfortably got the chocolates with more than a bit to spare. To put it in context it made the Mem feel a bit like the San Siro. It was just a massive ugly carbuncle of a ground with odd shaped incomplete stands, floodlights in each corner that didn't match, masses of low-covered terracing and some of the foulest toilet facilities known to man or beast.

The away end was a big old covered terrace behind one of the goals with a fetid brick wall for a latrine and a heavily fortified eight foot high replica of a Kenco coffee jar to provide what they classed as catering in Swansea. The 150-odd Rovers fans didn't exactly do the sizeable terrace justice, but at least it was one of those big old echoey stands with a low roof that meant if you got a few of you singing it sounded like a decent racket regardless. And if you scored you could charge kamikaze style down to the front and jump up onto the fencing.

This style of celebration got put through its paces almost immediately when Nathan Ellington scored in just the second minute of the match, sending the away terrace into delirium. Goals were pretty few and far between supporting the Gas in those days, and so they were celebrated with gusto *[Editor's Note - understatement alert - only two Gas goals in the previous 11 games]*. When the chants of "Duke Duke Duke..." had subsided 'Irene' rang out across the stadium, echoing under the tin roof of the away end and heartily winding up the Swansea lads on the North Bank. We eventually returned to our positions higher up on the terrace and then settled in for the expectation of 88 minutes of 11 men behind the ball. Marvellous.

I can honestly say in retrospect that I wish I'd left right there and then. If you discount my surprise at having used the toilet block and escaped without contracting any form of life-threatening illness, then seeing the Duke score his goal was pretty much the only high point of the entire trip. We conceded the equaliser within fifteen minutes and two minutes later Swansea were ahead. As always seemed to happen we'd capitulated under the slightest pressure and it was already hard to see a way back.

The North Bank went mental both times and even though the Vetch was sparsely populated in those days (only 2,734 present), the Swansea boys came charging down to the front of the terrace in a well-practiced manoeuvre giving it large to us in the corner and offering the impression that they were fairly keen to make our acquaintance face to face. We were outnumbered 20 to 1 and it looked fairly unlikely that all 150 of us would be able to squeeze into the giant fortified Kenco jar for protection.

I had scoped out the steel-caged catering facilities at half-time and decided that in fact they were part of an elaborate trap by the Swansea firm to weaken their prey with gastroenteritis. We don't do much well at Rovers but it has to be said that our pasties look like a King's banquet compared to what's served up at Swansea and a lot of other places. Every cloud and all that...

Amusingly Kevin Gall hadn't even made the starting 11 and sat contritely on the bench for the first half. Fortunately for Kev he got a run-out in an uneventful second half, although it would be hard to say that he added to our attacking threat as we didn't really have one at any point.

The full time whistle went and after a limp chorus of 'Irene' we bolted for the station. Scarves hidden, mouths shut, legs pumping. The area around the Vetch was doubly horrible in the dark. Small, tight terraced streets with plenty of dead-ends and dark alleys. We jumped on the first train back to Cardiff. Huh, from Swansea to Cardiff - that's what you call 'out of the frying pan into the fire' I think.

There were a few unpleasant looking blokes wandering up and down the aisle in a fairly menacing manner. After a couple of minutes one of them stopped at our table, looked at me and told me in no uncertain terms that if I wanted to get out of this unscathed I should hide my scarf pretty sharpish. I thought I already had! Anyhow, mentally searching for my third pair of metaphorical clean pants for the night I stuffed my scarf further down my jacket and tried not to make any more eye contact.

Five minutes later he came back and decided to sit on the other side of our table. He'd even brought a mate with him – both of them large, skinheaded, and hammered. I tried to look calm. They were as rough as guts and it was pretty clear from their talk that in the normal course of events we'd have been sliding down the wall in a crumpled mess by this point, but for whatever reason today they just wanted to chat.

It turned out they were from Bridgend and travelled home and away with Swansea. I always remember the most poignant moment in the conversation when one of them told us how gutted he was that Swansea were falling down the Leagues and could go out of business soon, but Cardiff were on the up. He said he only wanted one thing in life and that was for his little boy not to grow up supporting Cardiff because they were higher in the League and doing so much better. He was adamant that Swansea were finished and would never make it out of the bottom flight.

Thirteen years on and Rovers are in the Conference, Cardiff have been relegated back to the Championship and Swansea are still flying high-ish in the Premier League. Back in 2001 you could have bet me a million quid that might happen, and I would have taken that bet and some. He must be like the cat that got the cream now. And I bet his son supports Swansea!

Even though we came from completely different backgrounds I had a total respect for this bloke trying to bring his little boy up to support Swansea who at that point played in front of 3,000 fans at that dump they called the Vetch. I never liked Swansea that much but I'm made up for him that they've got to the big time now. Even if he was a bit scary.

The lads got off at Bridgend and told us not to get the scarves out until we were back over the bridge (yeah, as if we were going to). We got into Cardiff to find the train to Bristol was just a poxy old single carriage job sitting in a neglected platform at the back of the station. The doors were all locked wide open and the lights and heating were off so it was icy freezing in there. We sat on the train with another 30 or so Gasheads and waited for what seemed like an eternity.

By this time it was getting close to midnight and people were getting a bit aggravated. Finally a driver got on the train, jumped in the cab and turned the lights on. We sat for another fifteen minutes and then without warning the lights went out again, the driver jumped out and a bloke in a fluoro jacket told us the train was cancelled and we were all getting a bus back to Bristol.

After more waiting a rickety old bus finally turned up. Mercifully the driver cranked up the heater and we eventually set off home after our disastrous night in South Wales. There was a final shindig as we went over the Severn Bridge when a few of the young 'uns up the back started a bit of handbags and the bus driver lost his marbles because people were standing up in his bus. "For **** sake sit down!" he kept shouting in his whiny Welsh voice over and over - but everyone just ignored him. I thought he was going to stop the bus in the middle of the Severn Bridge and tell us all to get off and walk, but instead, without warning, he started pumping the brakes as hard as he could sending Gasheads flying all over the bus like confetti. Fair play to him, it seemed to do the job, and he got us to Temple Meads some time between 1 and 2am, where I trudged off up the hill to Totterdown to get home and get some sleep.

I was hoping when I woke it would all seem like a bad dream that never actually happened .

LET THE TRAIN TAKE THE STRAIN!

BY PAT STOKES

Ipswich Town - F.A. Cup 5th Round - February 1979

The 70s were dark days for football away fans. As I trudged through Eastville Park I used to watch the away addicts who were coming to Eastville being herded through the M32 subway. They were under Police escort from Stapleton Road railway station. Looking back it seems fairly barbaric tactics but I guess it was the way things were in the 70s.

We had similar treatment on an F.A. Cup trip to Ipswich Town in February 1979. The game was postponed on the Saturday so we bunked off school to take a mid-week 'football special' train to Ipswich. Two trains were organised as I recollect – a 'pink' train and a 'blue' train.

When we got there we were marched straight to Portman Road. Woe betide anyone who stepped outside the general throng. We were deposited into an empty stadium - it was still early. We sang our hearts outs to keep warm. We were armed with ticker tape (it was post Argentina 1978 World Cup). The teams came out, we cheered and we dispensed the ticker tape. Full of expectation, we settled ourselves, and then watched Rovers get thumped 6-1.

The bad icing on a bad cake was the four hour journey home. A logistical cock-up between the trains meant that our train was crammed to the hilt. It was an unofficial world record attempt to see how many footie fans could get on one train. Sadly Norris McWhirter was not there to witness and verify our attempt. In those days there was no buffet car, no wi-fi, no quiet zones and for me, no seat. I stood all the way back contemplating our general collective misery.

I've never been back to Ipswich!

[Editor's Note - This Ipswich side were the holders of the F.A. Cup and finished sixth in the top division that season. Scorers included household names Alan Brazil, Mick Mills, Arnold Muhren, and Paul Mariner.]

AWAY THE GAS Q&A

Imagine you are at an Alcoholics Anonymous meeting. Please stand up and say...

My name is **Matthew Foster** and I have supported Bristol Rovers for 12 years (first match vs. Cambridge Utd, 24th February 2001 - Won 2-1).

We were in League 2 when I starting the Gas /~~Rovers~~ / ~~the Pirates~~

My first away match was the Johnstone's Paint Trophy final against Doncaster Rovers at the Millennium Stadium (1st April 2007).

I have been to 12 away matches at 9 different grounds

My favourite away ground is ...(and why)

Griffin Park (Brentford FC). It has a pub on each corner. 'Nuff said.

I remember my worst ever away journey ...

Swindon Town. Ultra slow moving Police escort to/from the ground / train station. 2-1 defeat. Late-ish winner.

The furthest I've travelled away is ...   Leeds

Best / worst boozer =

There are 2 contrasting Thai restaurants-cum-pubs in Oxford. 'The Old Tom' is good, 'The One' (that's what it's called!) - into which a load of us were herded, straight from the train station - is not.

Best / worst half-time 'entertainment' =

I went to Portsmouth twice last season [2013/14] - once to watch Rovers and previously to watch Exeter City (my mate supports them). During the Exeter game some shouty blonde sort came on-pitch at HT to lecture us about Charles Dickens. More yawn-inducing than the football, if that were possible. Every other HT entertainment was 'best' compared to that.

My favourite home fans are ...(and why)

Portsmouth, although that tattooed hat-wearing bloke with the cow-bell - clearly seen from the opposite end of the ground - can do one.

The best[clean] chant has been …

Umm, are there any clean ones?? The JP Kalala one was funny - to the tune of Queen's Radio Ga Ga - "All we need is, JP Kalala".

The best away goal I've seen was …

Either of Eliot Richards' crackers in the abandoned game at Wycombe. If they don't count, then Craig Hinton's headed equaliser at Craven Cottage. There's a great 30-second video of it on You Tube under the title 'Fulham v Bristol Rovers FA Cup 3rd round 07/08'. Just as a spine-tingling blast of Goodnight Irene subsides, the 7k travelling fans behind the goal are jumping as the ball hits the net.

I really, really wish I had gone to these away games …

All before my time, but I love the You Tube footage of legendary games at Blackpool, Villa Park, Anfield, Ashton Gate, the Madejski etc. Memories of away games that stick in my head, despite me not actually being there, include watching the Play-Off Semi Final win at Lincoln in a bar in Hanioti, Greece, and hearing that we'd beaten Wycombe - and, so we thought/hoped, secured safety - whilst dressed as Keith Lemon at Bishop's Stortford vs. Maidenhead United. The pitch invasion at Adams Park still makes me laugh, despite it being tarnished somewhat by our subsequent relegation.

I regret … we didn't sign a half-decent target man to replace Ricky Lambert. Maidenhead United, at the time, had a striker called Mustafa Tiryaki who went on to play for Tranmere Rovers and now plies his trade in the Turkish First Division. Hardly prolific at League level, admittedly, but someone of his physical stature would've helped us stay in League One, methinks. Instead we had midgets like Jo Kuffour feeding off scraps.

Have you ever worn fancy dress? Not to a Rovers game yet but I have done fourteen years in a row to the last Maidenhead United away game of the season.

Our worst shirt sponsor was Eurocams (red on the kit, plus forever associated with relegation from the Football League)

Rovers at the old Wembley for the Leyland DAF Cup Final vs. Tranmere Rovers - 20th May 1990

Note that Devon White has just scored the equaliser in the middle photo!

All photos courtesy of Rick Weston

The 1989/90 Third Division Championship winning team in an open top bus procession in Kingswood [May 1990]

Both photos courtesy of Rick Weston

Play-Off Final win in May 2007 at the new Wembley.

TOP - Mike and Ian outside the stadium

MIDDLE - Far to Front - Mike, Phil, Scott and Russ King, in the Rovers shirt

Both photos courtesy of Russ King

BOTTOM - Gashead young 'un

Photo by Martin Bull

Montage of photos (broken foot no obstacle) from the Play-Off Final win in May 2007 at the new Wembley. The Gashead doesn't look very impressed by the horse!

All photos courtesy of Chris Bull

LEFT - Gary Collins, Will Bradley and Wayne Collins before one the more recent London away games.

ABOVE - Noddy ticket for first ever visit to AFC Wimbledon. Library photocopier job?

BELOW - Tom Hurd, Wayne Collins and Gary Collins soaked at Stockport County.

All photos courtesy of Wayne Collins

BOTTOM - Hereford's 'Executive' boxes.

Photo by Martin Bull

All photos by Martin Bull

TOP - 'Say No To Drugs' at Hereford United thrashing - March 2009

ABOVE LEFT - 4.47pm: Spot the waterlogged pitch & driving rain at Wycombe!! - August 2012

ABOVE RIGHT - Carlisle Utd fancy dressers - February 2009 - It was a thriller of a game...

BELOW LEFT - Wondrous Barnet sunset - Better than the match - August 2012

BELOW RIGHT - 'Sauce Station' at Doncaster Rovers - March 2008

ABOVE - Colin Clark and his sister Linda celebrating arriving back (alive!) from a 2-2 draw at Cardiff on 12th April 1975. Note Severn Bridge in background as if they daren't stop until they got over it. For photos of Colin, and son, 24 years later please see page 158.

Photo courtesy of Rich Clark

BELOW RIGHT - What a mess! Crewe's Gresty Road in 1995. Both photos below courtesy of Glen Young

BELOW LEFT - John Taylor being greeted off the pitch by Gasheads on the Isle of Wight pre-season tour - the first one in 1994?

ABOVE - Shrewsbury Town v Rovers - 29th December 1979 - Gary Emmanuel about to put in a cross in the gloom of Gay Meadow.

BELOW - Swansea City v Rovers - 5th April 1980 - Phil Bater preparing to take a free kick at the Vetch Field.

Both photos courtesy of David Maddy

YOU WON'T BELIEVE THIS MATE...

This chapter includes anything super interesting and vaguely outlandish that doesn't clearly fit elsewhere.

It's a smor**gas**bord of fantastic short stories and tall tales, including thrashing Reading in 1999, Rovers fans standing on a freezing concrete terrace in just their socks, the steward with serious vertigo, the day Steve Yates almost scored a goal, a meeting with Malcolm Allison on a train, and why only five Gasheads arrived at Swansea City on a 52 seater coach.

WASTE NOT, WANT NOT
BY PETE WEBB

So many memories, and probably so much I've forgotten too.

Luton Town on the supporters club train. I can't remember how far it got but I remember being stuck on the train for a long time while we waited to go home. We had stopped on a bridge overlooking a random High Street somewhere. Someone threw a toilet roll out the window. It hit the pavement with still a fair bit of it left. An old lady came over, picked it up, tore off the streamer and put it in her shopping bag.

Preston North End away in the F.A. Cup Third Round on 3rd January 1981. It was the season Terry Cooper was in charge and we had only won once all season at that point. We romped to a 4-0 lead; even before half-time! The heavens opened though and we thought the game was going to be called off. Thankfully the second half got underway. Preston got three back, but we held on to win 4-3.

Bristol City away on New Years Day 1987. Of course we'd been out the night before until the pubs shut and then carried on at home. There were a few regulars missing at the match that day because of hangovers. But what a game. It had it all. Admittedly they were all over us. Timmy Carter going off injured. Boris taking over in goal. And then Gary Smart's goal. Being slightly hung over myself I was just beginning to feel a bit better when the goal went in and I had to jump up and down to celebrate. At the end of the game we were able to pick up enough coins that were thrown way too short at us from the Dolman Stand to be able to go and have a pint on the way home to celebrate.

Wolves away in March 1989 with Dennis Bailey's goal. The car broke down, and just got home in time to be able to go to work next day.

Away games that didn't happen - **Wigan Athletic** was once called off about ten minutes before the game was due to start. I'd travelled up on Thursday and stayed with a mate up that way.

HOME AND AWAY – ALL IN A SINGLE GAME
BY MARTIN BULL

My most visited away ground is surprisingly Leyton Orient's Brisbane Road, a legacy of living in or near London for eight years and not having many other fixtures in the area to go to.

My six visits there haven't been particularly eventful though, except for the September 2004 match when somehow my mate Mike got separated from us Gasheads and ended up in the home section where he enigmatically stayed until half-time. We waved and gestured at each other across the divide, as if arranging a mime fight with Marcel Marceau's firm, or having a weird mute bromance.

To this day neither of us can adequately explain what went on, why we got separated, why there wasn't proper segregation between home and away stairwells, and why he stayed there for a whole 45 minutes of footy.

We think it was something to do with his ticket. I had my ticket in advance and in my hand, whereas Mike's decision to come to the match was too late to get the ticket in the post, so I bought one over the 'phone and was told to collect it from Brisbane Road. When I asked at the ground they told me to go to what seemed like a back door or a VIPs entrance. I half expected to have to utter a secret password and learn a Masonic handshake to get in. Once the door opened they pulled my ticket out of a wooden pigeon hole, as if I was in a medieval Oxbridge college, rather than rubbing shoulders with Leytonstone, the porn capital of London.

However, after getting through the 'away' turnstiles, we somehow got separated and as Mike followed the instructions on his ticket, and I did on mine, I ended up with the Gas lads (as expected), whereas Mike seems to have gone behind Mr. Benn's magic curtain because he ended up in the home section, and he swears to me that he was in the seat numbered on the ticket.

At half-time we met up and he came over to the away end. We then lost 4-2. The Jonah should have stayed in the home section!

11 GOOD MEN AND TRUE
BY MIKE JAY

My friend Colin and myself decided to visit all the 92 League grounds, so opportunities to visit new stadiums were always on our radar. We of course had seen Rovers play Reading at their old and rundown Elm Park ground several times, so the prospect of seeing a new purpose built all seater stadium was a real bonus.

We set off from Bristol early on the morning of Saturday 16 January 1999 down the M4 motorway towards the Madejski Stadium.

Rovers had been beaten 4-3 at home by Burnley the previous Saturday so we travelled to Reading only in hope. The Royals themselves were fresh from a 4-0 win over Wrexham and included a familiar debutant in their starting line up; former Rovers full back Andy Gurney. Rovers included Andy Thomson, a new signing from Portsmouth, for his debut.

The first half was pretty much even Stephen but who could predict such a remarkable second half. Six goals for Rovers in one half! We found it hard to take in. The main difference was that Rovers moved up a gear whereas Reading entirely failed to keep up with the increasing speed of the game.

The first came from a ball played through the middle of the defence. Cureton, always a threat, ran onto it, Scott Howie came out and Jamie stuck it into the back of the net. The second goal was comedy gold; two defenders bundling over Jason Roberts for no good reason for the most obvious penalty you're ever going to see. Up stepped Cureton again putting the ball low to Howie's left. Reading's Clement then lost it completely and was lucky to stay on the pitch for getting way over physical with Roberts who gave him the run around throughout the half.

More defensive mistakes gifted Rovers their third. Caskey made a bad pass, the ball bounced back leaving Cureton with yet another opportunity to take on Howie. 3-0. Moments later Roberts, who was on fire, set up

Cureton again inside the penalty area and he hit his fourth goal home - all in the space of 20 remarkable minutes. Shades of Germany v Brazil in the World Cup semi final 2014.

Reading's spectacular collapse was still only two thirds of the way through though. Howie pulled off a couple of spectacular saves to keep the score down and a few shots narrowly missed the target. After his set ups for Cureton justice was done when Roberts completed the scoring with two late goals which made up for those first half misses, and sent the Gasheads wild. More shocking defending by the dispirited home side helped him on his way, Roberts was able to simply walk past three defenders like they just weren't there. Both Cureton and Roberts were later in their careers to join Reading for large fees, while the Reading goalkeeper Scott Howie later joined Rovers.

Rovers won 6-0 watched by 13,286 fans, including about 3,000 delirious Gasheads. Those loud away fans contributed to Reading's second highest League gate of the season and we were informed afterwards that we were "without doubt the loudest fans ever to visit the Madejski". But we did have plenty to get excited about; 6-0 away wins don't happen too often, although I did see a 5-0 win at Wigan Athletic in 1983 with an inspired performance by Alan Ball, the famous 1966 World Cup winner.

That afternoon we left the stadium in a real daze buoyed by such an amazing performance by these players:

LEE JONES, STEPHANE LEONI, TREVOR CHALLIS, ROB TREES, STEVE FOSTER, ANDY THOMSON, IAN HOLLOWAY, DAVID LEE, MARK McKEEVER, JAMIE CURETON & JASON ROBERTS.

As we got into the car we switched the radio on and awaited what the footballing world thought about this incredible feat. We joined a long line of cars streaming home to Bristol, and as we reached the broadcasting area we heard fans recall their emotions on Radio Bristol.

A super day out, a new stadium to chalk off, and a memorable win against a decent side.

THESE BOOTS WERE MADE FOR...

COLLECTING AFTER THE GAME MATE!

BY MARK COUSINS

- We went to Luton Town for a game on a bitter night. The coppers were testing Gasheads boots for steel toe caps by standing on them. A couple of lads who had them on were made to take them off and stand on the freezing concrete terracing in their socks for the duration of the game.

- I can't remember what game it was but we were returning from a London game and pulled into the services near Newbury. We'd only been there a few mins when the Cardiff mob pulled in. It was decided we would leave pretty quick and in doing so poor old Oscar* got left behind.

  - Any Rovers fan of a certain age will know Oscar. He was part of the furniture at Eastville and was Rovers through and through. He sold programmes at home games, and scarves and rosettes etc., and also went to the away games.

- Whilst coming home from Derby County (the Baseball Ground) on the coach, we pulled into Frankley services and while we were in there some scallies got on the coach and pinched my mum's bag and blanket! I remember the Police caught them somewhere as I had a phone call to say I could pick the stuff up at Bromsgrove Police Station of all places.

I OWE ELIOT RICHARDS AN APOLOGY

BY MARTIN BULL

The night game at Huddersfield Town in January 2010 was not surprising-ly rather sparse in the cavernous away end. As my brother and I tried to while away the pre-match calm behind the stand we noticed a white board with bookies odds on it (see dreadful photo below).

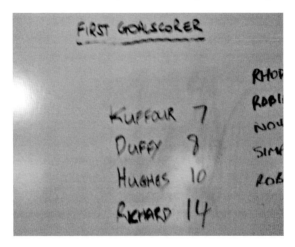

As my bro had a replica shirt with 'Kuffour - 17' on the back, he was quite happy to see little Jo's name at the top of the 'First Goal scorer' list, at 7-1. Darryl 'Powder Puff' Duffy was next at 8's, and Jeff 'where am I supposed to be playing boss?' Hughes was a decent bet at 10-1 as although he never seemed to know where on the pitch he should be, and certainly would never stick to it anyway, he did know where the goal was. Finally the name 'Richard' completed the list at 14-1. We both looked at each other and said in unison, "who's Richard?". "Never heard of 'im" was the classic reply; in sibling stereo.

As well as suffering the ignominy of two vaguely grown up brothers not knowing who the hell he was, that was probably also one of a thousand times that poor Eliot had his name spelt wrong. Over the years we regularly saw in the press 'Elliott Richards', and 'Eliot Richard'. Ok, so it's not exactly as bad as my school classmate Richard Head who quite happily cruised along at school until the mid-1980's when by using a certain version of his first name his whole name was turned into a new term of abuse that had swept in from America, but having your name spelt wrong is one of those de-humanising aspects of existence that just goes to prove that modern life truly is rubbish.

Then at Swindon Town in October 2010, I was buying a cup of tea [manly!] from the heavily fortified refreshments area, when the young lad serving me said "Do you have a guy called Eliot Richards in your team?". "No", I said, "I don't think so...". "Oh, really? ... he's a young lad, I used to know him at xxx [insert random, peripheral place of non-inti-mate encounter, such as college, or youth club], he was a really good footballer". "Maybe... he's a youth player then..." I limply replied, trying to be vaguely magnanimous to the spotty burger flipper. Inside, however, I was screaming 'NEVER heard of him mush. Either you Sir are suggesting I am not much of a knowledgeable fan, or you've been conned into fawning over some jumped up trout who used to do bountiful keepie uppies in the school yard and in jest swindled you into thinking he was a professional footballer!!'.

Needless to say it was the former. I really wasn't that clued up over our young players, and hadn't bothered to learn my lesson from Huddersfield. Doh.

If I had denied Eliot one more time before a cock crowed it would have rivalled Peter in the Bible.

So, I have to say sorry Eliot.

Or is it Elliott?

Or Elliot?

2-1 TO THE R-OOO-VERS

BY MARTIN BULL

Between 1998 and 2003 Arsenal won 1-0 an incredible 242 times.

Ok, that's a lie but I'm sure you do remember how Arsenal were famed for their ability to grind out a narrow win, by means of a lone goal and a watertight defence, accompanied by the chant 'one nil to the Arsen-al' from the stands.

This story is not quite on a par with that but we did famously enjoy six 2-1 wins in a row in our march to the Third Tier Championship in 1989/90, and I was honoured to be there for the first three of the series.

Those six wins were all within 22 hectic days. People talk about fixture pile-ups now but in that spring of 1990 our fixtures were piled up higher than an EU butter mountain, and this made the achievement even more marvellous.

In January and February 1990 Rovers managed to play just seven games. In contrast, from 3rd March to the famed season closer at Blackpool 64 days later we ploughed through 18 games. This consisted of two games every week for over two months, except a solitary week with a well earnt mid week break, and a crazy week where we played Monday and Thursday, in between the regular Saturday matches of course. What the Lord giveth, he taketh away; and double usually!

When I ventured to Fulham in March 1990, it was not only my first ever visit to Craven Cottage but was also only my third ever away game. I was at Uni at Reading and although I had been to London for several trips to West Ham United in the massive old North Terrace, as they were childhood favourites of mine, this was my first away game outside of my two trips to Reading F.C.

I didn't know London well at the time, but I knew that their neighbours Chelsea had a bad reputation, so I went to the game (on my own) under the erroneous belief that Fulham must be a rough lot as well. I faintly remember meeting a fellow Gashead or two at the tube station and as we all seemed to be rather clueless and slightly apprehensive we shared a taxi to the ground, something I've never done before or since, in the 24 following years. I distinctly remember gazing out of the window as we took the short trip, and as we went passed a boozer lots of colossal looking guys seemed to be on the pavement outside jeering us with glasses in their hands as we went past. They probably weren't of course, but all of this went to reinforce my feeling of foreboding, and later, whilst making my way back to Putney Bridge tube station on my own, I remember looking over my shoulder whilst walking though the riverside park with my Rovers top on.

Years later, around the turn of the Millennium, I became firm friends with Chris Brooks, a Fulham supporter, and he laughed his socks off at my little story, before describing his own fans as "a bunch of pansies". In fact his memory of Rovers fans is centered on when our lads apparently went to take over the home end in a match at the Cottage in the 1980's. Chris recollects that the Fulham fans 'parted like the Red Sea' and practically invited the Pirates to come on board, eat their food, take their seats and have their wicked way with their women folk. With no-one interested in a fight the Gas lads were probably so confused they didn't know what to do with themselves!

If Fulham was the start of an impressive sequence, what was truly astounding was that in each of the next five games we went behind first, yet came back each and every time to run out 2-1 winners.

The best of these upturns was against Cardiff City in front of less than 5,000 fans. We were 1-0 down with barely minutes remaining. Lots of Gasheads had already trooped out of Twerton as it seemed like it was just one of those days where we weren't ever going to breach their resolute defence. But Paul Nixon (on as a sub) and David Mehew (as ever!) scored two incredibly late goals, in 11 minutes of injury time (yes, that's not a typo, **eleven** minutes!) to keep our run going. It was like Fergie time, and it really seemed like the ref was just going to keep on playing until we won! :-)

Cardiff were relegated that season by a solitary point, so looking back at it, those late late goals sadly cost them dearly. As a nostalgia trip it's amazing to remember Cardiff in the bottom division and us promoted to what is now the Championship. It's easy to overlook that Swansea City, Reading, Hull City, Fulham, Blackpool, Wigan Athletic, Bolton Wanderers, Brighton & Hove Albion, etc. were regular visitors to Rovers in the Third or Fourth Tiers. Yet where are those awful teams, with their shocking decrepit stadiums, now?

TRUMPED UP REASON NO. 154 FOR EJECTING A FAN - TAKING THE P...

BY BLUEGLOSS54

Plymouth Argyle - Not sure of the year but it was before the ground was redeveloped. A regular stream of fans from both sides were being escorted out of the ground for one thing and another. As the game was rather lifeless a couple of Rovers fans at the open end decided to burn their match day programmes. Along came the Police to stamp them out, accompanied by a rendition of the 'Z Cars' theme tune [a TV cop series to you young 'uns] and a few boos and hisses. Myself and two others were ejected from the ground. The reason they gave me, to quote one of the Police escorting me out, was "for taking the p*ss"!

Ipswich Town - A F.A. Cup 5th Round match mysteriously played on a Monday night in February 1979. A rubbish journey on the coaches to the middle of Suffolk, but a tremendous turn out by the Rovers and non-stop singing all game during a 6-1 defeat! Spirits on the bus were high considering the result. There was loads of singing going on and some rather dubious acts happening in the rear of the coach to the chorus of "gumbelina gumbelina I am next". We stopped at a service station and then found we had to push start the bus as the driver had left the lights on while having his break!

[Editor's Note - This Ipswich side were the holders of the F.A. Cup and finished sixth in the top division that season.]

CONFESSIONS OF A COACH DRIVER
BY ADE MONNERY (GASSYADE)

There are two away memories that will stay with me forever.

The first was on Boxing Day in 2002 when we visited the Vetch Field. I was a coach driver at the time and was on a Christmas tour with some oldies. The itinerary revealed a morning tour of the Rhondda Valley, due back by 12 noon. The brain cells went into overdrive thinking about the possibility of getting to the match, so I raced around to finish the tour. My friends were told to meet me at our hotel on the outskirts of Cardiff and I would use the coach to take just the five of us to Swansea.

When we turned up at the Vetch with crimbo decs up on display and only the five of us on the coach the local old bill almost had kittens assuming we had dropped the rest of the group in the City centre for drinks. The best bit was that as a coach driver carrying 'passengers' I got in free to watch Rovers, and also to see my mates splitting their sides at what we had done.

At the end of the game we found our own way out by driving up a no entry to get out of Swansea. The other coaches went the official diversion and from what we were led to believe were ambushed on the M4 with various items raining down on the coaches from Jacks fans waiting on one of the bridges. It was a lucky escape not only for us but also for me personally as any damage to the coach would have been hard to explain!

[Editor's Note - a 1-0 away win (courtesy of Paul 'Goal Machine' Tait) probably didn't help their mood. It ended a club record eight consecutive defeats for us that stretched back exactly two months, and had included four games in a row where Rovers didn't even score. During this period Rovers not surprisingly fell to the bottom of the bottom division, for the first time in our history.]

My second away memory was the famous F.A. Cup Third Round tie vs Derby County in January 2002 which became the Ellington show.

Once again I was driving a coach and made it perfectly clear to the fans boarding that I was a Gashead too. We put on videos to keep the masses entertained. Before departure I was told that we all had to meet up at the last services to run "in convoy"... Pah, that was not for me, so as the last coach to depart we decided to play motorway coach rally, a.k.a. coach bingo. We passed the other coaches at an amazing rate which the punters enjoyed as their pre match entertainment. We passed the final coach on the M42 and sensing that there was no point in pulling in to the services as we were all needing liquid refreshment, we barrelled on to Derby. There were a few drop offs on the way in for those who thought they'd be fit enough to walk after a few pints.

Nobody gave us a chance of success but Ellington became a man that day. Struggling at the wrong end of the table and under the caretaker management of Garry Thompson we were gifted the opener, and 'The Duke' banged in three in succession. It was only in the closing minutes that we let in Derby's Ravenelli to score a consolation. This Premier League team of underachievers just lost to lowly Bristol Rovers, who if I recall correctly remarkably set an away attendance record of over 6,500; bear in mind that at the time we were close to going out of the Football League and only had Halifax below us.

The journey home was a joyful one that I shall remember for a long time.

QUITE INTERESTING AWAY STATS

Bruce Bannister is the only Rovers player ever to have scored a first half hat trick at an away game, during the infamous 8-2 win at Brian Clough's new club, Brighton & Hove Albion, on the 1st December 1973. Alan Warboys trumped him with the final four goals of the game, but his came split between both halves. That result was the worst home defeat in the entire Football League since Wolves thrashed Cardiff 9-1 at Ninian Park in a First Division match in 1955-56.

THE HOME GAME THAT BECAME AN AWAY GAME
BY WRECKLESS

Chelsea - Tuesday night game at Eastville - October 1976

I had hitched down with my friend, a Chelsea supporter. He wanted to go in the Chelsea end. Given that he was wearing his scarf and had a broad London accent, I thought this was probably the safest place for him to be and agreed to go with him.

We went one up (Bruce Bannister) before Ossie equalised around 70 mins. The Chelsea fans had been a bit restive, not helped by the fact that their team weren't playing well and that we were out in the open and it was raining. I had been hiding my smiles and laughing inwardly. Then five minutes from time, right in front of us, Dave Staniforth heads into the net.

Dead silence, except for yours truly who jumps briefly in the air to celebrate, before remembering where I am. The Chelsea fans were not happy (to say the least) and my friend suggested that we leave, which we did, to great abuse.

By now it was chucking it down, but at least we were first to the M32 slip road and got a superb lift back towards London in one of the biggest Jags I have ever seen, driven by a Chelsea fan who picked us up thinking we were both Chelsea supporters.

It was somewhere around Swindon that he twigged that I was an alien, by which time he couldn't really chuck us out.

My favourite away game though was the 5-0 win at Oxford in January 2000 where Jamie Cureton bagged a hat trick.

This was my younger son's first game. His name is Jamie. He dropped off at one point, but woke up to the sound of us all singing "Jamie, Jamie."

He thought it was for him. I didn't dare bring him down to earth by telling him that this was as good as it was ever going to get...

OUT FOR A DUCK?
BY CRAIG R

Northampton Town 1990

Rovers on course for promotion, a really hot day Spring day and most Rovers fans stood behind the goal on the Spion Kop. Really odd setting, in those days part of Northampton's pitch was used as the Northampton-shire County Cricket Ground in the summer, so it was one of the most quirky, half made grounds I have ever seen.

Rovers went 1-0 down but made one of their famous rallies of the time to come back and win 2-1, with Christian 'Crazy Legs' McClean equalising and 'Ollie scoring the winner.

What really stands out for me (and a few other Rovers fans of my genera-tion) was a bullet like shot by Steve Yates in the second half. It may not sound that amazing I know, but this effort was about 30/35 yards out and it was if Bobby Charlton himself hit it, staying about three feet off the ground the whole way before the 'keeper tipped it round the post. I never saw Yates shoot at goal before or after, although it's strange that later in his career he scored 14 goals for another Rovers, Tranmere.

[Editor's Note - Steve Yates, one of my favourite ever players, never ever scored for Rovers despite 196 League appearances, 41 Cup appearances and 1 sub appearance. Not surprisingly that is a record for a Rovers outfield player and I strongly suspect it will never be beaten.]

FEEDBACK & MORE CONTRIBUTIONS

Please send any feedback to me at - hello@awaythegas.org.uk - and please keep contributions coming in just in case there is a 2nd edition.

Martin Bull

www.awaythegas.org.uk

'R' IS FOR RELEGATED &
YOU'LL NEVER GET RID OF THE HORN
(12" MEGA MIX)

BY MARTIN BULL

I went to Millwall's old ground, the Den, once, in November 1991, when we were enjoying a resurgence under Dennis Rofe, and were once again holding our own in the Second Tier after the brief, and rather disastrous, reign of Martin Dobson. I don't remember much about it apart from lots of fences, vast swathes of bog standard terracing (as most old grounds still had), and a huge floodlight pylon plonked right in the middle of our away bit. Recent triumphs at challenging places like Wolves and Barnsley must have done wonders for our confidence as the record books show we won 1-0, from yet another David Mehew goal (the most under-rated goal scoring 'midfielder' I've ever seen). Unfortunately I have no recollection of anything match related   No change there then!

We seemed to have had a hoodoo over Millwall for a short while. We also went there on the final day of the season after, didn't read the script, and ruined their final ever game at the Den with a resounding 3-0 win. This was particularly bewildering because we had already been relegated and were a pretty feeble team. A quirky fact is that we were also the opposition when Millwall played their first ever Football League match at the Den, on 28th August 1920, the season both of our teams joined.

It had actually taken me three weeks from that 3-0 drubbing to even know that we had been relegated. In fact as we had been mathematically relegated 15 days earlier, on 24th April 1993, in actuality I had gone a startling 36 days before learning of our sad end to three exciting and battling seasons in the Second Tier. I had almost matched Jesus, with his frankly sluggish 40 days and nights in the wilderness.

So, how did this 36 day delay happen I hear you ask? And is it a Gashead record? Or can I sense snoring at the back?

I had been in a coma since February and after a family request for his potent presence by my bedside, I had miraculously awoken to the dulcet tones of Malcolm Allison twittering away next to me. As I sat bolt upright, like in a low budget horror movie, I turned to Big Mal (nurses tutting in the background as he offers me a huge stogie and a glass of Dom Perignon) and asked him, "How did the rest of the season go Mal?". He delicately breaks it me that we had been relegated over five weeks ago, and that he had been usurped by a young upstart no-one had heard of, named John Francis Ward. I wept profusely as I gripped the lapels of his sheepskin coat, pulled his face up to mine, and pleaded in my hammiest American accent, 'Tell me is ain't so Mal? Tell me it ain't true!'. As he tipped his Fedora to me and pursed his sad, ashened lips, I slipped back into my coma...

That would be a first-rate fable if it were true.

I reality I had been travelling on an overland truck in North and West Africa, and in that uncomplicatedly quaint age before the Internet and cheap international calls, information was slow and came at a premium. No-one on our truck had bothered to bring a radio and most were too busy skinning up to have been physically capable of finding a tuning button anyway. British newspapers were hard to come by, and VERY expensive for a budget traveller, especially when in the Francophone countries that dominate the West African interior.

I can't remember where I finally saw the Millwall result, but I remember it was in a random capital city, it was exactly three weeks after the paper had come out in the UK, and that it came via a friend on the charabanc who was even more desperate than me to read a British newspaper and to remember the dear old Blighty we had left behind some three months previous.

British papers could usually only be found in posh hotels, which was an obstacle in itself as we looked abysmal and could easily be mistaken for dirty street dwellers. In a strange way though it was nice to see that the 'ism' people faced when going into a posh international hotel in 'Black' Africa, wasn't racism, because hard-up unkempt people of ALL colours would be looked down upon, and a midget in a Colonial style red uniform and fez would probably follow you along the marbled halls liberally squirting air freshener behind you as you walked.

Usually we just wanted to go there for the chance to visit a toilet that didn't resemble an open sewer that a man with amoebic dysentery had just sprayed his faeces around in an epic circle, like a drunk yokel on a Somerset farm operating a disobedient slurry spreader.

The paper was therefore a bonus and given the hideously inflated cost I was quite happy that my friend had bought it and not me. The down side of this godsend was that you'd certainly have to wait for your chance to get to read it, and you may also need to 'contribute' a shekel or two for the privilege. It was the Sunday Times I think and was as thick as a thousand inhabitants of the Dolman Stand. I had to wait a full day to get my turn as the owner not only picked over every morsel of information like a tramp going through a discarded bag of chips, but flatly refused to even let me just peep at the footy results for one minute and then give it back to him. It was agony knowing that that simple wodge of ink black-ened paper right in front of my eyes held all the information I had craved for about three months now!

When I finally got to see it all my dreams of a fight back and a rise up the table whilst I'd been incommunicado evaporated within seconds. I scanned down the results and seeing that we had beaten Millwall 3-0 on that last day gave me some hope... which was then quashed a millisec-ond later as I looked at the table below and our proud name was there listed last; rock bottom of the table. Bristol Rovers (R). R for relegated.

It looked so harsh like that, especially without knowing any of the results for the past three months. Little did I know that after leaving Britain in February we hadn't ever turned the season around, and had been bottom since March, resulting in an effortless relegation on a miserable tally of just 41 points.

I do actually have a genuine Malcolm Allison story though, from those heady few months when he was in charge.

After the home game to Sunderland in January 1993 I was rushing off to Birmingham straight after the game and roped my Mum into ferrying me straight to the train station after picking me up from the Herman Miller building by the River Avon (years later I found out this building was a revolutionary design classic, whereas all us school kids who had passed it every day in the 80's thought it was just a hideous plastic blob that needed a good flood to wash it away). As I waited for the train I noticed a large man in a beige trench coat and fedora hat (I kid yee not) arrive on the platform. I almost did a double take as I realised it was Big Mal himself. It was barely 5.30pm so I really didn't expect him to be there, and he must have left the ground very abruptly after the match, as I had skedaddled the second the whistle went and had also cunningly avoided a lot of the traffic by being picked up on the opposite bank of the Avon.

I'm not the sort of person who finds it easy to talk to 'famous' people so I didn't speak to him. From my memory no-one had spotted him, and I don't remember any other Gasheads there anyway, as they would still be on their way from Twerton. As the west bound train came it was one of those little two carriage sprinter things that plied their trade between the South Coast and Wales. We got on at different doors but after I walked up the carriages I realised it was really full. I could see the last seat in the distance and as I got closer I realised it was next to some big guy who hadn't taken his trench coat off yet. I really didn't want to fawn over Big Mal (a coach who had won the First Division, European Cup Winners Cup, F.A. Cup, and League Cup remember!), but equally I wanted to sit down after standing on the Popular Side terrace for two-plus hours.

Not long after I sat down I realised a few Gasheads must have made it onto the train at the last minute, as one young lad, proudly wearing his replica shirt, came up to our seats and hesitantly asked Big Mal if he'd "sign this" for him.

'This' was today's programme, which he had shrewdly pre-opened to a double page spread containing the official squad photos from both teams on facing pages. Mal seemed to be... um... how shall I say this politely... on another planet inhabited by pixies and elves and as he went to sign it I could see he was aiming for the Sunderland page. I respectfully turned to him and whispered "I think the lad would prefer it on the Rovers page", to which he shifted his aim and gave a low grunt of acquiescence.

Unbeknown to us at the time, this was the last time we would ever face Sunderland in the Football League, which seemed slightly unthinkable at the time as we had got quite used to playing them and hadn't actually lost any of our final seven League encounters against them.

It wasn't always like that though. We played 12 times at Roker Park in the League and never won once. In fact we took regular beatings, including 6-1 in 1962, 5-1 in both 1974 and 1977, and 5-0 in 1978. We did however inexplicably win our only ever Cup game there, a 1-0 win in the F.A. Cup Third Round in 1978, less than two months after being trashed 5-1 in the League game for that season.

I didn't get to go to the New Den with Rovers until August 2005, when a few hundred Gasheads turned up for our one and only ever League Cup meeting so far with the Lions. As the crowd was as sparse as a First Round match befits, we had the entire West Stand to ourselves, although we were corralled into just one section of the steep top tier.

As we lost 2-0 and were never really in the game we had to make our own entertainment in the stands. The old Victorian piano from the parlour couldn't be squeezed into the ground to allow Mrs Mills to bash out cheesy mockney songs, so we had to make do with the second best thing; an air horn. This smuggled contraband parped away in unison to our songs as the stewards watched us like hawks to try to find out where it was. Several times they 'went in' like Commandos to try to confiscate it, but each time they were foiled by Pirate delay tactics and some nifty slight of hand work that cunningly passed the offending horn around a group of wily mates.

This seemed to go on for ages, and songs sprang up to taunt the stewards even more; "You can't find our horn, tra la la la la", to Boney M's 'Brown Girl in the Ring', and "You don't know where the horn is" to the tune of the 'You don't know what you're doing' chant that is usually reserved for clueless refs.

As if this couldn't get any more comical (no-one was watching the game by this point), extra stewards were sent to spy their beady eyes on the naughty schoolboys on the metaphorical back seat of the bus. One tall, very overweight newbie steward, presumably chosen as a match for the stereotype of a nightclub bouncer, immediately caught my eye as he shuffled from foot to foot and looked strangely uncomfortable on the lower slope of the gangway. As their supervisor barked at them to walk up the steep steps towards the miscreants, this lads head seemed to be spinning.

Within seconds he was down on the floor, as if licking the cold grey concrete. His orange jacketed colleagues tried to find out if he was ok, and it became clear that it was just a bad case of vertigo. Presumably he'd never done this job before, or maybe didn't even know he couldn't handle steep inclines. He did now!

As slowly as an asthmatic snail he started to crawl backwards down the steps, not daring to look behind him or down. This seemed to last forever, and seeing a big lad like that rendered utterly helpless by nothing more than man made concrete fabricated altitude was hilarious but also agonising, all at the same time. I was waiting for a heartless Gashead, the class clown on the back row maybe, to start up a chorus of the 'beep beep' tone you get when ginormous lorries are reversing.

The vertigo incident made me take my eye off what happened to the horn. I have a memory that they found the horn and triumphantly confiscated it, only for a second horn to be produced to provoke them yet again. This may well be a totally erroneous memory, but if true I think it would be a fitting end to this ripping yarn.

AWAY THE GAS Q&A

Imagine you are at an Alcoholics Anonymous meeting. Please stand up and say...

My name is MARTIN BULL and I have supported Bristol Rovers for 25 years

We were in Division 3 (3rd TIER) when I starting supporting ~~Rovers / the Pirates~~ / the Gas (which do you prefer?)

My first ever away match was READING FC - 21/11/1989

I have been to approx 95 away matches at 58 different grounds

---

My favourite away grounds are ... (and why)
- HEREFORD - CRAZY STADIUM WITH LOUD FANS.
- BOTH ELM PARK & THE MANOR GROUND [READING & OXFORD'S OLD GROUNDS] BOTH HAD A CERTAIN RUN DOWN CHARM!

I remember my worst ever away journey ...
HEREFORD (AGAIN) - 2009 - GOT MY TIMING WRONG - GATES WERE LOCKED. FINALLY GOT IN ALMOST 1/2 HOUR LATE (SEE BELOW).

The furthest I've travelled away is ... PROBABLY ONLY MANCHESTER TO NORWICH (VIA LEEDS) BUT IT SEEMED TO GO ON & ON & ON FOREVER! 420 MILES OVERALL.

The earliest / latest I ever got to a match was ... @HEREFORD
- VERY RARELY EVER EARLY. HA HA.
- LATEST - WAS WALKED OVER TO THE GAS END AS RICKIE LAMBO CRACKED HIS FIRST GOAL IN [26th MINUTE]

Best / worst grub = AS A VEGGIE I'VE GOT USED TO EATING THIN AIR OR EATING WAY OUTSIDE THE GROUND. SOME GOOD CHIPS (eg. LEEDS) OR A PASTY IS ABOUT THE BEST I EVER GET.

Best / ~~worst~~ boozer = BURTON! COOPER'S TAVERN, A TINY VICTORIAN BREWERS TAP FROM WHEN BASS WAS A PROPER BREWERY. BEERS SERVED DIRECTLY FROM THE CASK. (☺)

Best / worst half-time 'entertainment' =

BEST = SOUTHEND PENALTI SHOOT OUT BETWEEN THE CLUB MASCOTS

WORST = ANYTHING INVOLVING PUBESCENT CHEERLEADERS LEARED OVER BY MEN OLD

My favourite home fans are ... (and why)

• OLDHAM [LATICS] - LOCAL FANS FOR A LOCAL CLUB

• HEREFORD - LOUD & LOYAL. THE 'BULLS'; ENOUGH SAID.

The best [clean] chant ~~████~~ has been ... I CAN'T REMEMBER WHAT MATCH OR EVEN WHAT MANAGER (PROB BUCKLE) BUT ONE GAS WAG WAITED UNTIL WE WERE ABOUT TO KICK OFF & THE SECOND WE DID HE SHOUTED "WE WANT BUCKLE OUT". CRUEL BUT FUNNY

The best away goal I've seen was ... SO MANY TO CHOOSE FROM!

• RICHARD WALKER'S BRACE TO SEND US TO ~~LE~~ AT WEMBLEY 2007 WERE BOTH BRILLIANT

• LUTON 1 - GAS 4: ROVERS RAMPANT IN 2002. 2 ~~██~~ FROM BOTH CURETON & ROBERTS

I really, really wish I had gone to these away games ... (1999)

WHERE DO I START?. BLACKPOOL (1990), READING 6-0, DERBY FA CUP (2002), LINCOLN PLAY OFF (2007)

I regret ... NOT TRYING HARDER TO GO TO SOME OF THE 'BIG' GAMES ABOVE. I OFTEN SEEM TO END UP GOING TO THE RANDOM LITTLE GAMES :)

Have you ever smuggled Weetabix into Shrewsbury? ~~YES~~ / (NO)

Have you ever worn fancy dress? WELL... A BIT OF PIRATE GARB (YES) / ~~NO~~

Have you travelled away on a supporters train? (YES) / ~~NO~~

Our worst shirt sponsor was - (Snack Box) / ~~Peter Carol / Elite Hampers~~

MY
TOP
FIVE*
AWAY
MEMORIES

* TERMS & CONDITIONS APPLY

THE FOLLOWING MEMORIES MAY
ACTUALLY BE 4 MATCHES, 6 MATCHES,
OR INDEED ANY NUMBER OF MATCHES.

YOUR HOUSE MAY BE AT RISK IF YOU DO
NOT READ THEM ALL. FOOTBALL TEAMS
CAN GO DOWN AS WELL AS UP; IN
OUR CASE IT IS MAINLY DOWN.

ANNUAL APR OF SOMETHING FRANKLY
IMMORAL AND REPULSIVE, SUCH AS 3,265%

As mentioned in the introduction that you skipped over reading (naughty!), I tried not to mete out restrictive guidelines to contributors and preferred to give supporters the freedom to present their memoirs as they wished.

Several contributors to this fine book (cough!) had a wealth of experience watching Rovers lose all over the country, so rather than just pick out one or two memories, they sent me reminiscences of a handful or more games that were extra special to them. I decided it was usually preferable to keep their memories together, so I created this section for them. Gasheads exiled 'up North' have their own, similar, section later on; rather like a cultural Apartheid.

I need to give a special mention here to David Colley. He actually did send me an email entitled 'My Top Five Away Memories' and suggested I get others to do the same. I agreed but funnily enough I then decided to split his five up as several were worthy of being on their own in other sections (see pages 10 & 172). That is an honour, not a disgrace. Well, that's what I told him...

WELCOME TO THE ROVERS SON!
BY DAVID COLLEY

HALIFAX TOWN VS. ROVERS – 18TH MAY 1963

We all waited at Temple Meads for the special train to take us to Halifax for the game we had to win to save us from relegation to the Fourth division, the bottom tier, for what would have been the first time in our history.

The circumstances were perfectly poised with either us or Bradford Park Avenue to make the drop depending on the result of this one game. It was anticipated that we would be well represented there with an equal number of Bradford PA fans making the short trip to cheer on the team that were usually their local rivals, Halifax Town.

I recall the journey up took the train some six to seven hours, presumably because it was a football special and the crowded railway timetables of the day probably gave priority to scheduled services.

I remember the train made an unexpected stop at Derby station and dozens of our fans jumped off to buy drinks etc. To our amazement the train pulled away with many of them struggling to make it back to the train on time. I recall that half a dozen of our fans failed to make it and I often wonder if they ever managed to make it to the game. Don't forget in those days there were very few motorways and in all probability they will have a different tale to tell about this game.

Once in Halifax our preconceptions of a dark, dismal and gloomy Northern town became a reality as the heavens opened and the rain came lashing in from the moors above. As for the game, there was a sense of thrill as we went in to a 2-0 lead only to be pegged back to 2-2. As time marched on, up popped Ian Hamilton to poke in what was his second goal of the game, the ultimate winner, and despite bitten off finger nails we all went home relieved and very contented.

MANCHESTER UNITED VS. ROVERS – 25TH JANUARY 1964

There we were, 'up for the cup' and our rare chance to visit the home of the mighty Manchester United. Two trains went up and the attendance that day was nigh on 56,000, the biggest gate of the day.

Well, we lost 4-1 and did we give them a game? We accounted for ourselves quite well really but the United side was classy and played to a level we could only dream of. You know, even you younger Gasheads will have heard of Denis Law, George Best and Bobby Charlton. Well Rovers away fans saw those players and the rest of the star glittered side at their very best.

I recall one of United's goals, a goal that will always stay there in the memory. We were on a rare attack and with one of our players about to pull the trigger in their penalty area, he was dispossessed by Denis Law who took two strides and found Bobby Charlton out on their touchline. Bobby in a mesmerising run beat two Rovers players down the wing before dropping a looping ball into the penalty area to see who else but Denis Law majestically rise unmarked to nod the ball into the roof of the net. The whole move probably took no more than ten to fifteen seconds and the whole crowd to a man, Rovers included, rose to acclaim a truly wonderful goal.

BRENTFORD VS. ROVERS – 31ST OCTOBER 1987

It should have been an uneventful trip down from Bicester to West London for me and son Paul (Roadman), but my planning was sadly amiss that day.

At the last minute I decided to take Paul to his first away game. Arriving at the ground only a couple of minutes before kick off I had no choice but go into the home section as the away section had been closed for security purposes. The only place I could put the young Paul where he could see the game was on one of the stone buttresses where the players ran out.

It was a very intimidating atmosphere and one which I would not readily repeat. After two minutes Brentford scored and I found myself involuntarily animated in order to avoid looking too conspicuous.

I remember Devon White taking Steve Perryman's feet from under him which very nearly took a leg off. Perryman's response was in today's environment totally unacceptable; suffice to say one of the words did make reference to Devon's parentage.

Imagine my delight when with two minutes to go big Dev popped in the equaliser. Wonderful.

A very smug look on my face and a pleasant journey home.

Welcome to the Rovers son!

[Editor's Note - See two more of Dave's top five away memories in other chapters of the book, on page 10 and page 172]

DO YOU REMEMBER THE FIRST TIME?
BY WAYNE COLLINS

I love away days! Travelling to the game, the excitement in the car, wondering what will happen and what the score will be. There is something magical about it, especially if it's a ground you haven't visited before. The drive home isn't always quite so fun, often dependent on the score and Rovers' performance, but travelling is all part of the fun.

I've been to many away games over the last 12 years, all over the country.

My first memory of watching a Rovers away game is that day up at Pride Park back in 2002 when Nathan 'The Duke' Ellington scored a hat-trick leading to Rovers knocking out the then Premier League Derby County.

I can remember the excitement of being in the car on the way to my first away game and my first big stadium. We got to the ground and had a walk around - it was so impressive to someone like myself who had only ever been to the Mem.

As we all know Rovers won the game 3-1. What a day! One that I will never forget.

Another remarkable game was Southampton away in 2009. What a strike by Andy Williams to win the game in the last minute! This was a Southampton side that contained Rickie Lambert, Adam Lallana and the sought after Morgan Schneiderlin.

I won't forget walking out of the stadium surrounded by Gasheads singing that Andy Williams chant! What a feeling.

One of the greatest goals I've ever seen Rovers score on their travels was Rickie Lambert's screamer against Luton Town at Kenilworth Road in September 2007. We were sat the opposite end to where the goal went in - the ball was in the air and Lambo hit it first time, straight in to the net! Such a great goal and the atmosphere was electric.

Unfortunately my away memories aren't all good ones. One of the worst experiences for me has to be our 6-1 loss up at Walsall back when Dave Penney was in charge in 2011. The only consolation was Jeff Hughes' goal, but that wasn't enough to numb the pain.

That was the first and only time I've ever left a Rovers match early. And the season ended with Rovers being relegated back into League Two.

Another terrible day supporting Rovers was that awful match at Crawley Town in the F.A. Cup. The game was televised on BT Sport, the weather was horrendous, and we got totally soaked through! In the end the referee abandoned the game with twenty minutes to go as the pitch was like a bog. It also wasn't a pleasant train journey back to Surbiton sat in my cold, damp clothes.

[To view some of Wayne's photos please have a gander at page 70]

TRAVELLING MORE IN HOPE THAN EXPECTATION
BY JOHN COLES

I started travelling to away games when I was about 16 years of age, and that carried on for about the next 30-40 years, but it's true to say that most of my away-days were during the 1960's, 1970's and early to mid 1980's.

The first ever away game that I can remember attending was against **Leyton Orient** at Brisbane Road. The match was played on Boxing Day in the mid-1960's, and I have only a vague recollection of it. What I can remember is that that we won (I think), and that Alfie Biggs scored (I think). What I distinctly remember is that the pitch had very little grass on it, I remember that the only areas that were grassed were around the corner flags. The weather was cold and damp.

[Editor's Note - it must have been the 2-0 win in 1966, with goals by Alfie Biggs and Richard Plumb. We beat them again the day after; 1-0 at home]

I remember an evening game at **Fulham** in the late 1970's, when we filled a car and drove to London. There are only a few memories of the game (again), but I do remember standing at the end closest to the River Thames and that a heavy mist came from the river and engulfed the pitch up to about the half-way line. We couldn't see the far goalmouth clearly, and I assume vice versa. Poor old Miah Dennehy (who was a bit erratic at the best of times) set off on a mazy run, and I assume that he thought that he was running down the length of the pitch, but in actual fact he was running across the pitch and ended up colliding with the perimeter wall.

[Editor's Note - it was most probably 10th November 1978. Lost 3-0]

An away game that never was occurred in 1969, when we were drawn against **Everton** in the F.A. Cup. I purchased two tickets for the ground, and two train tickets. The weather at the time was very bad (snow), and the game was called off on the morning of the game. But what a surprise, Rovers organised cash refunds on the Saturday morning, and I received mine from Bert Tann himself. We spent the money on a day trip to London, and it was snowing there as well.

[Editor's Note - The match did get played in February 1969, in front of over 55,294 fans - the sixth highest crowd we have EVER faced]

Talking of trains, we travelled to **Plymouth Argyle** by train at about the same time, when the big hit tune was the song by Steam, Na Na Hey Hey Kiss Him Goodbye. I'm quite certain that you'll be able to remember the Rovers fans version of the words. Funny ground Home Park, literally in the middle of a public park, and the inside of the ground was painted all in green.

[Editor's Note - The Steam song was a big hit in America at the very end of 1969 so I think this game was the 2-2 draw in April 1970]

I remember another evening game at **Huddersfield Town**, when they played at Leeds Road. My first sight of the playing surface was breathtaking; absolutely immaculate and very very wide.

Newcastle United versus BRFC at St James Park on 1 April 1991. Rovers won 2-0 in front of an Easter Monday crowd of 17,509, many of whom were leaving well before the end of the game, to the sound of the Rovers supporters singing the Monty Python song, 'Always Look On The Bright Side Of Life'. I believe that this was Ossie Ardiles' first game as Newcastle manager after leaving Swindon Town.

[Editor's Note - It was, and as we had already done the double over Swindon in the season, Ardiles had the dubious distinction of losing three League games to us in one season!]

I particularly remember (for some reason or other) that the team coach passed us on the motorway on the way home. It was pitch black, but their coach slowed down and the players, and Gerry Francis, all waved to the supporters coach. Nice touch that.

I'll mention my away day to **Reading**, not that I can recall too much. It was in the 1980's and the weather was lovely, so it was probably spring or summer. The things that stand out for me were the crowd, who were very partisan and vocal, together with the ground itself. From what I remember Elm Park was constructed in wood, certainly the stand in which I was sitting was wooden, just like the old South Stand at Eastville. And just like Eastville when their team were attacking the crowd stamped on the wooden floor and made one hellavu noise. I'm pretty certain that we lost the game though.

Gillingham was one hell of a drive. We took the Supporters Club coach for that very reason, and found the Priestfield Stadium to be nothing special, no character but built smack in the middle of a residential area. Predictably we lost, but I seem to remember that Kenny Ronaldson scored a nice goal for us. Ken went on to play for Gillingham when he left us. He was a very skilful player, but a bit lightweight.

I remember our trip to **Carlisle United** in 2007, when Andy Williams had just been signed from Hereford United and everyone was excited. We were all over them in the first half, and went in at half-time one up. The second half was a completely different story, Carlisle equalised, and then Andy Williams came on. In the closing minutes he had a great chance to win the game, but tried to back-heel the ball into the goal, and missed the target altogether. Then on our way from the ground to the motorway, some bright spark lobbed a brick into the coach window, smashing the outer skin but leaving the inner one intact.

Before the game I was looking around Carlisle's supporters club shop, and in the brickwork was a scroll of honour to former players. One of the players mentioned was Hughie McIlmoyle, the B*FC player.

It was not unusual at that time for me to take the family with me to away games. We would always drive and my wife and children would spend the day shopping (or sitting on the beach), and when the time came we would join up and come home. In time of course the children grew older, and they would come with me to the games. I took various children (and their boy/girl friends) through a lot of the 1980's and early 1990's, culminating in our visits to the Millennium Stadium and the new Wembley Stadium, when we even had a couple of grandchildren with us.

But it always seems to me that BRFC supporters travel more in hope than expectation.

Devon - the capital of cheesy shop names

I got to Plymouth a bit early for the evening game in September 2012, and as befits a nice late summer evening I had a wander to find some nosh.

Apart from the obligatory rubbish chip shop name (I had seen many 'Codfathers' before but never a 'Codmothers'), I also found a hairdresser inventively entitled 'Herr Kutz', and an 'Embassy Club' that had this waggish advert outside, offering to be a 'Husband Day Care Centre'. I never expected Plymouth to be so full of wit.

BELOW - A sticker on a Janner's car proudly telling us it was from 'Crapstone Garage' topped off my time wasting foray.

LEFT - A week after the Plymouth match I spotted this unspeakable pun fiesta just around the corner from Exeter's 'St. James' Park'.

All photos by Martin Bull

107

ONE PERSON'S HEAVEN CAN BE ANOTHER'S HELL
BY PHIL COOK

What is it about following Bristol Rovers at away games that is so enjoyable?

- I love watching football and in addition passionately supporting one of the teams involved. Add to that many years of Rovers support and it still feels great.

- There are a number of football teams that are in their own way unique and I think we are one of them. Blue and white quartered shirts, 'Goodnight Irene', the Gas nickname ... it can only be Rovers and they are my team.

- I usually meet up with friends and as we all live in different places it's a great chance to meet up.

- ... and following on from that, the fact of attending the match gives a shape to the day that just meeting with no purpose couldn't do.

- I've visited a lot of places in the country following Rovers and with a lot of them I don't think I would have visited them otherwise. There are often pleasant surprises when you visit a town or city.

- I've been to a lot of different pubs pre-match and post-match and it's been great. In general the locals are welcoming and discussions about football are generally enjoyable.

CARLISLE UNITED - 7TH MAY 1977 (WON 3-2)

Rovers played their last away game of the 1976/77 season at Carlisle. Both teams were at the wrong end of the table so this was a key match in terms of relegation. A friend of mine decided to drive up so four of us set-off on the trip north. For 85 minutes Carlisle completely outplayed Rovers. They were leading 2-0 at that point and Rovers were lucky that they weren't further behind. The Rovers fans had in reality given up on getting anything out of the game. And then ... with two minutes of the ninety remaining we scored.

In added time we scored again and then in the last minute we scored the winner. It was just wonderful and the Rovers fans on the open terrace were ecstatic. The home crowd quickly went from a happy atmosphere of satisfied contentment to extremely unhappy despair.

We walked around the ground to the car after the game desperately trying to look glum, drove out beyond the city boundary and then laughed all the way down the M6.

One of our number had a seat in the stand and got talking to a Carlisle fan who was sat with his young son. An enjoyable conversation bubbled along throughout the match. At the end of the game my friend wished Carlisle well in their next [final] match. The Carlisle fan's reply was suddenly extremely unprintable.

Many years later a national newspaper ran a weekly series of questions and answers with fans of less fashionable clubs. In reply to the question 'What was your worst experience in football?' the Carlisle fan cited this game – which proves that in football one person's heaven can be another's hell.

[Editor's Note - before this match Rovers had only won two matches in 1977 and were 20th. Carlisle were 17th, but we had a game in hand and finished 15th after a seven match unbeaten run. Carlisle only lost this one game out of their last nine but were still relegated on goal difference. Their season ended on the Saturday (14th) but due to a huge fixture pile-up Leyton Orient played their last game on Tuesday (17th). Knowing they only needed a home draw vs. Hull City to stay up, they achieved it, thus relegating Carlisle whose fans must have been gutted at the end of a radio.]

QUEENS PARK RANGERS – 26TH OCTOBER 1971 (DREW 1-1)

My first ever away game was at Loftus Road in the League Cup Fourth Round. In those days there weren't away sections of the ground and this resulted in the Rovers fans being spread throughout the ground. Rovers played well with Jarman outstanding and at 1-0 up a ghostly 'Harrrrooolllldddddddd Harrrrooolllldddddddd' echoed around the ground. Rodney Marsh equalised late in the game from a free kick and we won a wonderful replay at Eastville by the only goal.

I was immediately hooked on away travel with Rovers – I guess it is tribal but somehow it always feels special.

CHARLTON ATHLETIC – NEW YEAR'S DAY 1974 (DREW 1–1)

This was played at night and was the first evening game to be played for some time – night games had been banned for a period as one of a number of measures brought in as a reaction to power shortages. The programme for the game had a mock cover in old-fashioned script describing the miracle of a game played 'under the wonder of electricity'. I still have a copy.

SUNDERLAND – 7TH SEPTEMBER 1974 (LOST 5–1)

I decided to hitchhike with a friend of mine from Bristol to Sunderland. We set off on the Tuesday and stayed in youth hostels all the way. This went well, except for the inevitable heavy defeat at one of the proper old grounds of English football. We stayed overnight in a youth hostel in the centre of Newcastle and walked down to the Cumberland Arms in Byker along street after street with every house pulled down as part of a slum clearance programme. We got in the pub and experienced the Geordie accent in its full glory – West Country met the North East and not a word was understood on either side.

BLACKPOOL – 5TH MAY 1990 (WON 3–0)

This was a short trip for me from Rochdale and just one big promotion party with thousands of Rovers fans there. I can't remember much about the game itself but what an occasion. I do remember talking in an animated fashion to a frightening looking guy with a 'better dead than red' tattoo. Let's hope that 24 years later he is neither...

WREXHAM – 2ND FEBRUARY 1974 (LOST 1–0)

This was the greatest season ever – I started as a student at Liverpool Polytechnic in the September and we didn't lose a game until February! Sorry to pick the one that broke the run but I just have to point out that we scored a perfectly good equaliser late on in the game ... I don't like to criticise referees but on this occasion I'll make it an exception.

OLDHAM ATHLETIC – 26TH FEBRUARY 2000 (WON 4-1)

When my daughter was seven years old I decided to take her to her first Rovers game – Oldham away (I live in Rochdale so it wasn't far to go). We sat in the away section with the Rovers fans. After half an hour we were 3-0 up and the away crowd was in full voice. My daughter turned to me and told me how much she was enjoying it. I had to tell her it wasn't always like that!

WIGAN ATHLETIC – 26TH FEBRUARY 1983 (WON 5-0)

We went to Wigan's old Springfield Park ground expecting to lose and completely dominated the game with a terrific classy performance from Alan Ball. I was stood with a friend on the terracing just below the directors box. Soon we were surrounded by Wigan fans who staged a demonstration against the Wigan chairman Freddie Pye. We felt obliged to join in and chanted 'Pye Out! Pye Out! Pye Out!' with the rest of the fans.

TOTTENHAM HOTSPUR – 22ND OCTOBER 1977 (LOST 9-0)

I was living and working in North London. A lot of my colleagues at work were Spurs fans so I was looking forward to our away game there. Before the match it was clear that Spurs had the better players, so I did expect defeat.

Nevertheless what happened was horrible. I was stood on a section of side terracing and at 8-0 the referee got carried away with the atmosphere and gave a clearly offside goal. I got into an argument with a massive Spurs fan about it. Why did I do that?! Fortunately he just laughed at me. My second to last memory is of our full back Tony Taylor arguing with the referee about it as the teams left the field. At least he cared as much as I did.

My final memory … drowning my sorrows in a local pub that night when Tottenham Hotspur v Bristol Rovers came on the television on Match of the Day. The whole pub (almost) cheered each goal as it went in.

BEING MARRIED TO A GASHEAD HAS BEEN EDUCATIONAL FOR MY WIFE

BY PAT STOKES

FIRST AWAY GAME — SEVERNSIDE DERBY AT CARDIFF CITY

My name is Pat Stokes and I have supported Bristol Rovers for 42 years. I was lucky in that soon after I started to watch Rovers we got promoted in 1973-74 with that marvellous team. My first away game was at Cardiff City (Ninian Park) in April 1975. It was also my Dad's first away game.

By then my Dad had decided I was old enough (11 yrs) to venture to an away game. Eastville was my footballing place of worship and will always be our spiritual home for myself and many others. However getting to watch Rovers away has always been a bit special.

He was unfamiliar with the ground and we ended up amongst a lot of very excited Welshmen indeed. Severnside derbies in those days were a bit spicy and the atmosphere was electric. Old football grounds have always interested me. The different shapes and sizes of stands and back then the towering floodlights that would signpost you to the ground. Colin Dobson put us ahead just after half-time but then Cardiff got two goals in two minutes. The guy behind me was having Welsh kittens and was screaming his head off "what a transformation of a game" I vividly remember him saying. It was hard to keep quiet especially when our own Welshman Frankie Prince came to the rescue with a late equaliser. We walked out quietly and relieved, my first away game chalked off!

BLACKPOOL AND OTHER NORTHERN ROCK

I wanted to impress my new girlfriend (Alison) and what better way than a romantic trip to Blackpool... on a cold and wet January in 1994 to watch Rovers of course. It rained and rained and rained. By the end we didn't care as Lee Archer had put us in a blue rainy heaven with the only goal to see us home 1-0.

Alison was impressed. It helped that she too was a football obsessive and supported her own blue boys, Everton. I think she saw my support of Rovers as her own footballing reality check on life. Lee Archer had sealed our fate; next year we celebrate our 20th Wedding Anniversary.

Being married to a Gashead has been educational for my wife. Under normal circumstances she wouldn't have gone near grounds such as Rotherham United where she leant on a recently painted red crash barrier that wasn't quite dry. That cost me a new jumper purchase. Oh how she enjoyed nearly freezing to death at Grimsby Town as Barry Hayles danced around their defence. Also some pretty grim games at Bury and Rochdale during the 'Graydon Era' or should I say 'Graydon Error'.

As a Gashead exiled in Manchester since 1986 I see more away games than home games. Rovers away fans are a special bunch – they have to be. Over the years I have seen the same familiar faces and their loyalty, passion, humour and commitment to supporting Rovers at away games has not wavered. Long may that continue.

OTHER HIGHLIGHTS OR LOWLIGHTS:

- What a game at Oldham in September 1997. Finished 4-4 after being 3-0 down early on. One of the best away games I have seen.

- Most bizarre game = Wigan Athletic in December 1997 when four Rovers players were sent off.

- F.A. Cup win over Derby County at Pride Park in January 2002.

- Away game I really wish I had gone to = the 8-2 win at Brighton & Hove Albion in December 1973.

[Editor's Note - This was the last submission to the book and due to space restrictions I've had to put two more of Pat's top away memories in other sections, on page 18 and page 63.]

MR. MADDY'S AWAY DAY DIARY

40 YEARS OF AWAY GAMES, MAN AND BOY

Editor's Note - When Dave Maddy sent me a complete history of his 40 years of away matches, in what was effectively a spreadsheet, I wondered how on earth to present this. Then it dawned on me. The 'entries' in the spreadsheet were almost like the crisp chatter of a diary, so here, with a smidgen of poetic license and hindsight, we present the best bits of Mr. Maddy's Away Day Diary.

1974 - 1980 : THE EARLY YEARS

30th August 1974 - Ashton Gate (Boo) - Gloucestershire Cup - We won on penalties. Age 12, I paraded my blue silk scarf in the East End on leaving the ground. I got a kick in the rear for my youthful bravado.

12th April 1975 - Ninian Park [Cardiff City] - Sat on the bench seats in the Canton Stand. Not segregated. 2-2 draw. Hurrah.

6th December 1975 - Manor Ground [Oxford United] - With Dad, brother and Mike. Marched unwittingly into the home end; swiftly encouraged to walk along the full length of the covered enclosure to get to the open end where the Pirates resided. Lost 2-1.

21st December 1979 - Craven Cottage [Fulham] - Tried to get to Fulham but encountered flurries of snow all the way up the M4 from Bristol. We heard that the game was off just as we reached Chiswick.

29th December 1979 - Gay Meadow [Shrewsbury Town] - See photo on page 73 of Gary Emmanuel in the gloom. Even in those days it was unusual to see Rovers wearing red socks! Lost 3-1. I blame the socks.

5th April 1980 - Vetch Field [Swansea City] - See photo on page 73 of Phil Bater taking a free kick. Tony Pulis is running away from him. Lost 2-0.

1980 - 1983 : THE UNIVERSITY YEARS

9th August 1980 - St James Park [Exeter City] - League Cup win on pens. Earlier in the afternoon we had seen Cardiff draw 0-0 at Torquay United. Football overload. Stopping at a Little Chef en route back to Exeter we met Bobby Campbell.

7th March 1981 - Abbey Stadium [Cambridge United] - Finally saw my first proper away win (3-1); only seven years after starting. Long walk from Cambridge station. Light rain, got steadily heavier. Luckily I had a collapsible umbrella - which the Police confiscated before entry to the ground. After the game, I got it back. It had a luggage label attached with the handwritten identification: "Youth with Spar plastic bag".

19th Sept 1981 - Elm Park [Reading] - 3-0 win. Followed up on the 23rd with a return to Exeter, and a 3-1 win there. Two away wins in five days - Oh My God! I wonder if they will still be saying that in 30 years time?

Boxing Day 1981 - Fratton Park [Portsmouth] - Goalless. The game was on Match of the Day. Not many highlights to show. Muh.

22nd March 1982 - Griffin Park [Brentford] - Lost 1-0, to a penalty conceded by Mark Hughes when the ball was slammed at him from about five feet away. Come on Mr Referee, have a heart.

27th March 1982 - Priestfield Stadium [Gillingham] - This may have been the day when Rovers (David Williams?) had a goal not given, as the referee thought the ball had hit the post when in fact it bounced back from the stanchion inside the goal. Saw Steve Bruce before the game, on crutches with his leg in plaster. That lad will go far, although surely you can't win anything with kids can you?

9th April 1983 Fellows Park [Walsall] - Last Tuesday we lost 1-0 to Oxford in the pouring rain. Many fans got drenched in the South Enclosure (where the South Stand had been before the fire). As some measure of recompense, Bobby Gould persuaded the club to lay on free coach transport for the following away game at Walsall. We lost 5-0. Thanks Bobby. He was so angry about the result though that he made the team get straight back on the coach to Bristol in their kit!

1983 - 1987 : THE RARELY ABLE TO GO YEARS

30th December 1983 - The Den [Millwall] - Kept a low profile. Paul Young "Wherever I Lay my Hat" played over the PA system. I prefer the original. I certainly won't be putting my hat down here; never went back there again.

12th May 1984 - Boothferry Park [Hull City] - A dull-all draw. Dad was scandalised that Hull got the Fire Brigade to use their hoses over the pitch.

25th August 1984 - Burnden Park [Bolton Wanderers] - Train from Bristol on the opening game of the season. Great away win. Police escort to walk back to the station, as home yobs kept pace with us asking, "where yer from, boys"?

25th Sept 1984 - Highbury [Arsenal] - League Cup - Sat well back in the West Stand. Roof was so low that we couldn't see the ball when it went high. It was a good Rovers side (Archie et al), but truly outclassed by the full strength home team. Maybe we can win the home leg by five?

9th April 1986 - Baseball Ground [Derby County] - 2-0 win with an outstandingly gutsy performance against strong home favourites. Young Master Purnell was clattered off the pitch near the dugouts. Mr. Gould jumped off the bench and ran over, but only to tell 'Percy' to man up and keep playing! At least that's how it looked to me from the away end. I am looking forward to reading about the win in the Bristol Evening Post tomorrow.

10th April 1986 - Gutted to see the headlines in the BEP are all about a recent player's criminal activities.

New Year's Day 1987 - Ashton Gate (spit) - Watching from the Dolman Stand, I stifled elation at Gary Smart's late winner.

9th May 1987 - Somerton Park [Newport County] - A famous win to save our proud record of never going down to the Fourth Division. That will surely never happen. Will it?

1987 - 1991 : THE FRANCIS YEARS

22nd August 1987 - Roker Park [Sunderland] - Left Bristol in bright, warm August sunshine. In County Durham we started to notice people were wearing heavy coats and the reality dawned about the climate in the North-East. Stood in home enclosure but got found out (possibly by only wearing summer clothes) and got jostled. How uncivilised. Drew 1-1. Won't be back.

5th November 1988 - Saltergate [Chesterfield] - Dad asked a young programme seller if he could "kindly direct us to the Grandstand", only to be met with the response: "Eeeehhh, that's formal!". As we were soon to discover, there was nothing grand about the stand at Saltergate. Won 3-0, including a Mehew brace.

14th March 1989 - Leeds Road [Huddersfield Town] - My only visit to Leeds Road. I sat in the stand, incognito. Behind me were Ian Holloway and Devon White. Rovers went two down, but came back to win 3-2. I turned round to see Ollie jumping up and down! This Dennis Bailey chap looks handy.

27th March 1989 - Molineux [Wolves] - A win from Mr. Bailey's wonder goal! As ever, I was slow to adapt to the Spring weather and almost fainted with overheating in the packed away end!

25th May 1989 - Craven Cottage [Fulham] - 4-0 pasting in play-off semi-final. 5-0 on agg. Jimmy Hill was magnanimous in defeat, waving to the Rovers fans. I later reminded him about this when Fulham beat us at Twerton some years later. He took it on the chin like a man.

28th October 1989 - Sealand Road [Chester City] - Hundreds of us Rovers fans in the stands were observed by a few Policemen, one of whom clearly had a black eye. The entire congregation sang "Shiner, Shiner, give us a wave". He didn't see the funny side, and (with several colleagues) simply waded into us and dragged a few out. Good job they didn't question his parentage as well. 0-0.

New Year's Day 1990 - Millmoor [Rotherham] - A rare defeat [3-2] so far this season. We were afforded our first view of the scrap yard next to the ground. Dad saw a Gashead buy a pie, take the lid off to have a look at the contents and promptly throw it on the ground in disgust!

10th February 1990 - Deepdale [Preston North End] - Deepdale is an incongruous mix of modern plastic pitch, yet Victorian architecture still in place. 1-0 win.

2nd April 1990 - Meadow Lane [Notts County] - A draw was enough in the Leyland DAF Southern Final to spark "Wembley, Wembley. We're the famous Bristol Rovers and we're going to Wembley". This made up for travelling all the way to Nottingham for the League match only to have referee Vic Callow call it off. Callow by name, callow by nature?

4th April 1990 - Springfield Park [Wigan Athletic] - Rovers' third game in six days, and third 2-1 win. Rearranged fixture. We had previously travelled all the way up to Wigan in heavy rain only to learn that the game had been called off as we arrived at the ground. Dad drove straight back to Bristol! A few years earlier we saw a friendly here against Rovers. We got there early, and I stood with my parents on the spoil tip that served as an away end. Referee George Courtney and his linesmen were walking round the pitch, looked up at my Mum and shouted "and I don't want any trouble from you"!

1991 - 2000 : LIVING UP NORTH YEARS

11th February 1992 - Anfield [Liverpool] - Went on the Supporters Club coach. Loudest and longest renditions ever of 'Goodnight Irene'. Home fans were gobsmacked, especially when Carl Saunders gave us the lead.

17th May 1995 - Gresty Road [Crewe Alexandra] - Play-off semi final - Silly me. Didn't realise away goals counted double, so was surprised how much we were celebrating the 1-1 draw! The sporting Crewe fans applauded us. Visited the great local fish and chip shop, with a sign saying "Welcome to Bristol Rovers". Surely you won't find batter hospitality than that?

Cheltenham Town FC · Tel 01242 573558 · www.ctfc.com

Coca Cola League One
Carlsberg Stand 1
Cheltenham Town FC
versus
Bristol Rovers FC
Tuesday 16 September 2008
Kick Off at 7.45 PM
Ref: 1457515383/39   Seat No.   D12
£18.00 Adult, £12.00 Concessions, £7.00 Junior

mira   MAIN SPONSOR

To Be Retained

CUP   e-on   **FIRST ROUND**
SPONSORED BY E.ON

Barrow
v
Bristol Rovers

Saturday 11th November
Kick Off 2pm
Adult £12.00 / Concessions £8.00

Visitors
Use Entrance(s) A or B

PHOENIX STAND
(AWAY)

WIGAN ATHLETIC
v
BRISTOL ROVERS

SATURDAY 2nd JAN'99
KICK-OFF 3:00pm

Nationwide 2

	ADULT		CONC.	TICKET No.	00212
£	10.00	£	6.00		

WIGAN ATHLETIC AFC LTD.
SPRINGFIELD PARK, WIGAN, WN6 7BA

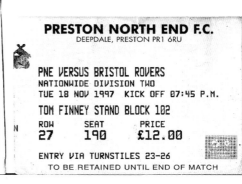

PRESTON NORTH END F.C.
DEEPDALE, PRESTON PR1 6RU

PNE VERSUS BRISTOL ROVERS
NATIONWIDE DIVISION TWO
TUE 18 NOV 1997 KICK OFF 07:45 P.M.

TOM FINNEY STAND BLOCK 102

ROW	SEAT	PRICE
27	190	£12.00

ENTRY VIA TURNSTILES 23-26
TO BE RETAINED UNTIL END OF MATCH

FA CUP 3rd Round Sponsored by AXA
DERBY COUNTY V BRISTOL ROVERS
Sunday, 6th January, 2002   Kick—off 3:00pm
McARTHURGLEN
SOUTH UPPER   PRICE
                                           £16.00
ENTER VIA TURNSTILES STAIR ROW SEAT
49 TO 50:   56   M   0644

Pedigree

The F.A. Cup 4th Round
BRISTOL ROVERS
Saturday, 27 January 2007 KICK OFF 15:00

TICKET SALES
www.shopderby.co.uk
0870 444 1884

SOUTH STAND LOWER Block F
ENTER VIA: TURNSTILE STAIR ROW SEAT
             55 to 58   63   KK   751
Receipt 0   £16.00
                        ADULT

Joma   Coca Cola

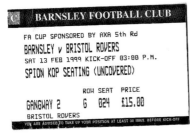

C | **BARNSLEY FOOTBALL CLUB**

FA CUP SPONSORED BY AXA 5th Rd
BARNSLEY v BRISTOL ROVERS
SAT 13 FEB 1999 KICK-OFF 03:00 P.M.
SPION KOP SEATING (UNCOVERED)

	ROW	SEAT	PRICE
GANGWAY 2	G	024	£15.00
BRISTOL ROVERS			

YOU ARE ADVISED TO TAKE UP YOUR POSITION AT LEAST 30 MINS. BEFORE KICK-OFF

PUMA   **Everton**   one 2 one

WORTHINGTON CUP 2ND RND (1)
20 September 2000 K.O 20:00

BRISTOL ROVERS
UPPER VISITORS

Block Row Seat
UV1   F   49

Enter by:Turnstiles 58-59

£10.00
VISITING SUPPORTERS

TO BE RETAINED

Various tickets from Gas away days

Scans courtesy of David Maddy

119

2000 & ONWARDS : THE DECLINE & FALL YEARS

17th February 2001 - Springfield Park [Wigan Athletic] - 0-0 draw. Mr. Referee fails to give us a blatant penalty and afterwards apologised to Rovers for getting it wrong. I wonder if those two extra points could prove important later in the season? I'm not yet sure about Mr. Garry Thompson. Having 2 r's in your name does seem rather ostentatious.

31st March 2001 - Britannia Stadium [Stoke City] - 4-1 defeat. Kevin Gall scored our consolation goal; his parents were sat in front of us. They celebrated the goal more than we did. There is no 'I' in team. But there is 'me'.

9th March 2002 - Victoria Ground [Hartlepool United] - 1 all - I thought, contrary to reputation, Hartlepool seemed a nice place, with broad avenues into the town from the south, and a sailing ship in the marina. Restarting after an injury to a Rovers player, Pools played the ball to our keeper Scott Howie, but Richie Humphreys immediately chased him down and put him under pressure to make a hasty clearance. Some sportsmanship! Shame on you Sir.

31st August 2002 - Glanford Park [Scunthorpe United] - 2-2 - *Stop Press* - Ray Graydon (who will surely lead us to promotion?) accepts the offer of a chip from a Gashead's take-away. No news yet on the battered sausage and scrumps.

26th November 2002 - Halton Stadium [Runcorn FC Halton] - F.A. Cup Replay - 3-1 win, but after extra time! Huff and puff. Geoff Dunford and Barry Bradshaw sat behind us, and started doing a hand jive in time with the music on the stadium PA system when some fans called to them.

17th December 2002 - Spotland [Rochdale] - F.A. Cup - Cracking fish and chip shop over the road from our turnstiles. Paul Tait brings us level at 2-2 and celebrates by running in front of us and pretending to play a trombone - vertically - backed by the sound of "Paul Tait is a goal machine"! Lost 3-2 though.

17th January 2004 - Spotland again - One of the senior ladies kissed Ijah Anderson before the game. Steady on love, there is a football match to play you know.

29th April 2006 - Spotland yet again - 2-0 loss. Hit on the back of the head by an inflatable crocodile. First time I've used that sentence in life.

28th October 2006 - Racecourse Ground [Wrexham] - I overheard a regular away fan say "I wonder if we'll ever win at Wrexham in my life-time?". In my five visits I haven't even seen Rovers get a single point yet: Aug 1999 2-1; Nov 2000 1-0; Apr 2003 3-2; Apr 2006 1-0; today 2-0.

11th November 2006 - Holker Street [Barrow] - F.A. Cup - 3-2 win - I stood near the corner flag, soaking wet and blown by a howling gale. Craig Hinton was warming up and volunteered to me that Sean Rigg went off because he had been socked in the jaw by some Barrow cad!

24th April 2007 - Moss Rose [Macclesfield Town] - My seventh visit to the only away match I can (and do) walk to from my front door, with only the aid of my feet. After my first visit in 1999 (4-3 win) little did I think that I would see five straight defeats before the all-important winner from Sean Rigg today. In fact we haven't beaten them at all, home or away, since that 1999 game (11 games).

3rd October 2009 - Carrow Road [Norwich City] - 5-1 loss. Delia Smith's influence did not extend to the catering for away fans. I got a cheese and mushroom pasty which had clearly been super-heated in the micro-wave. The scalding sauce dripped onto my shoes and it took weeks to clean off. If I had bitten into it, I would have had to go to A&E.

31st October 2009 - Stadium MK [MK Dons] - 2-1 loss - Saw Nick Higgs parking before the game; he mentioned he was taking the chance to gather information about the stadium, which was built by Buckingham. Is our one next?

14th Sept 2013 - Victoria Road [Dagenham & Redbridge] - Train down to Euston from Cheshire, cappuccino, then spent the morning in the National Gallery, focusing on British artists from 17th to 19th Century. Poor show from Rovers. 2-0 loss. Noticed some fungi behind the goal.

ENGLAND, SWEET ENGLAND

The good old English weather!

If you don't like it wait ten minutes and something different will be long.

Either that or it will just carry on raining for what seems like forever.

ARK AT 'EE UP ON YONDER 'ILL WITH THE GERT BIG SINCLAIR BEARD & LOADS OF FUNNY ANIMALS

BY MARTIN BULL

If there is one thing guaranteed to cause a bit of controversy at a match, either on the terraces or on the pitch, it is torrential rain.

I wrote the following away memory in the mid 1990's when I lived in Ethiopia and had a lot of time on my hands. I rediscovered it only recently.

"For the last seven years I have never lived in one place for long and this usually makes away games challenging and interesting. Challenging because I'm nearly always an exile without Rovers friends in the town, and interesting because I have to bungle my way to the ground by whatever means necessary. Have you ever seen a Buster Keaton film? Well, that's me trying to get to away matches; with British Rail, dodgy directions and a complete lack of previous knowledge of that town contributing to my traditional 'hanging off a clock face' scenario. It usually means I'm either two hours early with no-where to go, or running to make the kickoff.

One Saturday in September 1991 the strangely named 'Sprinter' train (an anomaly as it sprinted like Bernard Manning) crawled its way through the Wiltshire countryside towards Brighton. I'm sure this wasn't how Stephenson had envisaged the future of trains. As I arrived at Hove so did Hurricane Git, imported by Brighton & Hove Albion from the Caribbean to force away fans to pay more to sit in the covered part of the away section.

After a healthy lunch of Mars bar and crisps I sheltered in a door way, then under some stairs that smelt of pee, and then under a railway arch. It was absolutely gushing down and I started to worry about the game even going ahead. At some point I had to make a decision. Do I risk waiting for it to stop so I can go on the terrace, or do I get a stupidly expensive seat and risk looking a right fool if the rain abates? As I procrastinated someone who claimed to be 'Devon White's mothers, sisters, husbands mate' offered me a cut price ticket. I was well suspicious but it looked legit and surely big Dev's 'mothers, sisters, husbands' etc. wasn't gonna rip me off?

Sure enough the rain stopped the second I sat down. I hate sitting down, even with a cheap ticket. I hate it, I hate it, I hate it! BAH! If they had big sofas to seat four fans per sofa then I wouldn't mind so much, and if they had a little kitchen where you could go and brew a quick cuppa when the game lulled, I could also enjoy that, but simple little plastic seats do nothing for my pleasure spots.

After the game (3-1 loss) I did more train waiting for the mammoth trip back to Bath. Sure it was boring but at least I had the comfort of a train... didn't I? At Salisbury we were hastily turfed off the train and told a bus was waiting for us. Oh, great! I pay for a train, not a bus, because I like trains. In situations like this I make sure the people in 'authority' realise I'm not happy with their shoddy service, so I stomped around the carriage letting off steam to various BR peons. I hate buses, especially ones borrowed from the local bus company (why not hire a proper coach?) and full of half-drunk kids and parents who should know better. On a train you can usually get away from this rabble, but not in a claustrophobic bus. We finally got back on a train at Westbury, which then sat in the station for a further 40 minutes just to take the mick out of us."

My next strong rain memory is our first away game of 1994, a 1-0 win at Blackpool on 3rd of January. I have no idea how that game ever started and even less idea how it ever finished. It was raining whilst driving there, raining as we got soaked walking to the ground, raining during the action, and top it all off it was do-do-do-do-loo-loo-loo-loo raining in my heart. Given the antediluvian state of Bloomfield Road at the time, pre-transfiguration, it was probably also raining inside the toilets, the dressing rooms and the hospitality suite.

Although Bloomfield Road had the away corner partly covered (see wonderful photo on the front cover from the 1999 match when it was still pretty much the same), about a third of the massive crumbling Spion Kop was given to away fans and was open to the northern extremes. Throughout the rain lashed match two lone Gasheads stood over there for no apparent or necessary reason. Banter flew back and forth between them and the ranks of sane Gasheads under the East Paddock shed.

I distinctly remember a sodden, puddle strewn pitch, although as usual I remember nothing about the actual match itself. The history books tell me that Lee Archer scored the decisive goal, that we were honoured to see Richard Evans' only start of the season, and that only 3,311 ~~crazy~~ brave souls turned up during this deluge of the North.

This game was the piggy in the middle of three successive wins at Bloom-field Road, which started with the infamous last game of the 1989/90 season. That game is without doubt included in my top five list of Rovers games I wish I HAD gone to. 5,000 Gasheads made up most of the 6,776 crowd as they descended on the kiss me quick town for a sun soaked holiday and a promotion party. Blackpool were already down and Rovers were already promoted thanks to the 3-0 mauling of the old enemy just three days previous (an event of such international magnitude that Goya created a famous painting entitled 'The Second of May'). But like a villain in a Victorian pot-boiler, City could steal only our second ever Championship away from us if we didn't match their result. They were playing at Trashton against yet another relegated team and won 4-0, so we really did have to win. The boys did us proud, cruising to a 3-0 win and being held aloft during an enormous, surreal invasion of someone else's pitch.

My next two rain debacles were strangely both in August, which just goes to show it's not just Scotland where you get all four seasons in a single day.

The match at MK Dons in August 2006 was our first ever match against franchise f.c. In the early days of their majestically lengthy history they played at the National Hockey Stadium in central Milton Keynes. The Stadium was a lop-sided soulless affair and was demolished in 2010. The old joke goes that a bomb dropped on it and caused £3m worth of improvements.

We were in a lonely stand on the West side that was a little like a smaller version of the Mem's Centenary Stand, except it had no roof and no atmosphere, and occupied just a small plot on either side of the centre line. There was nothing else on that entire side of the pitch though, not even a burger van, resulting in the pictorial equivalent of the old 'throbbing thumb' in a Tom & Jerry cartoon, where Jerry invariably whacks his digit with a hammer and it swells up to the size of a balloon in an otherwise empty room.

As a freezing rain storm hit us I hoped to find some solace on the pitch. Unfortunately it never happened (we easily lost 2-0) and I got so cold, wet and depressed that I left my seat, and my mate Mike, and stood behind the stand for a good 10 minutes to try to thaw out and mop myself down. It was one of those rare times when you genuinely wanted the game to finish, so you could get out of there and return to a vaguely normal life.

We've played MK Dons away four times now and lost all four, with them scoring a brace each time. I saw the first three of these games. They are one of my least favourite away days! The 2-1 defeat on the last day of October 2009 was one of the most mind-numbing performances I have ever witnessed. I almost fell asleep in the comfy seats they have at their posh new ground on the outskirts of the city. Although I have respect for Paul Trollope he did produce unbelievably soporific football at times. The record books show we scored in that game, yet I have no recollection of it. Maybe I was asleep? I bet it was a futile consolation goal.

The less I say about the abandoned match at Wycombe Squanderers in late August 2012 the better probably. Let's just say it was one of the most bizarre away trips of my life, not helped by a sozzled old Gashead who came in late and wanted to have a fight because I dared to ask him to let me watch the match in peace. Our strangely turbulent rivalry with the Chairboys just seems to go on and on, not helped by many Gasheads thinking our dramatic win there in late April 2014 was karmic payback and was going to relegate them back to non-league! The old idiom proved true though, that 'he who laughs last, laughs longest', as they pulled off a remarkable escape the following weekend to relegate us... AGAIN (cf, 2001; when the our proud memories of the date 'the Second of May', got tarnished). Whilst we are on ancient ~~cliques~~ proverbs, I just hope we do get our revenge one day as revenge truly is 'a dish best served cold'.

This rivalry is particularly worrying because when I lived in Bath I used to watch a few Bath City matches every season. I remember the Romans playing Wycombe and thinking that although their quartered shirts were an alarming rip off of ours, I could forgive them as they were a club in non-league and wouldn't trouble our unique claim to fame. In fact they had been an irrelevance to us for most of our long history and it shows how low we have since sank, and how well Wycombe have done, to have meet them regularly in the Third and Fourth Tiers in the new Millennium.

I won't go into all the details of the abandoned game at Adams Park as they are well travelled, but when I was digging around in my various mobile phone photos for this book I was shocked by the photos I took just as the match had been abandoned (see page 71). As you can see for yourselves the scoreboard is there, stopped at 3-1 in the 68th minute, and the pitch is lush green and utterly pristine in the sunshine, as you would expect in August. Not a puddle on it, nor a cut up patch, or a muddy clod in sight. To any reasonable person I needn't write any more.

As we drove back towards Bicester, still in a state of disbelief, we noticed that the countryside just a few minutes outside Wycombe was bone dry, and we later heard that the game at Aldershot, 25 miles away as the swan vesta flies, also had a deluge and lightning, but continued to completion after an eminently sensible 10 minute break. Fortunately those three stolen points made no difference that season, but any chance of good relations with Wycombe are now about as strong as a comedy balsawood chair built by a crooked Buckinghamshire sweatshop.

WALSALL MINI PITCH INVASION
BY PAUL BRADBURY

It was the 18th March 1986, a Tuesday night game away at Walsall. I was living in Bristol but my trusty car was unavailable. A mate of mine picked me up in an old banger and we went to Fellows Park in the pouring rain. It really was a terrible storm, and as the away end had no cover all the Gas were soaked to the skin.

It was either the Police or the stewards that took pity on us at half-time, as they moved some of the Walsall fans down one of the covered side terraces and let us stand under cover beyond the fences that normally separated the fans. We were saturated and getting stuffed so it was a bit late but was a fine gesture. Near the end of the game we were losing 6-0 (nothing much has changed has it...) and me and my mate said enough was enough, so we agreed that the next time the ball and the play was down the other end of the pitch we would hop over the barrier, cut across the corner of the pitch, hop back into the away end and get off on our way home.

We waited for the right moment, hopped over the barrier, cut across the corner... and then heard a roar behind us. There were another 30+ Gas following us thinking it was a pitch invasion! Luckily the Police and stewards saw the funny side of it and nothing came of it; well not as far as we were concerned - what happened after we left is any body's guess.

When we got back to the car we found that his old banger had a flat tyre. We changed it in the pelting rain and then got onto the M5 to finish off this evening from hell. We just got past Gloucester before we found that the car brakes had totally gone. My mate worked for a haulage company and was not a member of any breakdown service so we had to wait for one of his own breakdown trucks to come and get us. We eventually got home about 2.00 am.

To sum up -

soaking wet   ✓

pitch invasion   ✓

lost 6 - 0   ✓

flat tyre   ✓

car breakdown   ✓

home at 2am   ✓

work next day   ✓

Now that's what we call a good away day!

SPECIAL FEATURE

GO MAD OR STOP CARING

Matthew Foster is (primarily) a Maidenhead United F.C. fan. More than ten years ago he changed Universities after meeting and falling for a girl studying at the UWE. They lived in Cotham, before and after graduating, and would often attend games at the Mem.

Matthew was thoroughly bitten by the 'Ragbag' bug and says that 'Tote End Boys' by Ben Gunstone makes the hairs on his neck stand on end, even though he's never known Eastville without the massive Ikea store on top of it. Having moved back to Berkshire (with the aforementioned UWE student, now 'the wife') away games are king now.

In August 2010 Matthew and two other Maidenhead United F.C. fans were (temporarily) banned from attending home games for 'crimes' they say they didn't commit. They became fugitives in the non-league underground and today, still stigmatised by the MUFC Ltd hierarchy, survive as supporters of fancy (not ground hoppers. Repeat, **not** ground hoppers). So, if you ever see a small group of Maidenhead fans on a train - following the Magpies, the Gas or whatever whim they are indulging that day - please feel free to have a chat and share a drink with them.

Matthew writes about their experiences on his blog - http://gomadorstopcaring.blogspot.co.uk/. Five of his Gas away day blogs are presented below, albeit with some minor editing.

I like his sense of adventure and, in a style reminiscent of the ancient Mummers plays of Marshfield & South Stoke (near Bath), I like how the same 'characters' crop up most away games, such as Murdo [a.k.a. Macleod (M)], Macleod (C), Craig, Willie, and 'the wife'.

AWAY DAY DIARY: BRENTFORD 1-0 BRISTOL ROVERS (26TH FEBRUARY 2011)

Whenever, as a youngster, we used to travel into London by road - on a family outing, a school trip or whatever - I used to notice the floodlights aside the start of the elevated section of the M4. From an early age I was aware it was Griffin Park, the home of Brentford FC. I'd always wanted to attend a game there, particularly of late after learning that it was a ground with a pub on each corner! Bristol Rovers' scheduled visits always seemed to coincide with something else, though, be it a not-to-be-missed Maidenhead United away game (becoming increasingly rare) or, as per last season's 3-1 win in September, a holiday to Lesbos. This season was different, however, with Saturday 26th February long since pencilled in as the day that I would make my Griffin Park bow. And with the wife in tow.

We arrived at the ground, with a packed 'New Inn' the first of the corner pubs. We walked down New Road past quaint terraced housing, a steady stream of home fans and then the second corner pub – a similarly decent-looking, if small, 'Royal Oak' – before entering the away end, standing in the lower section of the Brook Road stand with the majority of the other 856 travelling Gasheads.

Rovers entered the match on the back of a 1-0 home win over Oldham, which had been preceded by five straight defeats. Entrenched in the relegation places, new manager Dave Penney was struggling to integrate a plethora of loan and short-term contract signings. As is the Ragbag way, there were rumblings off-the-field as well, with some supporters wearing black and gold scarves in an anti-Glazer-esque protest at the continued incompetence of the Board.

The game was a decent one, albeit with clear-cut chances few and far between. It was settled by a soft first-half penalty, converted by Brentford captain Gary Alexander after Rovers keeper Conrad Logan was adjudged to have brought down Bees winger Myles Weston. There looked to be minimal contact and one away fan - who carried himself in a manner befitting a mention or two in Chris Brown's 'Bovver' and stood alongside me in the toilets at half-time - was so incensed by the penalty award that he was imploring anyone who would listen to invade the pitch and get the match abandoned.

The aforementioned Weston was impressive early on although he later drifted out of the action as his every touch - after the dive for the penalty - was met with boos/insults from the Rovers support, and new right-back Danny Senda seemed to get up to speed with the game. Home keeper Richard Lee was MoM, which was indicative of a decent Rovers display that deserved a point, characterised by a committed performance from rotund loan striker Rene Howe.

One player who didn't leave a positive lasting impression, however, was Brentford's diminutive winger Sam Saunders who seemed inclined to needlessly incite the away support at every opportunity and clearly thought he was a better player than his frequently miss-controlled first touch would suggest. Speaking to Macleod (M) in the days afterwards, it transpired that Saunders acted up in a similar manner when Leeds United visited Griffin Park last season. Small man syndrome, methinks.

Despite Howe exhibiting superb touch and great hold-up play throughout - and top scorer Will Hoskins going close on a couple of occasions - Alexander's penalty was the only goal. The Rovers players - and the manager - were applauded from the pitch at the end, however, by a noisy away crowd and I left hopeful that this encouraging team display could be built upon in subsequent games. Instead, the Gas would lose 1-0 at home to Colchester United and then 2-0 to Dagenham & Redbridge during the next week, also at home.

Penney was sacked less than two months after taking the reigns, having lost nine of his 13 games in charge. Captain Stuart Campbell has since been appointed player-manger until the end of the season and Rovers have taken ten points from his first five games. The players obviously wanted the authoritarian Penney gone. Not very professional, but at least it looks as if Rovers now have a fighting chance of completing a 'Great Escape'. I really hope so, and not least because it'll mean another trip to Griffin Park.

If we do get to return next season, then I'm sure that the wife won't need much persuading to accompany me again ... so long as I promise her another visit to the splendid 'Ealing Park Tavern', en route. I'd also like to actually have a drink in some - if not necessarily all - of the corner pubs. After the final whistle we turned left at the away end exit in order to complete a circle of the ground, and observe the two boozers we hadn't yet passed (to make sure it wasn't a myth). 'The Griffin' (complete with large plasma screens and heaters in the patio garden) looked the best of the bunch. 'The Princess Royal', in contrast, looked the type of place that you might want to give a wide berth, especially when with the missus.

Not your usual away day, then (despite the result being a let down, as is often the case these days), but enjoyable nevertheless. If Brentford weren't a contender for 'everyone's favourite second team' - i.e. they're a proper family club, all nice and quiet (I honestly didn't hear any noise from the home crowd until an uninspired chant of "Brentford, Brentford, Brentford" in injury time) - then I'd certainly consider going to a few more games at 'Four Pub Park'. As it is, here's hoping Rovers beat the drop and/or Maidenhead United have a decent run in the F.A. Cup, resulting in an away tie in TW8.

Sadly, I'm not sure which scenario is more likely...

[Editor's Note - Currently (summer 2014) Brentford are in the Second Tier, the Gas are in the Fifth and Maidenhead in the Sixth. Hmmm. Wasn't it BRFC who were supposed to be in the Championship within five years, not the Bees?]

AWAY DAY DIARY: OXFORD UNITED 3-0 BRISTOL ROVERS (8TH OCTOBER 2011)

When the League Two fixtures were announced, both Macleod (M) and the wife expressed interest in accompanying me to a Rovers game or two. The former is keen on increasing the number of League grounds he has visited and so early season fixtures at Macclesfield and Morecambe were highlighted, only to be ruled out as they clashed with a wedding and a birthday respectively.

The wife was luckier (or unluckier, depending on your viewpoint). Having enjoyed our day out at Brentford last season and being a fan of Oxford as a place (she's been on two hen parties there in the last couple of years), the Pirates visit to the Kassam Stadium coincided with an otherwise free weekend. It would prove to be yet another case of 'good day out ruined by 90 minutes of football'. Or, as the wife was to point out, a 'good day out slightly stained by 90 minutes of football'. Trust the women in our lives to put football into perspective!

The wife was my guide as we left the train station and walked over a bridge towards the main shopping centre, past a pub thronged with Rovers fans inside and riot Police outside. After locating the relevant stop for the 106C bus to the out-of-town Kassam Stadium we entered the nearby Old Tom to kill time, with a couple of drinks, before our 13:50 departure. The 'pub' part of this venue was rather small, the Thai restaurant part much bigger. It was fairly busy with, perhaps unsurprisingly, a 50/50 mix of tourists and students. There was also an eye patch-wearing old man (drinking real ale with a navy rum chaser) who would scorn at my ordering of a Mixed Fruit Kopparberg, saying that cider should be made from apples and nothing else, plus a 'Big Chris from Lock, Stock'-lookalike Geordie, who could barely stand and for whom another pint of Scrumpy Jack was definitely ill-advised.

There was a reasonably-sized queue at the bus stop, opposite an impressive looking Christ Church, containing more than one group of 'merry' Gasheads. One of these groups began talking to those behind us in the queue. The conversation would continue when they all sat in-front of us on the surprisingly single-decker (and therefore unsurprisingly full), but reasonably priced, Thames Travel 'football special' bus. It transpired that the three 'other' gentlemen (who hadn't met previously and just happened to be standing next to one another in the queue) the Rovers group were talking to were a Danish scientist, an American academic from Albuquerque - both of whom were en route to the Kassam, for their very first experience of live English football - and a German businessman from Nuremberg who didn't like football and was merely returning to his hotel, which happened to be next to the ground.

As we passed Magdalen College, the Roger Bannister running track, Littlemore psychiatric hospital, and other sights, the Rovers group continued to talk with the foreign visitors. I was, at this point, reminded of times when I have travelled on public transport to football games in Germany, particularly the occasion when - during my Stag weekend - a few of us were returning to Düsseldorf city centre on a packed train following the Bayer Leverkusen vs Werder Bremen match at Fortuna Düsseldorf's ground. A bespectacled Werder fan mistook our bemusement - at the loud, alcohol-fuelled banter between the rival fans, allowed to travel together - for fear and attempted to re-assure us with the now-immortal line - "Don't be scared you Englischer fans".

Both the wife and I lived in Bristol for a number of years. I absolutely love the place. And the people. And the accent. I love the accent. But I can't help feel that, sometimes, the accent can make a person sound slightly less intelligent and sophisticated than they actually are. I couldn't help but smile, wondering what the Dane, the American and the German made of it all, as they were bombarded with questions (some insightful, some not) and invited to join the Rovers lot for a pre-match pint. The American – who, unsurprisingly, was the most extroverted and talkative of the foreigners – let on that he had a ticket for the home end, which he was thereafter repeatedly encouraged to swap for one in the away end. At various points throughout the journey he was also serenaded with lusty renditions of the theme tunes to Happy Days, Dallas, Mork & Mindy and other American TV shows, plus 'The King of Rock n Roll' by Prefab Sprout (as aforementioned, he was from Albuquerque...).

I think he was secretly relieved when it was announced - by a bearded member of the Rovers group, who was wearing a St Pauli t-shirt (one of two that I saw day) - that, as the roads leading to the stadium were completely jammed and the journey was taking longer than it should, the pre-match drinks would have to be postponed. Why the main roads to a purpose-built, out-of-town stadium don't have a designated bus lane is beyond me. As it was, the driver let everyone out early - with the bus still marooned in traffic - and we walked the rest of the way. As we neared the ground I was again reminded of Germany. Twofold, in fact. Firstly, the paths seemed to disappear, forcing us to walk on the road itself, and on grassy verges, not unlike when the wife and I went to Eintracht Frankfurt vs. 1. FSV Mainz 05 and we had to trek through a forest to get to the Commerzbank-Arena. Secondly, a pub to our left ('The Priory') had erected a marquee in their garden and put on a BBQ for away fans. Beer and sausages in a tent outside a football ground? Germany in a nutshell.

Macleod (M) had already been to the Kassam (with Willie, to see Exeter City) and had mentioned that the ground was three-sided. Inexplicably, I had thought he meant only three sides were covered, not that were literally only three sides. As we walked through the car park of the adjacent Vue Cinema you could clearly see - because there was only a wooden fence behind one the goals - the seats of the three stands quickly filling up. This game had been nominated as a 'Gas On Tour' match by fans, an 'if you're going attend one away game this season, make it this one' type-of-thing, and so a large turnout from North Bristol was expected. And it wasn't hard to fathom where the designated away end was, as almost half of one of the stands was already a mass of blue and white.

After paying £20.50 each for an adult ticket (Murdo had mentioned that the Kassam was expensive, and I knew the price before departure, but actually handing over two purple notes plus coins for two tickets really brought home how ridiculously over-priced football is in this country) we took our seats. Or took someone's seats. Everyone was sitting (or standing) everywhere and anywhere they could. And the Gasheads kept coming. Not long after kick off the black tarpaulin that was covering a swathe of seats between the rival fans was moved across – I'm not sure whether by Rovers fans or the stewards – to make more room. The hitherto continuous chants of "Goodnight Irene" and "If you all hate City..." stopped, as sections of the away support charged across (some half-jokingly 'offering out' those beyond the Police line, others not so jokingly). The Police seemed happy to stand and record images using their video cameras.

The opening goal of the game came almost instantly, quelling any further disturbance. Up until this point, Rovers had controlled the game without looking overtly threatening. That said, it had taken a superb reaction save by ex-Gashead Ryan Clarke to keep debutant on-loan striker Scott Rendell's effort out and the scores level. Then, with 15 or so minutes gone, and the away end only recently expanded, an Oxford midfielder (Simon Heslop, it transpired) began a snaking run towards goal. The Rovers defending was poor; at least three players had a clear opportunity to tackle (or foul) Heslop. Instead, the ball ended up at the feet of the prolific James Constable, inside the area, and he made no mistake with a fine left-footed shot across the keeper.

There were over 1,600 in the away end apparently (it is said that double this would have travelled if form had been better) and the noise was decent. Going one down seemed to knock the enthusiasm out of the fans, and the players, however. The most vocal amongst the travelling hordes spent the rest of the half sporadically bellowing "Oxford's a ####hole, I wanna go home" to the tune of The Beach Boys', 'Sloop John B', rather than getting behind the team, whilst the players withdrew ever further into their figurative shells. Oxford United, meanwhile, appeared as mediocre and as uncertain as Rovers.

During the early stages of the second half I became quite frustrated by the Maidenhead United-esque tactics repeatedly employed by Rovers; lump it forward and see if 5ft 9in Scott McGleish can win headers against Michael Duberry, a centre half who - although much-maligned - has played over 100 games in the top flight and cost more than £5m in combined transfer fees. During one exasperated "stop hoofing it onto the head of their centre half!" plea, the bloke sitting in-front of me turned around and began to agree. He would miss an Oxford player being put clean through and then scythed down in the box by Rovers' whole-hearted but error-prone centre half 'Lord' Byron Anthony, who was playing out of position at right-back. Anthony could've walked but was instead merely yellow-carded. Former FC Franchise man Peter Leven expertly dispatched the spot kick and the game was all but over with more than half an hour to go.

I saw Rovers twice last year. They lost both times. They played well away at Brentford and were unlucky to lose to a disputed penalty. At home to Exeter City, however, they were out-played and comfortably beaten by Paul Tisdale's pass-first, hoof-second side. In the former fixture they had the rotund but powerful Rene Howe leading the line. Against the Grecians, they had the 5ft 7in Jo Kuffour. Coincidence that they performed better with a bona fide target man upfront? I think not. Obviously everyone would like their team to play delightful football and win but, given the choice of playing delightful football and losing, or playing ugly and winning, I'm sure we'd all prefer the latter. If your players are of limited ability, and/or you only have 'meat and potato' defensive midfielders such as Stuart Campbell (easily Rovers best player on the day, incidentally) and Craig Stanley fit and available, then I see nothing wrong in playing long ball tactics. But you need to have a big lump upfront.

The irony is that, in summer signing Matt Harrold, Rovers do have a reasonably decent big lump. Yet Harrold was on the bench on Saturday, apparently being rested by increasingly unpopular manager Paul Buckle. After the second goal went in, cries of "Harrold, Harrold" and "We want Harrold" became louder and increasingly prevalent. There was then a chorus of "You don't know what you're doing" when the promising Northern Irish wing-back Michael Smith - on for the aforementioned Anthony - was the first substitution. Harrold would replace the ageing McGleish not long after, and unsurprisingly caused the hitherto imperious Duberry some difficulties, but the damage had already been done.

Oxford visibly grew in confidence as the game wore on and went close to stretching their lead further before the impressive Constable (who should've been awarded MoM instead of 'had it easy' Duberry) notched his second, and Oxford's third, with five or so minutes to go. It was then well and truly open season, as far as the away supporters were concerned. Many of those who remained (a load who upped and left not long after the second goal had, judging by the looks of them, a pub to 'take' and riot Police to occupy) turned on the resident scapegoat, Chris Zebroski. Unfortunately for him, he was playing right-wing and so occupied the flank directly beneath us. Now, the away fans were understandably annoyed, and Zebroski doesn't seem to be the most appealing of characters and does resemble a lower-league Theo Walcott (pacy, albeit with suspect control and little or no footballing nous), but the rather venomous atmosphere didn't do anyone any favours. The final whistle was, predictably, greeted with much booing from the away end. To their credit, the players (led by Campbell) and manager did come over to recognise the travelling support. The feedback wasn't positive, however. 'Poisonous' would be a bit strong, but you get the gist.

Some of the Rovers fans were held back outside the away end, but the wife and I were allowed through (another advantage of taking her to the football). The bus journey back to town proved to be one of the more entertaining parts of the whole day; the Kerthney Carty-lookalike driver of the single-decker was obviously determined to get everyone who was queuing onto the bus, which meant that it was absolutely rammed and well over capacity (see photo on page 155) when it finally got going (after the driver had deliberately stalled ... twice). The Rovers faithful on board were in good spirits, calling for those standing to duck when we drove past the multitude of riot vans outside the Priory, in case the Police stopped us on grounds of 'elf n safety'.

In conclusion, and as aforementioned, a good day out slightly stained by 90 minutes of football. We will hopefully attend at least one more Rovers game before the season is out (and I wouldn't mind a night out in Oxford). Paul Buckle, meanwhile, needs to sort out his tactics. Put a big lump upfront if you're gonna play long ball, don't go with two defensive players in midfield if you're gonna try and keep it on the deck, stop playing guys out of position (e.g. centre half Anthony at full-back, full-back Gary Sawyer at centre half) and cease the incendiary remarks in the Press. Otherwise, the title of my blog - Go Mad or Stop Caring - will rather rapidly apply to even more of the hardcore Gas support than it evidently already does.

AWAY DAY DIARY: WONKY WANDERERS 1-3* BRISTOL ROVERS (25TH AUGUST 2012)

MATCH ABANDONED AFTER 67 MINS DUE TO 'ELF N SAFETY'

It dawned on me, in the run-up to this game, that Adams Park must be one of my most frequently-visited Football League grounds, mainly due to the fact that I've seen Maidenhead United play three Berks & Bucks Cup Finals there. I actually like Adams Park, the ground, but its industrial estate location leaves much to be desired. Indeed, a pre-match thread on the Rovers Alternative Forum suggested this was among the worst away days in the entire Football League. Hard to argue with. Pessimism abounds on that particular forum though, albeit perhaps with good reason; Rovers summer preparations hadn't gone smoothly, with pre-season expectations dampened by the departure of talented but temperamental winger Mustapha Carayol, on/off transfer sagas involving an Oxford United striker and a Faroe Islands defender, plus the seemingly-annual goalkeeping crisis; hopefully resolved by the loan signing of Sam Walker, protégé of recently-appointed part-time goalkeeping coach Dave Beasant.

Rovers' start to the League season had been unsurprisingly underwhelming; a 2-0 reverse at home to Oxford and a 1-1 draw at perennial strugglers Barnet. My two previous visits to watch the Gas at Adams Park had been a 2-0 Johnstone's Paint Trophy win (en route to the final) with Gav Villa in 2006/07, and a 2-1 League One defeat with Macleod (C) in August 2009. I was fully expecting a repeat of the latter score line as we set off on the relatively-short journey up the A404. The weather forecast was for intermittent heavy showers but it was sunny and humid as we parked the car. We debated whether or not to leave our jackets, eventually deciding to take them but leave the umbrellas ...

After a reasonably-priced pint (£2.80) in the small but smart clubhouse and paying £40 combined for one Adult and one OAP ticket (eventually; the ticket office operators were slower than Pat Baldwin turning) we took our seats in a three quarters or so-full away end. My Dad commented on one of the more 'interesting' tattoos on display, and also remarked that Rovers' rotund centre half Adam Virgo - who would go on to make a couple of decent blocks - "looks like a Sunday League player".

Rovers dominated the initial proceedings and deservedly led when Dave Clarkson (a goal scorer for Scotland against the Czech Republic in 2008 ... as witnessed by my mate Craig) drove down the left and Lee Brown neatly finished the cut-back. The Gas were passing it around nicely, with Wayne Brown and Matt Gill patrolling the midfield, and new signing Tom Parkes looking assured at the back. Wonky equalised, however, when Parkes and full-back Jim Paterson combined to leave former Exeter City ~~lump~~ striker Richard Logan free to head home at the far post.

Diminutive ex-Didcot Town and Weymouth striker Stuart Beavon had a hand in the equaliser and he looked lively as Wonky came back into the match with the scores once again level. Rovers would regain the lead around the half hour mark, however, with a hit every bit as good as Brian Connor's famous winner for Maidenhead United against Reading, on this very ground, in the 1997/98 Berks & Bucks Cup Final ("Royals rocked by Connor strike"). Target man Matt Harrold, who held the ball up effectively throughout the afternoon against one of his former clubs, caused confusion in the Wonky defence and, as the ball broke, recent Wales U21 international call-up Eliot Richards took a touch before leathering the ball into the net from fully 30 yards. A truly great goal.

Richards would soon score again, to put Rovers two ahead, with another almost as good; a first-time effort from inside the box after a poor defensive header. Word on the street (or, more accurately, the forums) is that Richards might enjoy the off-field trappings of being a professional footballer a little too much. If he applies himself properly, then League Two (and above) had better watch out. Rovers were again in complete control at this stage and, as the half-time whistle sounded in glorious sunshine, I looked forward to them possibly extending their lead. Regardless, three well-deserved points were surely in the bag. I really should have known better, though... this is Bristol Rovers after all!

With the players back out and lined up, the referee - Andy Davies, your name shall go on the list - prepared to signal the start of the second half. The skies had darkened rapidly and the heavens opened. The rain poured down noisily and the scene was almost apocalyptic. The referee hesitated, for what seemed like ages but probably wasn't more than a minute. He eventually decided to continue. A mistake, in hindsight. If he had taken the players off at this point, I could have understood it. Instead he played on, as the rain got heavier and the conditions increasingly problematic for the players. The ball was still rolling OK(ish), but they were sliding about; Clarkson falling over when it would have been easier to score. As lightning forked in the sky, rain lashed down and into the stands; fans clambering back from the exposed front rows. After one particularly loud clap of thunder (the last?), the referee spoke to someone on the touchline and then took the players off. The electronic scoreboard showed 67 mins.

Ironically, it had started to brighten and the rain almost immediately subsided (there would be no more thunder and/or lightning). The tannoy announcer declared that the match WASN'T abandoned and instead the referee was going to take time to 'assess' the conditions. Wonky sent out a member (just one) of the ground-staff with a miniature garden fork - to much laughter from the away end - while Rovers sent out their subs to knock the ball about. Then, after about 20 mins or so, and with the referee not once having emerged to 'assess' the conditions, Mark McGhee signalled to the Rovers support that the game was off. Cue a loud chorus of boos and chants of "We want our money back" from the away end as the Wonky fans, complete with drum (quelle surprise), celebrated.

Eventually we filed out of the ground, rather miserably so (see photo on page 152 - typical Wycombe, they can't even spell). Some took their frustrations out on advertising hoardings and wheelie bins. Later a Police car with sirens wailing whizzed past us, heading towards the ground, as we walked to the car in the rain (sans umbrella). Subsequent photos in the Sun newspaper apparently show a Policeman being pushed back / over and ticket office windows being thumped. While such behaviour cannot be condoned, it can be understood. The decision was an unfunny joke. Not as farcical as Anthony Coggins calling off Dorchester Town vs. Maidenhead United after 86 mins in March 2008, but close. At Dorchester, there was standing water on the pitch and the ball was barely rolling; my issue was not with the game being called off, but waiting until 86 mins to do so. At Adams Park on Saturday the ball WAS rolling, however, and the referee had played through the worst of the storm. The official line from Wonky - which explicitly mentions Bristol Rovers fans when it doesn't need to, and so reads to me like an attempted justification - is as follows...

"Flooding in and around the Adams Park stadium and a bolt of lightning which struck the Dreams Stand - where the Bristol Rovers fans were housed – left no other option but to cancel proceedings".

So the referee abandoned the match on the advice of the ground's 'elf n safety' officer ... who is, presumably, a Wonky Wanderers employee? I imagine Davies would (now) say that he had to stop, initially, because of the lightning and then couldn't re-start - after the lightning had passed - because the incessant rainfall had subsequently made the pitch unplayable. I very much doubt, though, that the same decision would have been reached if the home side had been 3-1 up. There were plenty of thunderstorms and heavy rain across the country on Saturday, but how many League games started and failed to finish? Just the one.

Rovers certainly have many positives to take from their performance, but in all honesty it is difficult to focus on that at the moment. As a Maidenhead United fan, my dislike of W@nky Wanderers (a term coined after their then-manager Martin O'Neill made some disparaging remarks about the Magpies when linked with the Nottingham Forest job in the early 90's) was already deep-seated. I now dislike them even more (if that were possible). As such, I'll feel exceedingly sore when they win the re-arranged game. Which they will.

[Editor's Note - Matthew's prediction was very apposite. As most of us Gasheads will effortlessly recall, as if laser etched on our retinas, Wycombe irritatingly won the re-arranged match 2-0]

AWAY DAY DIARY: OXFORD UNITED 0-2 BRISTOL ROVERS (9TH FEBRUARY 2013)

Starved of recent live match action, largely due to the weather (Winchester City vs. Cinderford Town, Maidenhead United vs. Dover) and apathy (Weston-Super-Mare away), Macleod (M) suggested we attend the Oxford United vs. Bristol Rovers game, despite the fact that we'd both been to the distinctly unappealing Kassam Stadium before. Back to something resembling full health after nearly an entire week in bed with sinusitis - and bearing in mind Rovers' excellent recent form under the returning John Ward (13 points from six games) - I didn't need much, if any, encouragement.

Topics of conversation on the direct train to Oxford included 'Against Modern Football', incorporating Christopher Samba's reported wage at QPR, Maidenhead United's proposed new stand, and Oxford United's old Manor Ground. The conclusion was that - as is often the case - things are 'fifty shades of grey' rather than simply black or white. I never had the pleasure of attending the Manor Ground (I'm not even sure where exactly, in Oxford, it was) - and I fully appreciate that I seldom pass up an opportunity to comment on how run-down Maidenhead's York Road is looking - but I'd wager that Oxford's former home is held in great affection, certainly when compared to the out-of-town, unfinished, soul-less Kassam Stadium.

A group of cap-wearing, middle-aged Rovers fans (with some youngsters in tow) disembarked the train, in error, at Appleford (and / or Culham?) before finally departing permanently at Radley. I mocked them, bewildered as to why they were spurning the delights of Oxford town centre. It transpires they were much cleverer than they looked ...

So much for a pre-match pub crawl of historic Oxford.

Straight from the train we were herded, with seemingly every other white male, out a side exit, past waiting Police video cameras, to a small and distinctly unappealing Thai restaurant-cum-pub. It was not even 11:30 am and already the place was near capacity, with Rovers fans prevented from leaving by a wall of fluorescent-jacketed riot Police (see photo on page 153). As I muscled (!) my way to the bar, Macleod (M) headed to the toilets where, he would later divulge, someone was already bringing up their breakfast. We stood outside, in the freezing cold, as it was too crowded inside. Apparently we were to be held there, before being transported to the ground, "for (y)our own safety and that of the public". Great. There was plenty of Stone Island and Aquascutum clobber on display, to be fair, but previously the Rovers fans had been held in the much nicer (and bigger) 'Duke's Cut'.

Thankfully, as we finished our pints, we managed to persuade one of the Policemen to let us go into town after explaining that we weren't from Bristol (true) and we wanted / needed to get some food (not true). After agreeing to remove our colours (I was wearing a Rovers scarf, Murdo a white, blue and yellow Carl Zeiss Jena one), we were allowed to break the line and head towards town. However, after less than a minute's walk we were held again, as we approached the railway bridge nearby. Another Policeman sprinted over to ask, with some incredulity, what we thought we were doing. It transpired that he was the Sergeant ... let's call him Sergeant Ali Affirmative-Action. After repeating to him exactly what we had told his colleague, who had let us go, Sergeant Affirmative-Action went and confirmed this conversation had taken place before demanding that we leave our details.

As such, our names and addresses went into a notebook, checks were done over the radio (Murdo was asked if he had any middle names!) and Sergeant Affirmative-Action also took close-up photos of us with his phone. I bit my tongue rather than comment on how I could now empathise with persecuted minorities. I also refrained, albeit just about, from asking if I could take his photo. Eventually we were allowed under the bridge and, as light rain began to fall, we passed the aforementioned 'Duke's Cut' and approached the Westgate shopping centre, now the (rather ugly) heart of this historic city.

I had been impressed with the 'Old Tom', on my last visit, and so we headed straight there. It was almost empty as we entered but quite the opposite when we left. Topics of conversation here, over further pints of Guinness, included The Doors (prompted by a BBC4 documentary I'd seen on the making of the 'LA Woman' album), 'Apocalypse Now' - greatest film ever?, and the impact of social media on the music industry. We were tempted by the delicious-looking and smelling Thai food but instead decided on pasties from the newsagents next door. Time for a quick photo of a freezing Macleod (M) outside the spectacular Christ Church (fact - Christ Church College, Oxford, has produced 13 British Prime Ministers) before we caught the 13:50 106C bus to the Kassam.

As per my last visit, the bus was stuck in heavy traffic as it approached the stadium. I asked the driver if we could be let out early, to walk the remaining distance. He seemed reluctant, initially, but then did pull over and opened the doors. The bus emptied. Unlike my last visit, we decided for a pre-match drink in 'The Priory'. I'm not sure if this is / was a designated away fans pub? Regardless, it was unsurprisingly busy. Again, there was plenty of Stone Island and Aquascutum on display. We sat on a window sill and had a decent view of the commotion outside as some Rovers fans reacted to being charged by a group of locals, and then scuffled with Police. The bar was promptly shut and, after a lengthy queue for the urinals, we headed to the ground.

As we traipsed a muddy path one middle-aged Oxford fan attempted to fight the group of Rovers fans in front of us. He was, unsurprisingly, accosted by the Police almost immediately. The rather childish - from both sides - 'hold me back, hold me back' posturing continued across the car park. It was at this point that Macleod (M) and I would bump, almost literally, into Sergeant Ali Affirmative-Action from earlier, looking rather panicky this time. 'I thought you two said you weren't going to the football' he screeched, sarcastically. If he didn't already have his hands full grappling one of the cap-wearing, Darti Brown-esque 'hard men' then I've no doubt we would have been in big trouble, despite the fact that at no point did we say to him, or any of his colleagues, that we weren't going to the football. He seemed like the type of egotistical, condescending, over-promoted, jobsworths who give the Police a bad rep. Where were his ilk during the nationwide riots of 2011? Hiding behind a desk or - at best - a video camera, one suspects.

Macleod (M) and I are, at heart, non-league football fans. As such, we much prefer standing at games. Fortunately, as a Leeds United follower, Macleod (M) doesn't often have to endure sitting, even at League grounds. Over 1,900 Rovers fans were in the away section on this occasion and, to my huge surprise, the stewards / Police didn't move to expand the available seating (the Rovers fans had done this, themselves, in 2011). This meant that there wasn't nearly enough space. £21.50 for a non-existent seat! Instead of being forced to sit, we had to stand in the yellow-painted gangways. We didn't mind; breach of trading standards notwithstanding - geddit?!

As aforementioned, Rovers have been in a great run of form since John Ward returned to the club. A striking turnaround, bearing in mind that they looked near certainties for relegation under the hapless and seemingly clueless Mark McGhee. Significantly strengthening the spine of the team with the additions of experienced goalkeeper Steve Mildenhall, assured centre half Mark McChrystal, midfield play-maker John-Joe O'Toole and promising target man Ryan Brunt, plus playing players in their correct positions, has worked wonders. The squad appears bonded and energised and, as is often the way, the upturn in results has seemingly gone hand-in-hand with an upsurge in confidence and good fortune.

Rovers were rather lucky not to concede at Oxford, as the home side (who's newly-signed keeper was booed throughout) *[Editor's Note - Luke McCormick killed two children whilst drink driving]* missed a good chance in the first half and then saw a header drop just wide in the second. Their left-back, Liam Davis, was also the game's stand-out player. But, roared on (albeit intermittently) by a tremendous travelling support, Rovers were determined, full of running, well-organised and, ultimately, successful. A re-taken Lee Brown penalty had put the Gas ahead shortly after the interval and, as Oxford huffed and puffed, the win was sealed after a quickly-taken free-kick put Eliot Richards through, one-on-one, just before the final whistle. Richards, and seemingly every outfield player, would celebrate his goal with obvious delight in front of the travelling hordes. Cue a mass exodus from the home supporters, some with less-than-honourable intentions.

Perhaps unsurprisingly, the away fans were held back from entering the car park after the game, for what seemed like an eternity. Perhaps understandably, some of them became increasingly agitated. A helicopter hovered noisily overhead, a cameraman took photos with the aid of the biggest flashbulb I have ever seen, dogs barked angrily and the Police attire - complete with batons and black, military-style helmets - hinted at an aggressive, non-conciliatory tone. I was in a good mood, however - not only had Rovers won, but also Arsenal (at Sunderland) and Maidenhead United (at home to Billericay Town).

By the time Macleod (M) and I had been allowed through the Police line, though, we'd missed our 106C bus back into town. As the next one wasn't for another 45 mins, we spoke to a steward and he directed us back the way we had come, past supporters coaches finally leaving for Bristol, and down an under-pass which reminded me (not in a good way) of Didcot, towards the infamous Blackbird Leys council estate and a bus stop with a more frequent service. In the short time that we would have to wait here, it dawned on me that the middle-aged bloke that Macleod (C) and I would sometimes bump into on nights out in Maidenhead, who we thought would drunkenly chant "Blackburn-Leeds, Blackburn-Leeds" over and over, was actually chanting "Blackbird Leys". Better late than never, eh? This bus ride, taking a completely different route to the 106C, wasn't overlong, but didn't seem to pass through the most desirable parts. Several Oxford fans were aboard. The ones I could overhear were bemoaning their club's supposed stagnation and discussing who they would like to hypothetically replace Chris Wilder as manager. One of them suggested Jamie Carragher. 'Nuff said.

We were dropped off on the same street that we would've been if we'd got the 106C and so, if / when I go to the Kassam again, I might consider getting this bus instead... if only I could work out which one it was.

After a 'stupid coloured drink' (or two) in the 'Duke's Cut', where we overheard an elderly, grey-haired, bespectacled American professor seemingly grooming his "favourite, most promising student", and witnessed a hen party hide something (Worst. Stash. Ever.) in a nearby bush - we made it back to the train station. With no carry-out to hand we headed to M&S, in hope rather than expectation ...

There was, unsurprisingly, no alcohol worth purchasing in M&S. There was, however, a celebrity present! The last time we were at Oxford station (travelling home after yet another Worcester City vs. Maidenhead United postponement?) we had bumped into Loyd Grossman. This time, Macleod (M) spotted and chatted to the "comedian's comedian", Stewart Lee, mainly about their mutual love of The Fall. The conversation continued on the station platform, where the photo on page 153 was taken. It transpired that Lee had been speaking at a lecture about the effect of government cuts on aspiring writers, comedians, musicians etc. (Can I have a grant to sit around and do some writing please? Thanks). I immediately tweeted the photo but, in an attempt at humour, and because I am a contrary so and so, I mentioned that we'd met with Richard Herring (the other half of the Lee & Herring double-act). Within minutes, Herring had re-tweeted the post (which surprised me, as I'd only mentioned - not hash-tagged - him) and I was soon getting countless other 're-tweeted' and 'favourited' notifications. Some of the accompanying comments were great - Lee was said to resemble Jo Brand, Dickie Davies and Morrissey, accused of plagiarising Angelos Epithemiou's carrier-bag shtick and (jokingly, I'm sure) described as both a "homeless guy" and a "tramp". Macleod (M), meanwhile, was likened to an "unwell-looking" Eric Cantona and a Leeds United scarf-wearing Vinnie Jones.

An amusing end to a good day ... one that not even Thames Valley's 'finest' could ruin.

AWAY DAY DIARY: PORTSMOUTH 3-2 BRISTOL ROVERS (19TH APRIL 2014)

I would have written this sooner (possibly) but it's taken me *that* long to get over ... nah, I can't even bring myself to say it! *[Editor's Note - He means the 'R' word. The word we shall never use...]*

I rather dislike the phrase 'sleeping giant', but genuinely believe that it can be applied to both Bristol clubs. Rovers have been shambolically-run (understatement alert!) for many years - check out how many managers they've had in recent times, and bear in mind that last season's playing budget was apparently bigger than a couple of Championship sides - but they weren't really going to drop out of the Football League. Were they?

Unlike Willie, who drove us down to see Pompey vs. Exeter City earlier in the season (see photo on page 152), the wife was more than happy to let the train take the strain. Good girl. She has previously accompanied me to Rovers games at Brentford (lost 1-0) and Oxford (lost 3-0). In hindsight, I really should've seen what was coming. On the train, neither the bottled water nor the ready-made M&S cocktails were mine. Honest. I was on the 'French Lager' from M&S. #manly

We arrived in Portsmouth with plenty of time to spare ahead of kick off, so meandered our way in glorious sunshine to the 'Good Companion'. It was packed, both inside and out, with Rovers fans. There were queues for the gents, blokes in the ladies toilets etc., and the atmosphere was electric with 'Goodnight Irene' reverberating throughout. I was reminded of the (now infamous) F.A. Cup First Round 'proper' tie between Horsh@m and Maidenhead United in November 2007. We had travelled in (relatively) huge numbers and the pub directly opposite their ground (the Queen's Head?) was spilling over, pre-kick off, with Maidonians. You could barely get through the doors, so some of our group went to the off-licence across the road and came back with a crate of lagers to drink outside. Memorably, an old boy showing off in his classic Ferrari convertible was left as red-faced as his car when it conked out - loudly and seemingly in slow motion - as he drove past the throng. Superb! We all deserved so much better that day than the lifeless display offered up by Drax and the boyz. It's hard to forgive and forget. *[Editor's Note - Maidenhead United's wonderfully entitled manager, Johnson Hippolyte, is voluntarily nicknamed Drax, for reasons unbeknown to most of the human race]*

The away end was (very) close to capacity. Officially 2,300 were in there. I reckon it was more. A plane flying overhead trailed a banner, reading "Forever Looking Up At Us - SAFC". Bristol City 1982 Ltd fans are apparently thinking of organising something similar for the first Rovers home game of next season. *[sarcasm font]* Hilarious! *[/sarcasm font]*

Rovers, undoubtedly hampered by early injuries to Danny Woodards and Michael Smith, and with top scorer John-Joe O'Toole only on the bench, attacked like Liverpool but defended like Hartlepool ... Reserves. 2-2 at the break, with Portsmouth centre halves Bondz N'Gala and Jack Whatmough the stand-out performers. As I visited the York Road-esque toilets at half-time (where a group of cap-wearing smokers were already planning - with a glint in their eyes? - trips to Grimsby Town and Lincoln City) my expectation was for a Rovers onslaught in the second period, shooting towards the away end. I should have known that I would be disappointed ... 3-2 the final score. 17,998 saw it. The away fans had been noisy throughout and chants of "We are staying up" rang out defiantly at the final whistle. I, conversely, had been fearing the worst since the 2-1 home defeat to bottom-of-the-table Torquay United, the previous Saturday, and this display - not a bad one, per se, but ultimately fruitless - did nothing to dispel my gut feeling that Rovers were in big trouble. They had been the better side in the first half, yet shared four goals. The Gas certainly didn't lack effort, but were bereft of creativity in midfield and pace upfront. They also conceded sloppy goals. A recipe for disaster, in my opinion, but the general consensus in the away end seemed to be that they'd have (just) enough to survive. Subsequent results might indicate that the players felt the same way.

Maidenhead United had also lost - 3-0 at mid-table Farnborough - to put them on the brink of relegation. *[Editor's Note - Unlike Rovers, the Magpies escaped the drop after a couple of near miraculous wins in subsequent games]* I drowned my sorrows with a large 7UP in a nearby McDonalds. The home fans were happy; their fifth successive win under caretaker manager Andy Awford meant that they were safe. Lucky them.

After a meal in Guildford and sprint across town, we missed our intended train by less than a minute. The wait for the next one, plus a flat can of lager that I shouldn't have bothered with, probably explains the look on my face (see photo on page 153). That and the plummeting temperature; hence my borrowing of the wife's woolly hat. Did someone say good day out ~~ruined~~ slightly stained by 90 mins of football?

#whosyourfavouritenonleagueteam?

ABOVE - The denouement of the Wycombe debacle in August 2012, with 'score' on the scoreboard. Typical Wycombe shambles, they can't even spell properly on the big screen.

BELOW - Spot the difference. Pompey greeting Exeter and Willie, and then later in the 2013/14 season Rovers and 'the wife'. Bless 'em. At least they tried.

ABOVE - Thou shalt not pass. Thames Valley riot cops won't let anyone vaguely 'football looking' leave Oxford Train Station in February 2013.

RIGHT - Murdo Macleod with ~~a random tramp~~ comedian Stewart Lee at Oxford Train Station after the match.

BELOW - Matthew Foster with wife's woolly hat on after Pompey game in April 2014.

153

Swindon Town
25th April 2009 -
Nice weather, but
slow forced cop
walk back to the
train station.

All photos on pages
152 to 155 courtesy of
Matthew Foster.

154

ABOVE - Packed Oxford Bus - November 2011

BELOW - In Brass Monkeys, an Irish pub in the delightful German university town of Heidelberg. The landlady - an Irishwoman - took it upon herself to get the scarf collection out. Unlike Fatty's Irish Bar in Düsseldorf's Altstadt, which has hundreds of scarves covering the ceiling (a spectacular sight), there were only two in Brass Monkeys. An Arsenal one, as she is a fan, and a Rovers one, as one of the regulars, Simon, is originally from Keynsham. Small world!

Note obligatory man behind hijacking the photo with large pair of oversized thumbs. Must be from BS3.

BELOW - NOTE - That is NOT a C*ty scarf!

LEFT

Photo from Murdo, a.k.a. Macleod (M), taken on the tiny Greek island of Halki, where there is a bar that has football scarves on the wall ... with Rovers above City!

Obviously as it should be.

155

Various shenanigans when we played
Barnsley in the F.A. Cup 5th Round on
13th February 1999.
All photos courtesy of Glen (Gas4life!!!)

ABOVE FOUR PHOTOS - Jamie Cureton's infamous last minute leveller (and hat trick) at Walsall in March 1999. Timeline = 1 - Goalie kicks it at Jamie's bonce, 2 - JC shows his match ball to travelling Gasheads [plus 1 man pitch invasion], 3 - Black power salute, 4 - It's a fair cop guv.

BELOW - Gasheads chanting 'Beaper Farm Barmy Army' (the campsite many stayed at... and got wasted at) on the Isle of Wight pre-season tour - the first one in 1994? Note obligatory ice cream van for nutritionally balanced summer sustenance.   All photos courtesy of Glen Young

LEFT and ABOVE - Rich Clark, and his father Colin Clark, at the Blackpool match on 24th April 1999. Note large Plasticine replica of the Eiffel Tower in the background to help them pretend they were in Blackpool.

Both photos courtesy of Rich Clark

BELOW - Marcus Stewart being greeted off the pitch by Gasheads on the Isle of Wight pre-season tour.   Photo courtesy of Glen Young

ABOVE - Gasheads flock to the crumbling Spion Kop terrace in the sun at Blackpool. Probably the April 2000 match (last time we played there).

RIGHT - Glen, Stuart Neely (RIP) and father Bob Neely, Glasgow Gasheads/Rangers.

All photos courtesy of Glen (Gas4life!!!)

THE ROVERS FAMILY

In the long run the sentiment behind this section makes it the most 'important' chapter of the book.

Being a Gashead is not an easy ride. There are no 'glory hunting' Rovers fans! In fact the opposite must be true; fans who have followed Rovers through thin and thin, over several decades, must be closer to mad than sane. And personally I'm beginning to feel especially sad for our younger fans, who haven't seen much success, and certainly won't have seen us in the Second Tier or even as a team commonly challenging for promotion in the Third Tier.

If we weren't 'a family' there would be no way we would survive. Without the precious moments of camaraderie, togetherness and gallows humour portrayed in the following pages I'm really not sure we could continue everyday to tell people, "I'm a Rovers fan...".

When you haven't got much at least you have each other.

A WIN, AND ONLY A WIN WOULD DO!
BY DAVID ROBERTS

The Beatles were Number One ('From Me To You'). I'd seen this popular beat combo at the Colston Hall earlier in the year; I think it was five bob (25 pence) for a ticket - I might be making that up. I was still at school and later in this year the American president will be assassinated. Then there was Profumo, Philby, and the Great Train Robbery ... quite a fun-filled year.

But for fun, tinged with just a soupçon of doubt, going to Halifax was right up there in my diary of momentous events.

Even though 'A' levels beckoned, my mind was full of football thoughts, unpredictable and erratic - would my football club survive the ignominy and shame of a double relegation and misery in the fourth Division? (oh the irony 51 years later, writing this in Summer 2014)

I am convinced that ditching the blue-and-white quarters after the 1962 season got us in this mess, and of course dear old Bert Tann had done his best work with the finest Rovers players in our entire history: the fab 50's team(s).

Blame it on my dear dad, for in 1949 he took me to a Rovers game* (a birthday treat - yeah I'll bet) and I've been afflicted with the Gas gene ever since.

I was brought up in sunny Lockleaze, a hotbed for Rovers supporters. A short stroll over Purdown and there it was, Eastville, my spiritual home for many years to come.

My inner compass persisted in nudging me toward an obsession with Bristol Rovers Football Club, and here I am sixty-five years later, my journey almost at an end, a one-sided love affair, unrequited love, but only one of us seems to be committed to the relationship.

So. My first away-day. The penultimate game of the 1962/63 season (excluding the Glos. Cup Final**) . Bring it on, we can meet this challenge, can't we?

There was what appeared to be a full train-load of Rovers fans ('Gas' hadn't yet been invented) setting off for Halifax, which I knew was in West Yorkshire (I did have an 'O' level in Geography!). Whether this train was a forerunner of R.A.T.S. I've no idea, but if not, it would have sown the seeds of a good idea.

With an air of uncertainty and nervousness the gathering hordes of Rovers fans seemed to mill around Temple Meads Station, in a confused manner with no particular purpose; all in anticipation of a great escape they hoped would come later that afternoon.

The train journey was an adventure of sorts, although by then I was an old hand at train travel as my dad being a railwayman (he was the booking clerk at Stapleton Road Station, nice 'n handy for Eastville) would get free passes for the family for rail travel, and it suddenly dawned on me - why hadn't I been to any other away games? Ah well.

We played cards, made a lot of noise, and generally messed about like teenagers throughout the ages, eager to get to our destination and learn our fate.

A win, and only a win would do!

The only thing I can remember about the game was after we took an early 2-0 lead, Halifax, with their relegation already confirmed, drew level, and then near the end Ian Hamilton scored the winner to give us a 3-2 victory, and thus avoid a double-relegation. There's a distant memory that could be playing tricks on me, but in the far corner of my mind I think the Shay had some sort of 'tip' behind one of the goals. It could have been the result of one of the coldest, snowiest, longest spells of Winter since 1947, and had been used to bank up the excessive amount of snow that had fallen.

(Ashamedly) There was another event that sticks in my mind, foolish stupidity by me in a Wimpy Bar (an innovation, the trailblazer of McDonald's). Although as a former Roman Catholic I would have unburdened my troubled soul in the Confessional (very convenient), my mum and dad were less than impressed that when I got home I produced from my coat pocket, a tomato-shaped ketchup container. The ill-conceived excuse I used: *"it appealed to my keen appreciation of all things Art-Deco ... "*, so I nicked it - stupid boy!

I didn't intend to bare my soul in this short memoir. But hey even at my time of life, I can still spot an opportunity for self-preservation.

Life, as I age, I realise was merely a memory. The recollection of moments often prove richer than the moments themselves. Could that be the case when I recall these memories of Bristol Rovers Football Club? (a purely rhetorical question...)

Too old to die young.

David Roberts aka darloGas

VeryGaslongbeforetherewasGas

Viva La Causa

* Bristol Rovers 2 Reading 1

** We beat the darksiders, 2-1

[Editor's Notes - 2,126 saw the match, including about 500 Pirates. We scored an impressive 70 goals that season. But we let in 88! Terrible snow that winter meant Rovers didn't finish a game between 16th December 1962 and 8th February 1963.]

DREAM A DREAM

BY WSMJOHN

I remember the dark days when we went to Twerton and were struggling under Bobby Gould. In October 1986 we went to Wigan, who had very low attendances and no smart new all seater stadium in those days. I travelled up with four friends from Weston. No one knew where the ground was and we assumed the Rugby League ground was their stadium due to its prominent size. Passing Northerners laughed at us waiting outside the ground but eventually gave directions to the football ground.

When we got to the ground it still had a typical non-league set up. Two old men started a conversation with us and invited us into their supporters club for a drink on the condition we did not cause any trouble and hid our colours. As we later left the club to go in the ground, we wished the two old men the best of luck and shook hands.

At that time we were only taking one supporters coach away, and there were about ten of us independent travelling Gasheads behind the goal. We heard that the coach had broken down on the motorway and was waiting to get fixed or replaced. We sang our lungs out, all ten of us, but we were losing 4-0 by half-time. The coach finally arrived with an extra 50 fans as backup. We made a hell of a noise on this grass bank with a little bit of terrace and Rovers managed to fight back to 4-3, with a Kenny Hibbitt penalty and David Mehew's first ever double for Rovers. Wigan were finding it hard to hold on at the end but it finished 4-3 and all these Northerners were applauding us.

To this day I hope those two old chaps managed to see Wigan in the Premier League. For some reason I have recently been thinking about our dark days as a club and thought about directors who did not always help Rovers, perhaps through their arrogance or for their own financial gains, but I believe we have to think positive now as how low can we go from here!? Let's hope Darrell Clarke can be our new Gerry Francis.

UP THE GAS!

THE EIGHTH WONDER OF THE WORLD
BY LUCAS SWAIN

Before writing this short memoir I had to delve deep into my mind as a Bristol Rovers supporter. I haven't been following the club I now love since the glorious days at Eastville, I didn't even witness a match at Twerton Park; I'm the current generation of supporter who knows nothing beyond the rusty turnstiles of the Memorial Stadium. Nonetheless, the memories I've collected in my span of supporting Rovers are precious, so picking one to write about was proving a challenge.

After much deliberating, I eventually decided that the most prominent memory I have as a Bristol Rovers supporter is the 3-2 victory at Southampton in the 2009-10 season. I was still fairly young at the time, but that just added to the magic of the game. It was my first highly exhilarating away day victory; nothing will ever beat it.

Southampton was then – and still are - a football club of significant size, so the match-up already had great appeal for Gasheads. It was a Tuesday night, Rovers fans flocked in their droves, and I coincidently had an appointment with the doctors which assisted me from escaping the clutches of school early, allowing me to attend the match. It was to be one of the biggest games of the season, but the match already had a narrative.

After selling Rickie Lambert to Southampton for £1 million I was initially bitter; it felt like the biggest act of betrayal feasible. Lambert was the all-conquering striker who was emblematic of Rovers during my years as a fan. Nobody was better, and chances are nobody will ever be better.

Despite what I naively labelled a side-step transfer, Lambert was still a Gashead in my eyes, and there's still a part of me that likes to believe he still is. Southampton may have acquired our prize possession physically, but the fans were still attached emotionally, that much was evident at St. Mary's Stadium.

Deep down everybody expected Lambert to come back and haunt us that night, it would've been natural. The age old unwritten rule in football:

ex-players must score against their old club, which Lambert did, but I don't think anybody expected what would later transpire.

Southampton: Kelvin Davis; Dan Harding, Radhi Jaidi, Neal Trotman, Lloyd James; Dean Hammond, Morgan Schneiderlin, Jacob Mellis; Papa Waigo, Rickie Lambert, Adam Lallana.

Bristol Rovers: Mikkel Andersen; Carl Regan, Danny Coles, Byron Anthony, Aaron Lescott; Stuart Campbell, Mark Wright, Jeff Hughes, Chris Lines; Chris Dickson, Jo Kuffour.

Looking at the starting elevens for the game, it's quite remarkable this Bristol Rovers side were once capable of competing with Southampton. With two future World Cup players and three Premier League stars, Southampton were streets ahead.

I remember arriving at St. Mary's Stadium and standing back for a moment to marvel at the stadium. Many supporters may argue it doesn't have the character The Dell had, but there's no denying Southampton's new residence is one Rovers supporters would love to see Bristol Rovers play in weekly, minus the red wash of course.

Approximately 2,500 fans crammed into the away end, creating one of the best atmospheres I had ever witnessed. It felt like Bristol Rovers had taken over Southampton; it was half an hour before kick-off but already 'Goodnight Irene' was whipping around the stadium at full force.

But as the game kicked off I, and even the most ardent Rovers supporters, knew we were facing an uphill struggle. The likelihood was we were going to lose, maybe steal a draw, and when Adam Lallana fired Southampton in front after combining with Lambert it sure looked that way.

Yet to our surprise, Rovers managed to churn up an equaliser. Chris Dickson, the man who will forever be remembered for playing his joker card in his first match for the club at Brentford, by this I mean he was fantastic for one game then nothing but mediocrity after, rounded Kelvin Davis to score from a tight angle.

After the celebrations it wasn't long before the noisy blue corner of St. Mary's were back planted in their seats. Southampton managed to put themselves 2-1 up just on the stroke of half-time, Rickie Lambert with the goal. For the sake of crowd reaction, it was great to see Lambert refuse to celebrate against the club he fused an unbreakable bond with.

The game was looking bleak for Rovers in the second half, but a flash of brilliance from Carl Regan, another player who turned out to be nothing more than average, saw him burst round Dan Harding before providing a low cross for Jo Kuffour to tap home.

This was uncharted territory for me as a Gashead. Going away from home was synonymous with losing; it took between 10-15 games before I even saw my first victory for Rovers away from the Memorial Stadium. Looking back on it I was crazy to keep going, but I knew when victory came it would be sweet.

Southampton wasn't my first away victory, but it was by far the best. The instigator of this fantastic triumph, though, was Andy Williams, transfer listed at the time. The winger-come-striker entered the fray just before the equaliser for Rovers and contributed, although not directly, to the leveller. But there's no doubting his contribution to the winner!

Running down the right wing, bravely cutting onto his weaker foot, Williams cocked his leg to fire and seemingly made time slow down. St. Mary's was silent for just five seconds, but it felt like five hours. The thud of the ball echoed into the stands as Williams struck it; you could hear a pin drop as this homing missile flew through the air. The ball whipped round a helpless Kelvin Davis as he swan dived to his right, nestling in the top corner and sending the Rovers fans into raptures.

My reaction? I'm not sure how to describe it. I was in such a state of shock I didn't know what to do. Initially I and hundreds of other Gasheads charged towards the Southampton fans to the stewards' dismay, rubbing every bit of what just happened in their face. Just from buying Lambert there was bitterness from me towards Southampton, so this felt like a war was won, not a football match. I then paced down the stairs frantically to get to the front of the pitch where the players were overflowing into the stand. Breathing uncontrollably, I stood, smiled, laughed, screamed, and turned around to see 2,500 people doing the same. Without question it was the best sight I've ever seen. That corner of St. Mary's, for me, was the 8th wonder of the world, and I'll never forget it.

That night was symbolic of Bristol Rovers, the club I grew up loving. We may lose our key players and have times of hardship more than any other club, and it may drive you to the point where you question your sanity. However, the unity and spirit of our fans will never dampen, and it's that what makes Bristol Rovers Football Club special.

IT'S NOT GOING TO BE A SHORT TERM THING
BY GASSHOLE

My best away match?

The 5-0 thrashing of Oxford at a locked out Manor Ground. I travelled from Australia for that one; straight from Heathrow. Ever tried getting into a football stadium with a suitcase?

Another memorable one for me was losing 6-1 to City in the Summer of '78. I was a kid on my own watching from the East End with a Rovers shirt on under my coat - I almost got heat stroke. I was raging on the inside at all those posturing ponces aiming abuse towards the open end. That was the day that confirmed it was not going to be a short term thing... Rovers 'til I die.

WE COULD HAVE COME IN A TAXI
BY NICK RIPPINGTON

I remember during my youth, when Terry Cooper was the man at the helm, that we were propping up Division Two (the Championship as it is now) and I was still going to every game, but with very little expectation or hope.

I turned up with three mates to get the coach to Burnley (the game in April 1980 I think), only to find that the coach had been cancelled due to lack of interest.

Rather than turn for home, another lost soul suggested that we climb into his Ford Cortina and drive to Turf Moor.

The Gas away support that day amounted to six of us. We had very little chance of a result, survival was no longer an option, and all we could do was show our support in the best way we could.

All match we sang our hearts out and, to be fair, after trying to lynch us midway through the second half, the home contingent actually developed some respect for us on the basis that they realised our plight and acknowledged our unswerving loyalty to a lost cause.

A group of them walked us back to the car to protect us from Burnley nutcases intent on doing us harm and waved us off on the long journey home.

Just outside Cheltenham the Cortina gave up the ghost. The prop shaft went and we were towed off to a garage in deepest Gloucestershire. We then had to share a couple of taxis back, costing us £7 each which, in those days, was a pretty penny and more than we had paid for petrol or our entry fee at the game.

Arriving back at 1am in the morning a bedraggled crew, our only consolation was we had proved our loyalty to the cause. And, against the odds, the Gas had managed a 1-1 draw.

On a separate memory, but a related theme of camaraderie and travel, I recall being on a train coming back from Fulham. I was a student just embarking on a journalism course in Cardiff. This must have been the November 1978 match as I clearly remember we had lost 3-0. Bobby Campbell, the then manager, insisted all the players travelled back on the train with the fans.

David Williams, my favourite player at the time, sat down with a few of us and I managed to get an exclusive interview for college. I don't suppose you would get that sort of thing nowadays. I don't remember much else about it, but the players certainly weren't abused even though their performance had been pretty dire.

WHEN HOME IS AWAY
BY FABGAS

One of my best away day memories was actually when we played Bath City in the F.A. Cup First Round at Twerton Park in November 1994.

As we were officially the away team some Gas supporters went into the away end, but with almost 7,000 there Gasheads were spread out everywhere. Some, like myself, stood in the same place as usual, often finding a Bath City fan or two in 'their' space.

We crushed our hosts 5-0, with Paul Miller bagging four, and Vaughan Jones on the 'wrong' side, but that was almost not as important as the whole experience, which was possibly unique and will probably never happen again.

It was all good natured and proved that it is possible to have a match where all fans can behave without the need for segregation (like those rugger fans manage to do every match).

THE SILENT SMILE
BY DAVID COLLEY

Ask any younger Rovers fan for their favourite away match and Reading vs Rovers on 16th January 1999 is probably in their top one, as Brian Clough would say. Well for me it's definitely up there in my Top Five, all of which I've written about in this book.

As I was Sales Director at the time of John Madjeski's print company in Oxfordshire, where his Auto Trader was printed, it was my responsibility to ensure the company's Corporate Box was always filled with guests in case he was ever to call in. This was very difficult on most occasions, particularly when it was a case of 'do you want to come and watch Reading versus Scunthorpe on a freezing cold, bleak February night?'.

When it came to our match there in January 1999 the thought of being in the box with typical prawn sandwich types was difficult to envisage. The possibility of them celebrating a goal against my beloved Bristol Rovers, plus hangers-on taking the mickey, would be too much to take.

So on the day of the match I feigned illness and took my son Paul (a.k.a. Roadman), then a kid, into the absolute back row of the away end with all my fellow Gasheads, directly diagonal to Madejski's box. It was 0-0 at half-time, but then came the deluge. I remember taking my small binoculars; imagine my delight as I saw the gloomy despondent faces in their box becoming more and more dejected as one after another Cureton (4 goals), Roberts (2 goals), and co, gave them a pounding.

It was incredible walking through the office on the Monday. My silence and smile said it all as I passed through.

Happy days!

50 + 30 = 1,000

BY SOUTHMEAD GAS

One away game that sticks in the memory was Chester City away on 5th March 1988, in the first season of the Gerry Francis era.

My old man drove three generations of us up. I can't remember the journey, but once inside the ground we chose to go on the open terrace behind the goal along with about 50 other Gasheads, with maybe 30 others up in the stand.

It was still virtually winter in England so it was no surprise when it started to rain just before kick off, and as the crowd was barely over 2,000 and there were very few of us away fans, they moved us out of the open end and under cover at the end of the enclosure, dead opposite the Gasheads in the stand.

Every time the ball ended up on the terrace behind the goal, my son would run and get the ball back as no one else seemed to want to bother, which he loved.

Rovers, with big Dev and little Gary Penrice up front, were starting to look good for goals and we were becoming a hard team to beat.

We dominated the game and won 3-0. I will never forget singing 'Gerry Francis' blue and white army' up to those 30 Gasheads in the stand opposite and them singing it back to about 50 of us, little knowing it would be thousands singing it in the not too distant future.

Dev, Percy and Boris got the goals, and we left the ground knowing Gerry's team was going to offer good viewing and exciting times ahead, never realising how exciting of course.

THE GRASS IS BLUER ON THE OTHER SIDE
BY JOSH SEARLE

I can barely remember my first Rovers game. I know the result, it was a 2-2 draw with Manchester United for Nick Culkin's testimonial match, but the details of the match have long vanished from my memory. However, it must have had some impact on my four-year-old self, as I began to follow Bristol Rovers, a team from the 'wrong' side of the Severn Bridge.

I only followed the Gas though, I didn't really support. Sure, I would attend a fair few home games each year, I would wear the shirt, I would sing the songs (those I was allowed to), but I didn't feel that joy and despair of really supporting a football team. To be honest, outside of match days at the Mem I was more of a Chelsea fan.

That was until my first away game on 29th April 2006; a three hour trek to Rochdale to witness Rovers succumb to a 2-0 defeat. A future hero of mine, Rickie Lambert, netted from the spot to put the hosts in front after Craig Hinton saw red just before half-time, and Ernie Cooksey added the dagger to the heart at the end of the second half.

When you look at it like that it's strange to see why it would have such an impact on me. However, from at least half an hour before kick-off I was part of a wall of noise. 'Goodnight Irene' rang out around Spotlands as various inflatable's came floating my way before being batted back into the vociferous Rovers contingent.

The atmosphere I experienced was what convinced me Rovers were the club for me, the only club. The Chelsea apparel I had acquired found its way to the charity shop the next day.

There have been special days on the pitch watching Rovers away, as well as in the stands. Fulham away in the F.A. Cup in January 2008 is a standout for me. Although, again, off the field events play a part, namely misplaced trust in modern technology, in making the day more memorable than others.

Despite Fulham having moved back into Craven Cottage many years before the fixture took place, our Sat Nav still believed Loftus Road was where we should go. And it was something we didn't notice until arrival. So, what to do with no map, and no real experience of London? Well, Chelsea is near Fulham, right? So let's head there and see what happens.

With Loftus Road to Stamford Bridge, somehow via Griffin Park, complete, we now find ourselves outside Chelsea Football Club, on an F.A. Cup Saturday, nearing 3 o'clock; two blokes in blue and white quarters wading through a sea of Chelsea blue, and what I believe was, based on memory, Scunthorpe claret and blue. Needless to say we got some strange looks.

However, four requests for directions and three buses later, we found ourselves, finally, outside Craven Cottage.

Was it all worth it? Of course it was! A 7,000 strong army of Gasheads out-sung, outnumbered, and watched their side out-perform Premier League Fulham, battling to a 2-2 draw and eventually going on to win the replay on penalties.

THERE REALLY WAS ONLY ONE RAY KENDALL
BY MARK COUSINS

We went to Fulham one Friday on the Supporters Club coach. When we got there it had been snowing and the game was postponed. It was freezing and Ray Kendall (God rest his soul) made us coffee from the machine on the players coach.

Enough said.

WARNING – GAS INVASION

BY MEADER

The first big away support I can remember as a Gashead would have been the first game of our promotion season, 1973-74, when an estimated 4,000 Gasheads saw us beat Bournemouth 3-0 at Dean Court in front of over 11,000 in total.

Then in late January 1974 there must had been 9,000 Gasheads at Aldershot when we won 3-2. The BRFC Supporters Club took 32 coaches to the game as it was played on a Sunday.

And you know what the official attendance was that day? It was a massive 13,196! About another 1,000 got in for free when the fence went down at the far end of the ground closest to the road. Looking at the ground today [official capacity = 7,100] you wonder just how 14,000-ish got in.

[Editor's Note - This game against the Shots marked a club record 17th unbeaten League away match in a row. Strangely we lost the next four away games though! The record attendance at the Recreation Ground came four years earlier in a F.A. Cup 4th Round replay vs Carlisle United, watched by a staggering 19,138.]

QUITE INTERESTING AWAY STATS

We've never lost away to Man City. Admittedly we've only played them twice (League Cup in 1992 and the League in 1998), but a draw each time is actually quite impressive.

Of all the older clubs Man City was the last one that we had never met in the League or cup, as it wasn't until that League Cup match on 23rd September 1992 that we had EVER met.

Ardent Rovers away travellers must be sick of the sight of striker Tom Pope, who has scored in 3 of his 4 away games against us. He scored for Barrow in the F.A. Cup game at Holker Street on 11th November 2006, then for Crewe Alexandra at Gresty Road on 29th January 2008, and finally bagged a hat-trick for Port Vale at Vale Park on 20th November 2012.

Our all-time record for scoring a goal in consecutive League away games is 21 on the trot. The run started at Reading on 6th March 1990 and went on for over nine months, through promotion and half way through our first season back in the Second Tier, to 12th Jan 1991. The run was Fulham, Northampton Town, Wigan Athletic, Huddersfield Town, Birmingham City, Tranmere Rovers, Notts County, Blackpool, Leicester City, Wolves, Ipswich Town, Notts County, Swindon Town, Middlesbrough, West Bromwich Albion, Watford, Millwall, Brighton & Hove Albion, Plymouth Argyle, and Charlton Athletic. It was finally ended by a 2-0 defeat at Hull City on 2nd February 1991. The run comprised of 9 wins, 7 draws and 5 defeats, which suggests that scoring in away games is a rather handy thing to do.

On a more sour note our all-time record for failing to score a goal in consecutive League away games is 7. The run started at Colchester on 5th December 2009 and went on through to 20th February 2010, taking in Tranmere Rovers, Millwall, Huddersfield Town, Leyton Orient, Walsall and Gillingham. Apart from 2 no-score draws, long suffering Gasheads had to endure 5 losses, via 11 unanswered goals.

A BET'S A BET!

BY RUSS KING

My road to Wembley, for the League Two playoff final in 2007, started quite a few weeks before even the Johnstone's Paint Final in early April, let alone getting into the Playoffs.

Sat in our local in Clevedon, Rovers' good run of form came up in normal conversation, as well as how good the newly finished Wembley looks. Ian (a former Man Utd season ticket holder) and Mike who is at university (token Chelsea fan) discuss the slim chances of Rovers getting there, as we were so many points away from the playoff places at this point. After a few drinks Ian then raises a bet that if Rovers make it to Wembley he'll pay for Mike to go.

During the final games of the season, Ian, Phil (another former Man Utd ST holder) and me are on holiday in Florida with me wandering round in my Rovers shirt whilst checking the scores after every game. The League table started to show just how close Rovers were to getting there.

Back in 'The Crab Apple' many weeks later we sat down to watch the playoff semi-final second leg. We were 2-1 up after the first leg and so close to Wembley. We're regularly reminding Ian of his agreement with Mike if Rovers were to get through.

The next thing we know, that Stuart Campbell goal hits the back of the net and all of us erupt, as with each and every Rovers goal that night. All except for Ian that is who is counting the cost of our expensive holiday being followed by an expensive day to Wembley, x 2. A bet's a bet!

Tickets in hand we leave Clevedon at silly o'clock to get to the Colston Hall to catch the coach; Me, Ian, Phil, Mike and Scott (another Chelsea 'fan' and my Brother-in-Law).

We arrive and are met by Shaun (an ex-Twerton and Blackthorn End ST holder) and his group. It's about 6:30 in the morning and Shaun hands us a can of Stella each, which nicely starts us off for a long day ahead.

After looking on the forum at where Rovers fans were heading we all head to Leicester Square and after breakfast are met by a sea of blue and white filling the famous square.

With kids outside the Yates seeing who can kick a football the highest by bouncing it off the windows of the Hotel next door, and 'Goodnight Irene' being sung loudly, we slowly see the Police turning up. It starts with a lone copper and his Vauxhall Corsa, but even though there's no chance of trouble it soon ends up being Police with full gear on and about 50 officers 'keeping an eye on us'.

We leave around midday and get the tube up to Wembley, joined by other Rovers fans. Another chorus of 'Goodnight Irene' starts and we get a lot of confused looks from fellow tube passengers.

One of the other Rovers fans around us at the end of the car turns round to us and asks, 'do you mind if I take a slash here mate?'. He then opens the window between the carriages leans through and taps a guy in the next carriage and asks the same question whilst reliving himself on the floor and then getting off at the next stop!

We get off ourselves a few stops later to find a proper toilet to use. Mike and Ian race each other up the steps of the station to get to the toilet first. Ian wins and has the obligatory Rocky moment at the top of the stairs.

We finally get to Wembley and me and Ian go off to meet Shaun at 'The Greyhound' pub. He warns us to get some drinks on the way to the pub as the garden is heaving and you'd never get served. We then hear Shaun's story of his journey up earlier. He'd seen an unattended back-pack and rather than reporting it as most people would post 7/7 he opened it up. Being the lucky git that he is, he found two bottles of champagne in there, which soon got finished.

As we head back to the ground, we put our bets on. I write down Rovers 2-1, and Igoe for last goal scorer, with £5 on each. Ian goes for Rovers 2-0, but then turns round to me and asks for a fiver as he had spent his last money buying the Strongbow Supers in the off licence. As I've now only got my last £10 in my wallet I throw the Igoe last scorer bet in the bin and just put the other two bets on.

As we are over the other side of the stadium to our seats, we seem to be walking through all the Shrewsbury fans. We ask an Officer for directions, whilst holding our cans in a 'no drinking zone'. I cheekily asked him to hold it when I need to do my shoe laces up, but he politely declines to help me out. *[see two photos of the day out on page 68]*

Rovers go behind after only a few minutes, so Ian's 2-0 bet goes straight out the window and it also quietens down the 40,000 Rovers fans in the ground. They erupt though at a Richard Walker brace, including a second described by the commentators as a "goal to grace the Champions League final".

We go into the break 2-1 up and with the Rovers fans in very strong voice. I go to get something to eat, as it's been a very liquid day, only to find it's £8 for a burger and drink.

During the second half I look over to Ian who is slumped in his seat and needs waking up. Later Rovers are still ahead, but you can feel the tension in the air as their keeper goes up for a late late corner.

The ball goes clear and falls to Sammy Igoe who runs from the edge of the Rovers box, past the half way line, and rolls the ball towards goal, where it is tackled into an empty net. The full time whistle goes and with that final goal the bet I put on has suddenly gone, and the bet I didn't have the money to put on would have been fulfilled; all in one kick.

As we head back to the coach at Victoria we meet Shaun who has a carrier bag full with another eight cans of Stella. The coach is fairly empty so we all spread ourselves around and get two seats each. I fall asleep up against the window and wake up somewhere along the M4 as the coach is pulling over onto the hard shoulder. Someone (possibly me) had fallen asleep on the emergency exit and the driver had a warning light and had to pull over.

Shaun is being whacked on the head by one of his family with their huge foam finger whilst he is getting through his cans. The driver sees him and warns him that he shouldn't be drinking but as it was a quiet coach and he knew who we were and what the result was, he'll let us continue. Shaun replies "no problems drive, cheers", then goes into his carrier and says "do you want one drive?", who reminds him that he needs to direct the coach.

Finally we get back to Clevedon, and fall into 'The Crab Apple' where the story all started.

What a day!

THE NIGHT WE OUT SUNG THE KOP
BY ALEX AUCHTERLONIE

I have been following Rovers for nearly 50 years. I was a member of R.A.T.S. (Rovers Away Travelling Service). I have seen some great games; Ipswich in the F.A. Cup - getting beat 6-1 and travelling on the scheduled train with R.A.T.S., getting punched in the ear from a City fan walking up Winterstoke Road (there was five of them and what they thought were three of us. There were actually 18 of us! My ear hurt for weeks but I believe it did not hurt as much as his nose), Wembley 1990, Blackpool 1990, Derby County when Nathan Ellington scored his hat-trick, Millennium Stadium 2007, Wembley 2007.

It is difficult to pinpoint a single game. Beating City is always good but Liverpool away in the F.A. Cup in 1992 was amazing. We out sung the Kop; not many do that. My son, then 9 years old, stood on the seat and never stopped singing from beginning to end. A fellow Gashead commented "he's bound for the Popular". He still supports them today with the same passion as me.

[Editor's Note - Liverpool went on to win the F.A. Cup. This happened to Rovers five times before but never since; yet another example of our demise]

CAN YOU PASS THE SPROUTS PLEASE CARL...
BY TREVOR EDWARDS

Blackpool in the 1989/90 promotion year was fantastic; the journey up, the brilliant win, denying Bristol City (1982) Ltd the championship - just great. We all went on the pitch at the end and I ended up on the cover of the 'Gerry and the Dream Makers' video produced to celebrate our super season.

After the game I lost my brother Neil after getting caught up in the celebrations. I was still wandering around a bit worse for wear at about 6 or 7pm. I was in the car park and finally found my brother talking to Billy Ocean! Carl asked him (as the designated driver for the day) if we could take a few ladies back to Bristol for him. Well, you couldn't exactly turn down Mr Saunders, so we took them back to lord knows where in Bristol at some ungodly hour and that was 'job done'.

A couple of years later, after another away game, I am in the Joe Banana's nightclub in Bath and even though I am, let's say bamjaxed, I spot a very nice looking girl and decide to make her night (not) by giving her the pleasure of my company. She asks me how my day has been and I tell her "Well, I've been to the Rovers" to which she pipes up "my sister is going out with Carl Saunders". Crikey. "Then..." I say to her, "I know your sister...", and to cut a long story short we talked into the night, exchanged numbers and not long after I moved to Bristol to live with her.

Christmas was approaching and she says 'would you like to go for Christmas dinner at Carl and Mandy's?'. Well, 'do you want pay rise?'!

So off we go for a Christmas feast and I'm sat with Carl Saunders passing the sprouts. Carl and Mandy were extremely nice, we talked a bit of footy (as much as I thought appropriate) and a good time was had by all.

It was a strange experience sharing a table on Christmas Day with someone who at the time was one of the stars of Bristol Rovers. It was particularly nice to see that these players are pretty down to earth and at the end of the day they are doing a job just like the rest of us.

ARE YOU A GASHEAD FANATIC?

BY MARTIN BULL & CHRIS BULL

Are you one of those eccentric fans who will do peculiar things as a Gashead? Most of this anti-social (but exceedingly funny) behaviour occurs at away games. If you want to find out if you are a true Gashead screwball, take our test below.

• If you answer 'yes' to **more than 6 of the following characteristics** you are a full blown cracker case, too far gone for any medical or psychological salvation. You would die for your club... and probably will.

• If you match **between 3 and 6 characteristics** then you are nicely peculiar but not dangerous enough to get deranged status, or to be dragged off in the middle of the night by the men in white coats, dressed only in your pants.

• **Less than 3 characteristics** and you are a bit sad basically and probably only used to watch a few games a year from the quaint Members Enclosure at Twerton.Anyway, watching Premier League footy on Sky with a nice milky tea and a sensible packet of Shortcake biscuits (nothing too extravagant) is more your style isn't it?

• **None?** We have a stinking Robin in our midst. Get the gang plank ready!

---

10 characteristics of a Gashead fanatic:

1) When asked if you are crazy you will probably reply in Cantona-esque style philosophising that, "I am normal, the rest of the world is mad".

The perfect answer... of a perfect lunatic.

2) You like to stand in the pouring rain for no apparent or necessary reason (e.g. Brighton September 1991 and Blackpool January 1994).

This usually transpires when there are two parts to the away end; a covered section and an open portion.

3) You stand on your own (or with a maximum of two mates) in a section of the away end that no-one else is standing in. No-one knows why people do this. It's a question that top psychologists have pondered for years and never found the answer, although being a victim of British Army mind experiments is high on the list of promising explanations.

Our guess is that you think that it makes you look well 'ard (especially if it is raining and it's an open terrace).

4) You won't give the ball back when it goes in the away end (e.g. York City, September 1995). People who do this are usually old enough to know better, obviously like entering into a panto spirit ('shall we give him the ball back boys and girls?') and probably still go scrumping for apples.

5) You are the BRFC teeny player who was complete guts in the 1995 Wembley Play-off Final penalty shoot-out competition, and who fluffed the kick which would have won it for us. This miscreant hit the most centrally aimed and softest kick (too tired from the run-up I suppose) seen since Gary 'Nice' Lineker's one against Brazil when he could have equalled Bobby Slap's England goal record.

Come back Diana Ross, all is forgiven.

6) You travelled north to both the Huddersfield and Bradford games in February 1995 despite it basically being the same journey within three days of each other. Or you went to Watford away [League] on 17th November 1991, and then on 20th November you went to, yes you guessed it, Watford away [Cup]! You could either be labelled 'demented' for these, or 'committed'. You decide which you prefer.

There is still the possibility though that the two tags are one and the same really.

7) You are that lone Gashead from the West Stand who risked getting lobbed out of Wembley before the 1995 Play-off Final had even started, by getting onto the pitch and running over to Andy 'Suntan' Tillson to give him a pat on the back and an inspirational quote or two from Vice Admiral Horatio Lord Nelson in his shell-like. Nelson's body was famously preserved in Brandy after his death at Trafalgar. That may be an alternate explanation of Andy Tillson's skin colour?

The Gashead in question then ran back to his seat but not before striking out at a balloon on the pitch in such a lackadaisical manner that it suggested he had either indulged in a few too many glasses of the old jungle juice, or else had been watching copious videos of Junior Bent.

If you watched this crank from your comfy seat and said "I wish I had the bottle to do that" then you lose a point for being a soft lad.

8) When goals are scored you whip off your top, bearing your horrible pasty flabby chest, and swing it around your head in a wind-mill style last seen in the grainy colour footage of Mick Channon's days.

If you continue to do this on huge crumbling wind-swept terraces in December you score an extra point.

9) You're the bloke who always used to wear that woollen BRFC sweater that was presumably hand knitted by a dying relative he didn't wish to offend.

10) Even on below zero winter nights you wear only a T-shirt or replica top to the match. This is called 'doing a Rofe', after Dennis Rofe, our greatest patron of this image. He was as hard as the proverbial brick outhouse.

Please Note - this was originally written in 1995, with some minor changes in 2014. The authors are not sure if they contributed to Andy Tillson being know as 'Suntan' to some Gasheads, or whether we were just adding a voice to a few mutterings we heard. It was almost 20 years ago you know. We had hair and everything…

SUN, SEA, & SINGING GRANNIES

A.K.A. THE BLACKPOOL & BRIGHTON CHAPTER

Unless you have the fortune to live on the coast but then got sedated to its magnetism, there is still something magical about the seaside, especially when accompanied by sun, sand, beer and a cracking footy match.

I have subtitled this chapter 'a.k.a. The Blackpool and Brighton chapter' as most of the memories come from there, including the 8-2 demolition of Brian Clough's Brighton & Hove Albion in 1973.

It's still early days for Morecambe memories...

Some five-star photos from Blackpool can be found in the second colour section (pages 158 and 159).

THE SINGING GRANNIES
BY COLIN EMMITT

After the 2-0 home victory against C*ty on Easter Saturday April 22nd 2000, which witnessed a fabulous goal by Wally Walters and kept us in the play-off hunt, a group of six of us set off for Blackpool for the match on the Easter Monday. We had pre booked rooms in a Hotel along the sea front (probably the last available due to the bank holiday).

We went out for the evening all kitted out in Rovers shirts had a nice meal and then hit the bars. Rovers fans literally took over Yates bar with constant singing and created a fantastic atmosphere. When it closed (or more to the point when the Police kicked us all out) the six of us headed back to the hotel bar.

The Hotel bar was actually in a large lounge and there was an elderly couple there, one playing an organ and the other singing to the Hotel residents whose average age must have been 75+. We, along with 4-5 other Gasheads who had booked into the hotel were propping the bar up and listening to the erm... entertainment. I asked the couple if they knew 'Goodnight Irene', to which they said "no". So the 10 of us started singing 'Goodnight Irene' to the room of elderly residents. Eventually the guy playing the organ picked up the tune and a number of the old folk started singing along until eventually we had the whole room singing it.

When getting into the lift to head to our rooms an elderly couple jumped in with us and thanked us for making their evening, saying what a brilliant time they had. As they got out the lift we could hear them singing away 'Goodnight Irene'.

This was the day we converted a room of pensioners into honorary Gasheads.

THAT WITHERING LOOK
BY REX

We used to run a coach to every away game from 'The Pied Horse' in St George. The pub would always open around 8am wherever we were going, and it's fair to say most of the regulars on the coach were just as interested in the 'day out' as they were in watching Rovers.

The driver of the coach was always Mike, a Rovers fan who I still spot at many away games. The great thing about Mike was that he didn't mind parking up for a couple of hours (that normally turned into several hours) on the way back from games, to allow us to quench our thirsts - and most of those on the coach had some serious thirsts to quench.

We set off from the pub at around 10 in the morning, most of us already having had a few pints at the Pied. The weather wasn't great, and by the time we were getting near Exeter it was absolutely lashing down, and there was the almost inevitable announcement on the radio that the game was off. There was a suggestion from a few on the coach that we should head for Torquay who were home to Hartlepool (I think) that day, but our chief organiser Stoner said that that game was off too (it wasn't) but we would head into Torquay town centre for 'a couple of beers'.

By the time we got to Torquay it was about one o'clock, and Mike the driver said we would have a two hour stop. We all knew a two hour stop would mean at least three hours by the time we had got all the troops together, so we all scurried off to various watering holes.

By this time, five or six of the soberer members of our group (a.k.a. The lightweights) had discovered that Stoner was in fact lying about Torquay vs. Hartlepool being off, and in desperate need of a football fix, went off to watch that.

Around about four o'clock as I was trying to round up everyone from various pubs, which, as these were pre- mobile phone days, was quite a task, especially as I had a drink in every pub I was going into, it became apparent that we would have to wait until at least 5.30 before those watching the game would be able to get back to the coach, so all the drinkers were told they had until six to drink up - but no later than that!

Six o'clock turned into seven, and we eventually started the journey back to Bristol. We had just joined the M5 at Exeter when a few of the lads at the back of the coach approached me with the question 'Rex, any chance of a beer stop?'

I did point out that we had just had a six hour beer stop, but they were adamant they fancied another, so I said we would put it to the vote, and proceeded to ask who was for said beer stop. Only four on a coach of 50 odd voted against, so we pulled off the M5 and stopped at the first pub we saw, which was in Cullompton.

The landlord - who was on his own - was a bit over awed to see 50 odd of us piling off the coach, but he was very welcoming, and phoned up a couple of extra staff to come in and help him serve.

By this time the beers were really flowing and there was a great atmosphere in the pub, helped by mates cheering on each other in a game of Killer on the pool table. A bit later a coach load of rugby players came in, which only added to the atmosphere with songs being belted out at every given opportunity.

The landlord knew he was onto a good thing, and come last orders said we would be alright for 'a late un'.

I have no idea what time we left the pub, but I got home around 2am. I woke my wife up as I fell through the door, and as our son was about one year old at the time, it's fair to say she wasn't overly impressed with me.

'Where have you been?'

'Football'

'The game was called off 14 hours ago, it was on the radio - WHERE HAVE YOU BEEN!

'Err, we stopped for a quick pint on the way home love'

And with that she gave me that withering look that husbands all over the world will know and turned over and went back to sleep.

I have had a few 'quick pints' on the way back from football in 40 years of watching the Gas, but I think Plymouth away remains the benchmark!

WELCOME TO BRIGHTON, SUCKERS
BY THE BLUEDEEMER

It was the Easter Monday game at Brighton's Goldstone Ground in 1979. Three of us aged between 18 and 20 went in my mk2 Ford Cortina rust bucket. The game was a disaster, lost 3-0 in front of 24,000, so us lot decided we'd find a B&B, have a night out in Brighton and then drive back the next day. We found one a couple of miles away but drove back to a car park in town to save walking a long way later.

After a good night we fell out of a nightclub about 1.30am to go back to the B&B. The problem was none of us could remember its name so we ended up having a very uncomfortable and restless night crammed in my car. I had had enough of it by about 7am so I got out to have a pee before driving home and noticed the petrol cap was missing. As I was still a bit green I cursed about having to go and get a locking cap now, not realising that the reason it was missing was because some delinquent had siphoned the tank while we were trying to sleep in the car!

First and last time I went to Brighton.

TAKING IN THE WATERS AT BRIGHTON

BY JOHN COLES

My family and I all love Brighton, so we loaded up the car and went for a day-out there, in the late 1970's I believe. The idea was for me to go to the match, and my wife and children would go to The Royal Pavilion. It absolutely bucketed down all day, and the Pavilion was closed for renovations, so my wife had to amuse herself and the kids whilst trying to keep dry. I went to the game and found myself in the uncovered end of the Goldstone Ground, and was like a drowned rat by the time that half-time arrived. From that moment onwards the sun came out, so I sat on the terrace and literally steamed. I was off work for about two weeks afterwards with bronchitis and no, I most certainly don't remember the score of the match.

It was not unusual at that time for me to take the family with me to away games. We would always drive and my wife and children would spend the day shopping (or sitting on the beach), and when the time came we would join up and come home. In time of course the children grew older, and they would come with me to the games. It was on one of these excursions that I went to the dullest ground that I have ever been to... Dean Court, Bournemouth. Perhaps I was just unlucky though, eh?

QUITE INTERESTING AWAY STATS

Rovers' first ever away hat-trick in the F.A. Cup was one of our most famous away victories in history. It was Nathan Ellington's trio at Derby County on 6th January 2002. 6,602 Gasheads were there to see it, and made up over a third of the total crowd. I unfortunately was in the car park of Ikea in Croydon when I heard snippets of it on the radio! Shopping vs. football. Hmmm. It was the first time a Fourth Tier team had beaten a Premier League team (the PL was created in 1992).

PUTTING THE BOOT IN

BY MARTIN BULL

One of the best half-time entertainments I have ever witnessed was at Roots Hall (Southend) on April Fools Day in 2005. It was the ubiquitous penalty shoot out competition, but the twist was that it was between the mascots of the two teams. For some bizarre reason Captain Gas had gone there, and he was playing Elvis J Eel, or was it Sammy the Shrimp?

Southend must surely be one of the only clubs with two significantly different mascots (as opposed to several clubs who have a male and female version of the same animal), and it's also particularly wacky that Elvis and Sammy symbolize pretty much the same aspect of local history, as if they needed them both because the eel enthusiasts might cause a ferocious riot if only the shrimping industry is represented.

Every time Captain Gas shot a penalty his stupid big boot flew off. It was funny at first but rapidly became just a tedious design fault. This display of comical ineptitude culminated in the goalie (the Southend mascot) actually catching his boot rather than the ball.

We lost the proper match 2-0, and were disqualified from the crucial mascot shootout.

Two losses.

All in a days work for a Rovers away outing!

PLEASE DO NOT FEED THE SEAGULLS
BY DAVID TITCHENER (TITCHTHEPHOT)

I have been a Rovers fan since 1971 and my first away game watching the Gas was against Brighton and Hove Albion. My Mum is from Hove and a lot of her family still lived there. My cousin was having a birthday party that weekend so we thought we would use it as an excuse to go there. My brother Neil, and best mates Alan and Jon were keen to go to the match so I got my Uncle to buy us four tickets. He did so... but unfortunately got us tickets with him and my cousins in the Brighton end!

We thought we had better not wear our scarves as although Brighton play in Blue and White as well ours had 'Rovers' printed on them... a bit of a give away! We couldn't change the tickets so I decided to bite the bullet and hope that if Rovers scored we could try to stifle our cheers. Boy, did we choose the wrong match to go to! It was the infamous 8-2 thrashing in December 1973, with Brian Clough as their new manager.

Obviously stifling our cheers was not something any of us were very good at and it soon became apparent to the thousands of Seagull fans around us that we were from the 'other side'. Bearing in mind how football was dogged with hooliganism back then, we were a bit concerned for our safety. We needn't have worried because by the time Rovers' sixth goal went in they started cheering with us. And when the seventh and eighth went in it was like their team had scored.

They were superb fans who took the game in the right spirit and caused us no problems at all even though it will go down as one of our best games ever. My cousin's party turned into a Rovers celebration and we rushed home on the sunday in time to watch it on 'The Big Match'.

ABOVE - Gashead larking about on the Prom at Blackpool. Probably April 2000 match (last time we played there).   Photo courtesy of Glen.

BELOW (left) - Sign that made me larf at Morecambe's old Christie Park ground.
BELOW BELOW (left) - 'elf and safety gone mad at Blackburn? 3 photos by Martin Bull

BELOW (right) - Mickey Evans; Plymouth Argyle legend, Rovers nightmare signing!

AWAY THE GAS

Q & A for the forthcoming book on the marvellous away game memories of Bristol Rovers Fans

Imagine you are at an Alcoholics Anonymous meeting. Please stand up and say...

My name is *Trevor Edwards* and I have supported Bristol Rovers for _28_ years

We were in Division _3_ *(OLD)* when I starting supporting Rovers / the Pirates / the Gas (which do you prefer?)

My first ever away match was _@ Ashton Gate._

I have been to approx _180_ away matches at _60_ different grounds

---

My favourite away grounds are ... (and why)
Shrewsbury Town (Weetabix) Craven Cottage and Blackpool for the famous win.

I remember my worst ever away journey ...
To Wigan in 89/90, the game got called off at 2.45, a long way for a bag of chips.

The furthest I've travelled away is ...
Rotherham United.

The earliest / latest I ever got to a match was ...
3.40 after being on the Stella in the Centur ion in Tiverton, not a great excuse.

Best / worst grub = Best : Crewe - gravy on the chips
Worst : Exeter - awful.

Best / worst boozer =
Swansea Jacks was best –
Anywhere in Rotherham was the worst

Best / worst half-time 'entertainment' =
IN THE BAR, RARELY SEE IT !

My favourite home fans are ... (and why)
Liverpool – they gave us a standing ovation
they know their football up there.

The best [clean] chant to home fans has been ...
Will you ever beat the Gas v B.City
Staying Up, Going down, Staying v Swindon (Tax fiddle)

The best away goal I've seen was ...
Paul Nixon v Blackpool 30 yards plus.

I really, really wish I had gone to these away games ...
Lincoln in the play offs.

I regret ... nothing. Supporting Rovers it what it is,
good or bad so be it!

Have you ever smuggled Weetabix into Shrewsbury? (YES)/ NO

Have you ever worn fancy dress?   YES (NO)

Have you travelled away on a supporters train?   (YES)/ NO

Our worst shirt sponsor was - Snack Box / Peter Carol / Elite Hampers

EXODUS: MOVEMENT OF GAS PEOPLE

In its own way this is a companion chapter to 'My Top Five Away Memories' [pages 99-121], although the difference here is that these Gasheads are exiled, invariably in the Northern wastelands [a.k.a. anywhere beyond Michael Wood services].

As a regular exile myself, including two years in Africa, I can completely understand the sentiments in this chapter, including those of one of my own brothers who swapped Bath for Leeds, lost the map and never returned, and writes, as if he is Eric Cantona, that at his sporadic Rovers games "even though I am away, I am nevertheless home".

The beauty of Northern games is seeing things like Alan Ball's master class, a dog loose on the pitch, candy floss being sold in the away end, Jim Gannon missing a penalty... twice, great fish and chips, a hat-trick goal from Jamie Cureton's face, lots of rain, and Worrell Sterling and Will Hoskins scoring long range stunners at the same stadium, separated by 15 years.

WHEN I AM WITH MY PEOPLE

BY CHRIS BULL

Having moved up North nearly twenty five years ago and having limited time and opportunities to visit back home each season, it means that my watching the Gas during that time has been focused more on the away than the home experience, and indeed, given the lack of miles travelled, what is defined as an away game by most supporters is more of a home experience for me. I'm sure that the majority of supporters in exile know this feeling.

At the end of each campaign I'm looking at the Leagues either side of us to see how my forthcoming season is going to be shaped by Northern teams either coming into or leaving the division, and sometimes I find myself way too immersed in the potentials because of it. For instance, me following York City's re-entry into the Football League at the start of the 2012/13 season via the play-off final with as much gusto as any of their own supporters was tempered at the end of the end of that same season when both Rotherham United and Bradford City got promoted, therefore severely damaged my chances to see Rovers closer to 'home' the following season.

It's because I mainly go to Northern away games these days that I savour my Rovers match day experience as they might not come up too often, even though being a realist – and Gasheads are nothing if not realists - I know that given our away record over the years, I go to these games understanding that there is a likelihood that we won't perform too well. Not to say that as soon as the Eagle coach leaves Bristol it's a guarantee to be spanked as easily as a poorhouse child, but time has taught me that as much as I'm excited to see the boys play away, it's the experience of the day rather than the result that I relish. Put it this way – as much as I might occasionally see 'Pirates plunder three points' in the back pages of local papers on Monday evening after a Rovers visit, it's more likely I'll be faced with a 'Pirates made to walk the plank' zinger instead.

I don't mind admitting for example that any trip to Crewe will be more in anticipation of the magnificent fishcake and chips served up at the Gresty Road chip shop than any performance on the pitch itself; that a memorable visit a few years ago to Boundary Park found me in a magical old cake and pie shop a mere stone's throw from the ground, serving up delicious home-made food at prices seemingly unchanged since the 1980s; that Halifax Town once had a supreme catering van in the away end that sold the usual cooked fare plus funfair food stuff like coconut ice and bags of brandy snaps, or that it was the pre-match sound of Tommy Steele's 'Any Old Iron' coming out of the rusty old PA on a visit to Glanford Park that put a smile on my face.

When things are not expected to be majestic on the pitch, then you take refuge in any other form of entertainment on an away day. And no, the definition of entertainment does **not** include the almost mandatory appearance in stadiums at 2.45pm of a local dance troupe of schoolgirls called 'Sparklez' gyrating to wholly inappropriate sexualised dance music, creating an endemic of lycra-clad Ebola across the length and breadth of the country. And no, your team predictably running out to 'Right Here Right Now' or 'Simply The Best' is also not part of the match day experience that I care about.

If your team was to run out to Melt-Banana's 'Cat Brain Land' and have Sparklez dance to it, then that would be something to report, but generally speaking I have to take my away day entertainment in other forms.

Away days sometimes bring up that 'I was there' moment for anyone who can't make it to many home games and its easy to feel denied of such home advantages. Speaking as someone who missed out on so many of Keith Valle's hilarious home match day introductions in years gone by, when you do get an 'I was there' moment at any away game it makes it all the more delicious. For example, I might not have been there to hear Keith announce the substitute arrival of a young Gary Flitcroft as 'Gary Flipflop' to mass hilarity at Twerton, but I was there at York City in the 1994/95 season, when a dog came onto the pitch and remained running free for about a minute amongst deliberately stationaary players and it was down to a theatrical Dean Kiely in the York goal to recognise the sheer glory of the situation, making an exaggerated comedy leap to try and capture it to mass pantomime cheers from the crowd. The 'pursuit' ended with a savvy Gashead from the away end luring it in with chips to get it off the pitch, while one wag sang "One dog in Yorkshire, there's only one dog in Yorkshire" (you can still see the scene on You Tube: http://www.youtube.com/watch?v=9_QNssmF88s).

Sometimes those 'I was there' moments appear more than once at the same ground. Barnsley's Oakwell was the scene of Dennis 'I should have been cast in 'Game Of Thrones', I'm that rock' Rofe's wearing of just a polo shirt and shorts on the bench during a sub-zero November game. It became so much of a talking point amongst Gasheads who attended the game that a photograph commemorating the event graced the next front cover of the sadly missed 'Second Of May' fanzine.

This was incidentally the same day when a few hours before I'd been overheard in a pub by a local and been subject to genuinely aggressive abuse suggesting I was inbred. If you'd ever been to Barnsley in the early 90's and seen the amount of people there with three eyes and a tail, then that's a bit rich, like Ritchie Rich is rich. It was a place that was so dated at the time that it reminded me of that joke where a motorist driving through a Northern town knocks over a woman's pram in the middle of the road and is relieved to see only coal falling out of it.

Anyhoo, in the same ground a season later I had another 'I was there' moment when, during a truly abysmal game, Rovers fans in the open away end had noticed that right behind the stadium there were a few games being played on the local pitches there. Soon enough everyone decided to rush en masse to the back of the stand and watch those games instead, roaring on our support for the pub teams below, much to their surprise and the rest of Oakwell's. For the rest of the afternoon our backs were turned on the game we'd paid money to go and see, and instead our hearty voices bellowed out cheers and chants for our newly found free entertainment. Every goal that went in we cheered, and we cheered again when the goal scorers of 'The Pig & Whistle' or 'The King's

Head' below applauded us for our involvement. I even recall us starting off by supporting a team playing in blue and white, and when we saw how utterly rubbish they were, we started chanting for any team on the pitches playing in the same colour as our away kit at the time instead ("Come on you bluuuuuuuuuues! *pause* Ah, you're guts! Yel-looooows! Yelloooows!"). It was one of the most fun away games I have ever been to.

I don't get to see Rovers win away that much, so when I do the occasion is imprinted, and when we win in a game that we have not only been under the cosh for 90 minutes but manage to nick a winning goal late on or deep in extra time, it's special. A few seasons ago we went to Huddersfield Town and as they hadn't lost a game at home so far that season, Rovers away in midweek against an in-form team generally equates to shoving a couple of tenners down your pants, pouring lighter fluid on your crotch and setting fire to yourself.

I was meeting a mate there who is a Terriers season ticket holder and he introduced me to a guy he knows who is a Gashead. He managed to get me into the away end for free by passing me some weird kind of Willy Wonka golden ticket through the railings. My friend laughed and said that at least I wouldn't have to pay to watch us be humiliated.

Throughout the game Town were battering us and we should have been 10 down by half-time but our goal led a charmed life. The second half was exactly the same but somehow we held out, until, in the fifth minute of injury time, we made a rare sojourn forward, and on the outside of the box, in front of travelling Gas, Will Hoskins looped a beautiful curled chip past the keeper.

Moments later the whistle blew and we were three points the richer from a game that we never ever should have won and we were going mental. Anyone there would say that justice really had taken a good kick in the seat of the pants that evening but those are the times you celebrate even more. I met my friend outside. He asked me if I wanted a lift to the station, and before I could answer he made a point of angrily telling me, "You can f off and walk" while his kid stood next to him crying at the nature of the defeat. Given that Rovers seem to be the masters of capitulation between the 80th and 90th minute, that game will stay in the memory.

There are however grounds where Rovers traditionally do well away. You might have to squint a bit to find them, but they are there. Rotherham United is one such club in recent years and the old Millmoor ground close to the start of the 1994/95 season was the scene of one of my favourite and most memorable away journeys. Rotherham at that time seemed not to be in great shape, the natives were restless and an end of game demonstration had been announced. The away end was wire-fenced and at the back of the stand there were areas that seemed to resemble corrugated iron which that was so old it curled at the bottom so you could see daylight and the feet of people walking past. I took a vague interest in this at the time but having been resident on the Popular Side at Twerton for years, it was hardly a unique dilapidation and rather something that represented a 'proper' football stadium in my eyes.

Rovers ran out convincing 3-0 winners, the final goal of which was a magnificent lob from distance that each time I think about it, it moves further back down the pitch to the degree that now I imagine it was lobbed from somewhere else in South Yorkshire entirely. Although the home fans had been grumbling for some time (it was still the first half!), the whole ground nevertheless rose to applaud it so that momentarily I received a vision of the entire ground turning monochrome and every-one attending wearing three piece suits, waving rattles and throwing their hats in the air while shouting "Huzzah!".

This rosy image was only going to last until the final whistle though, at which point home fans came onto the pitch to demonstrate. I don't know what the plan was but as they piled out of the Kop end, they seemed to be coming closer and closer and they weren't the happiest. We could hear home fans walking behind our stand and could see the feet of them through the curled metal and realised that they could enter our stand with little effort. I suddenly got this weird vision that all of what was happening in front of us and behind us was some kind of pre-arranged two prong attack on an away end of fans who were fenced in with nowhere to go (hey, don't blame me – Brimson brothers books had a huge market share back then).

As the organised throng chanting 'Sack The Board' approached past the penalty area in front of us, I can't remember seeing any Police or stewards near them and in my mind's eye now, if there was any Police presence that day it would have been some 1950's parody of a fat panting copper blowing his whistle and trying to find a Police box to call for help for his other portly chums to huff and puff running to the ground. Some Gasheads were climbing up the fence with a bit of bravado and a few choice words of humorous banter aimed towards the approaching group, so I wondered what was going to happen next.

What did happen next was a huge chorus of 'Sack The Board' suddenly rang out from our end, to which the home fans responded in kind and so began a unified chant from both sides. Millers were at our fences and climbing up to meet Gasheads at the top, but rather than nefarious deeds being committed, hands were vigorously shaken, applause was given on both sides of the fence and appreciation and understanding was shared. For any club which can only dream of being in a top League and which year after year operates on a tight budget and might have at best, if lucky, very limited and relative forms of success, 'There but for the grace of God go I' is a mantra that we all understand.

When we face other clubs having a bad time of it we recognise that they could just as easily be us, and, given finances and costs in the lower Leagues, then statistically speaking it probably will be one day. That visit to Rotherham made for a memorable game, result and performance but it was also something that cemented the common themes of being a lower League football supporter, and I will always think fondly of Rotherham fans as a result of that day.

Away days are not usually destined to become the best days of your football supporting lives, but the landscape changes and with it often the nature or context of the experience, and so it becomes something entirely different than a comfortable home game, even if some of those memorable events we hold onto could just as easily happen at a home or away experience. Going to away games, you are numerically in the minority, you are financially worse off, you are entering a universe where quite often the hope of a win or even a draw will not even enter into the equation of the travelling supporter, and so it will generally make no sense at all – both fiscally and psychologically – why you choose to do it when there seems to be very little return for significant financial and emotional outlay. But perhaps that's precisely why we do it. It takes a person who is both hardy and yet also foolhardy to commit to away travel and so to be amongst other like-minded souls on matchday is a reminder that we are not alone, that we crave endeavours and challenges, and although we don't expect much for our input and sacrifice, occasionally we will be rewarded.

It might be a reward in the form of something that happens on the pitch – Worrell Sterling's 25 yard pile driver against Huddersfield Town in front of the travelling Gas support is one of the finest goals in away colours (green and yellow quarters, I seem to recall) I have ever seen - or it could equally be something that happens off it, such as a sunny evening trip to Hartlepool United where a beautiful Jo Kuffour daisycutter on the edge of the box and a rare away victory was more than equalled by the reward of hilarity that ensued when, on the way to the ground, one member of our party [me; the editor!] stood in the biggest single piece of dog poo I have ever seen and how it covered the bottom of their shoe like a dirty brown blanket.

So that's what I have in terms of a few choice memories of Gas away days in the North of England, how I rely on these games to keep connected, and how these games act as home games in a sense. Whilst on that note, I am constantly staggered how many Gas manage to get to midweek evening games in Yorkshire and surrounding areas, I really am. It's a reminder how special an away day is and how dedicated any away supporter is, and even if a good deal of those games are made on my own (we sometimes forget that for many, travelling to games can be a very solitary, lonely experience), I only have to enter the away end of a ground and hear the burrs and nuances of a West Country accent and dialogue to know that I am with my people and even though I am away, I am nevertheless home, regardless of wherever that ground might be.

Finally, an apology to Norwich City. I'm sorry for splitting the back of one of your seats in rage at the Gas 1-5 defeat at Carrow Road in the 2009/10 season. It's a bit out of character for me, and to be fair, I only kicked it twice and you really should make them a bit more sturdy, but even so, I'm sorry. On the plus side, I did get a right lush pizza before travelling back up North. *[Editor's Note - Calm down bro. It was only Pizza Express you Northern savage]* See what I mean? Go to an away game and the pizza afterwards is just as important when it comes to the memory banks. Proper job.

Chris Bull is a keen half marathon runner and avid follower of the undisputed best band in the world - Shonen Knife, from Osaka, Japan.

He is hoping that by 2020, all Yorkshire people will finally understand that wasps are not wasps but jaspers, and that if Yorkshire really is 'God's Own Country', then God has neither visited Bradford nor been stuck in Church Fenton.

THE ROAD TO WIGAN (BUT NOT TO THE PIER)
BY NICK HODGSON

In September 1980 at the tender age of eighteen, I left Bristol to head 200 miles north to start studying at Lancaster University. The South Stand fire at Eastville had happened a few weeks earlier, Terry Cooper (complete with perm) was the manager, and I'd had to watch Rovers play a home game against Grimsby Town at Ashton Gate of all places, so I kind of realised that the 1980/81 season was going to be a tough one.

Even then, being a Rovers fan wasn't easy! I'd chosen Lancaster over Hull, despite knowing that there was no local professional football team to follow. My geography at the time wasn't great, but when I arrived 'Up North' I soon realised just how close I was by train to many famous football grounds. Also literally just down the road was Morecambe, where I was to live in my second year, but The Shrimps at the time were no more than a solid Northern League outfit (I have since taken three trips down memory lane to see the Gas play there).

Football has always been my great passion, and the Rovers are at the heart of that passion. My plan of action at University was to have a great time, go to as many grounds in the North West as possible (ideally watching the Rovers) - oh, and maybe get a degree at the end of it.

By and large, the plan worked, helped by heavily discounted train fares thanks to my student rail card that made travel unbelievably cheap. As well as watching both the Liverpool and Manchester derbies, and the odd match of interest (Swansea City being promoted to Division One at Deepdale, Rochdale beating the City at Spotland - inevitably I was a Rochdale fan for a day - and going to a packed Maine Road), I did get to see quite a lot of the Rovers.

This included going to one of coldest grounds in the country, Boundary Park, to welcome the re-signed Paul Randall off the bus. He wasn't entirely fit and I'm sure nearly tripping head over heels as he walked down the steps off the coach probably didn't help! We lost to Oldham

Athletic 2-0 that day and relegation beckoned. We always seemed to do quite well against Preston North End, but I remember travelling back from Bristol at the start of one term via Wrexham and watching us capitulate at the Racecourse Ground.

The best match of all in my three years in Lancashire was in 1983 at Wigan. It was my final year at university and I'd managed to borrow my mother's car for the entire academic year (how I got away with that I'll never know). The trouble was that the loyal old white Mini Clubman was prone to the occasional mechanical disaster. Now I'm no car mechanic, but it had been dawning on me for a while that the brakes were becoming be a bit dodgy. By the time I had set off on Saturday lunchtime down the M6 to Wigan, a journey of only 40 miles, I realised that my only hope in getting to watch the mighty Rovers was to be very gentle on the accelerator and make liberal use of the handbrake, because the middle pedal was just not interested in responding. Remarkably, apart from one near miss (or should I say near hit) into the rear end of the car in front on a one-way section in Wigan whilst looking for signposts to Springfield Park, I made it in one piece.

Now if you never went to Springfield Park when it existed, let me try and describe the scene for you. The ground made Twerton look palatial, and the away end was literally a grassy-cum-muddy bank. The main stand was a smaller version of the Dribuild at the Mem. The crowd that afternoon was a faithful 3,288, with probably no more than 50 or so Gasheads. Rather like most folk in Lancashire, the welcome from the Latics fans was a warm one, but what I'm sure none of us, home or away fans, were expecting that afternoon was a midfield masterclass from a 1966 World Cup winner.

More knowledgeable Gasheads than me will know the story behind the signing of Alan Ball, but all I can say is a big thank you to whoever did that deal. His display on Saturday, February 26th 1983, is one of most breathtaking performances I have ever seen in a Rovers shirt. 'Bally' had of course reached the highest level that any professional footballer can achieve by being part of England's World Cup winning side, aged just 21.

Now at the final club of his 20+ year career and his legs 'gone', especially on the heavy muddy pitches of the era, he relied on the youthful vigour of Tony Pulis and Geraint Williams to do the running whilst he used his brilliant football brain to make incisive passes, splitting open the hapless Wigan defence all afternoon.

It was truly a honour and privilege to watch someone perform like that for the Rovers. We won 5-0, one of our best away results - ever! For the record, the scorers were Randall (2), Withey (2) and Platnauer. Current physio Phil Kite was in goal and Ian Holloway was the sub (remember, only one substitute allowed in those days). The car journey back was remarkably uneventful, probably fuelled (every pun intended) by the excitement of the result and Alan Ball's performance.

Today I am writing this just days after we have been relegated to the Conference. Wigan, complete with their state-of-the-art stadium and F.A. Cup victory in 2013, are in the Championship play-offs trying to return to the Premier League at the first attempt. What contrasting fortunes. Alan Ball is sadly no longer with us, and following the Rovers continues, as ever, to be a roller-coaster ride for us fans.

I did get my degree and have been living in London since the late 1980's. I manage to see the Rovers at least twenty times a season, almost always with my 17 year-old son Ed, who may be a born and bred Londoner but is 100% Gas, like his father, grandfather and (although he never knew him) great-grandfather.

There are plenty of other stories I can think of about Rovers away games I have attended, including abandonment's (both at Crawley Town and the infamous Wycombe Wanderers health and safety debacle), being snowed upon (numerous locations), and dodging flying bricks (Swansea City), but the 5-0 win at Wigan Athletic in 1983 will stay with me vividly until I finally have to hang up my metaphorical boots.

[Editor's Note - At 37 years and 262 days of age Alan Ball became the third oldest debutant for Rovers when he played against Chesterfield on 29th January 1983. The oldest is Harry Smith, at 38 years and 36 days, who played in 1946/47 when teams were still readjusting to post war life]

365 BLUE & WHITE AWAY DAYS A YEAR
BY MARTIN BULL

This isn't an away game memory as such, but is about my exile in East Africa, and given that I lived close to Shashemene, the fabled home of Rastafarianism in Ethiopia, I think I should be allowed to enter into this émigré chapter, which after all is named after a Bob Marley song.

Yes, you heard right. Whilst people whinge about living as far away as London, or Wales, I was exiled in Ethiopia for most of 1995 and half of 1996. Just in case your geography is sketchy, to get to Ethiopia you take the A2 from London, hang a right at Gillingham, and then continue 5,838 kilometres.

It wasn't really the distance that made exile tough, as many Gasheads have lived far further away than me, it was more the lack of communication, my own lack of money, and simply the bygone age we then lived in.

In 1995 Ethiopia was still recovering from a totalitarian Marxist government and a prolonged Civil War that had only ended four years previously. The atmosphere was still a little tense (especially after an attempt to assassinate the Egyptian President Hosni Mubarak in the capital Addis Ababa) and investment hadn't yet returned to the country. Communications were poor and expensive, and the Internet was still just the stuff of a pornographers dream. As a semi-volunteer I didn't have much money, and no disrespect to Rovers but phoning home to find out footy news wasn't high on my financial agenda. I got my Rovers news mainly via letters from home, and the press cuttings that accompanied them. On average I'd say I found out the details of a match (and sometimes the score itself!) about 10 days after it was played. Every few days I itched to be able to go the Post Office on the other side of my dusty town to see if there was anything for me (there are no home post deliveries in Ethiopia, or most of Africa) and it was the highlight of my week to get a letter, or even better the occasional package crammed full of cuttings. If a package was from my Mum it would probably also contain some food I missed, and if it was from my brother it would most likely have a wicked mix tape in it. These simple pleasures were a rare lifeline.

This is starting to make me sound like I was a prisoner in jail. I wasn't. That came later in life.

Ethiopia now (2014) is a very different place and is in the grip of an urban economic boom and Premier League fever. Matches are shown in bars everywhere, many people have 400 channels on satellite, several of which are showing football from all over the world (often obscure Middle Eastern stuff), and mini-buses regularly show off their allegiance to Arsenal, Man U etc. But back in 1995 most people had to make do with ETV (Ethiopian Television), which was one channel of biased news, ancient American repeats, and one decent film a week. They also quaintly finished the night around 11.30pm with a grainy old recording of the Ethiopian flag flying, whilst the typically scratchy national anthem played behind it. The climax of the sporting week was an hours highlights from the Premier League, three weeks after the matches were played, and 'Gillette Sports Special', an hour long smorgasbord of various sporting flimflam that was six months old (I kid you not, it really was almost the gestation period of an elephant; but beggars couldn't be choosers).

During my first month there in 1995 Rovers hardly played any games due to country wide floods and snow, which gave me time to organise my weekly rituals. I bought a radio that could receive all the guff in the universe and listened to the BBC World Service sports news once a day, and the results on Saturday. I started to receive regular match reports in the post and every Saturday I went through my 'psychic power' ritual, without really knowing if we were playing or not, especially after games had been postponed. Looking back these were beautifully innocent days, and I guess I wasn't an obsessed fan. Going to the actual match was still the real point of being a footy fan for me. The rest was just stats.

The ritual was nothing elaborate, just a bit quirky. After a morning shower I would stand in my scant room and put my Rovers T-shirt on whilst willing the team to win today and humiliate the opposition. The Rovers T-shirt had to go on first (nothing else could sully my body) and my body had to be pure and freshly cleansed (hence the shower). The T-shirt was from the geezer down the little alleyway at Twerton Park, between the main turnstiles at the Bath End and the Gateway / Somerfield on the High

Street (now there's a name that takes me back... ahhh, good old Gateway - West Country and proud). It was thinner than a waif with ringworm and probably only cost me a few quid. YGWYPF, as the kids might say [you get what you pay for]. It just had a large BRFC logo from that era on it; you know, the most boring logo ever known to humanity, two interlocking squares and a quarter of a football. Zzzzzzzzzzzzzzzz.

But it was MY T-shirt and it was the indispensable focal point of MY ritual when 6,000 kilometres away. In fact without the T-shirt I doubt there would have even been a ritual. The only other Gas memento I had brought with me, and fit for such high-level pagan worship, was an old 'Design Windows' home kit (the one where the sponsor was actually on a sew-on patch), but I'm pretty sure I gave that away quite soon after my arrival to a friend I made in Ethiopia. See the photo below of Metaferia Negash and me in our respective Rovers attire in my favourite restaurant in Awassa. I'm the one on the left :-) The poster is wonky, not us...

And it seemed to be working, as Rovers were slowly clawing their way up the table. One day I got confirmation in the post that Rovers were in the play-offs, after beating Cardiff by a late goal. My home-made League tables had already pointed to this likelihood but I needed hard journalistic proof before I celebrated too wildly.

When we played the second-leg of the play-off at Gresty Road I was in a small town with the unfortunate name of Soddo. Foreigners usually embarrassingly pronounced it So-do, rather than the reality, which was the full on Sod-do. I set my alarm for 6am and thrashed around in my bed when the radio informed me that Rovers were going to Wembley!

This was a big problem though. I felt very left out being a Gashead a million miles from Wembley. I jokingly asked my boss to pay for an air flight and give me time off; I seem to remember the words 'off' and 'bugger' being in the reply somewhere.

Even worse was the fact that the BBC World Service didn't give a monkeys about the most important match for a squillion Gas years. Why couldn't they provide live coverage? Or at least interrupt programmes with the latest updates? Why couldn't Andy Warren be allowed to scream and rant over the world airwaves, giving heart attacks to old grannies in Western Samoa who accidentally tuned in whilst channel hopping? Why wasn't anyone interested in my most important day for years? Why why why!? I had lots of whys, as the BBC sorely underestimated the huge BRFC supporter base in Ethiopia (two... at a rough count).

I found out the result in a very cold and cruel way, by having to wait for the evening's 15 minute Sports Round-Up when they drolly gave me the terrible news in one monotone sentence. I think I heard it about three hours after the final whistle which in those days was a minor miracle.

That one dull sentence was a killer. I had nervously waited all day for that one utterance. How do you prepare yourself for such an all of nothing piece of news? It took years to build up to that day yet a mere three seconds to execute all your hopes and dreams. 2-1. And it was those bleeding Huddersfield kick-donkeys as well.

It wasn't until the press cuttings arrived, plus my brothers indubitably impressive report, that I learnt the full horror. Marco van Stewart, avec headband, revealing his full skills to the nation's stadium and hitting a screamer against the bar in the last minute yet coming home a loser, Gareth Taylor missing an open goal, Andy 'God' Tillson having a strangely ineffective match and later seen scuffing around the Wembley seats distraught at his poor performance, wearing the dreaded away kit, and worst of all my brother evidently bearing his pasty chest in public in a Mick Channon windmill celebration at the dreamy sight of Marco's goal.

I still have the T-shirt somewhere, minus the sleeves as the underarms were castrated in order to rescue the rest of the holy relic. I haven't worn it for a very long time as it is now more fragile than the Turin Shroud.

Having 365 away days a year was hell when Rovers were doing well, bearable when they were floundering, but never a gratifying state of affairs.

QUITE INTERESTING AWAY STATS

We've never lost at Hereford United in the League, notching up 2 wins and 3 draws at Edgar Street. However, rather bizarrely we've never won there in a Cup match, and never even scored, losing 3 out of 4 easily (8 goals to nil), and then also 'losing' the September 2009 Johnstone's Paint Trophy 1st Round match on penalties after a tame scoreless draw.

We've never won at Barrow in the League, with three games between 1967 and 1969. We did however win (3-2) the infamous F.A. Cup 1st Round match there on Remembrance Day 2006. I write 'infamous' because their player James Cotterill punched Sean Rigg so hard, in an off the ball incident, that it gave Sean a double fracture of the jaw and meant he drank through a straw and ate from a teaspoon and will have metal plates in his jaw for the rest of his life. Cotterill later told Police that earlier in the game Rigg had "barged into him". Ooh diddums. Thankfully this wasn't swept under the carpet like a lot of on-the-field sporting violence (cf. it's a man's game... yeah, but it's not a thugs game!) and he was not only banned by the F.A. until March 2007 but was also sentenced to four months in prison after admitted Grievous Bodily Harm. Pea brained Barrow apologists lined up to say he was a scapegoat. Coin throwing at Steve Phillips was also reported to the Police. There must be something about post-Industrial dock towns (Gillingham, Southampton, Cardiff, Liverpool, Newcastle anyone?) that has bred microscopic brains and Popeye style arms into too many of the local men, who will fight their own shadows if they turn around too fast on a sunny day. That's if their stupid pit bull dogs don't eat their babies alive first.

ROVERS UP NORTH 1998/1999

BY JOZER

In 1998 I was living in Sheffield, finishing College and working in a brake shoe factory in Chapel-en-le-Frith. I had a simple but reliable VW Polo and used it to commute 50 miles a day to Chapel, and to go to Rovers away games when I could.

1998/99 was the season when we started well, flirted with relegation after selling Barry Hayles, and then went up and down again before finally pulling clear of bother by going unbeaten for the last five games of the season, as Roberts and Cureton clicked and we plundered 11 points from 15.

Stoke City - Back then we were Stoke's jinx team for a couple of years. Driving to work early one morning in October 1998 I picked up a couple of hitchers. The bloke was a Stokie who was going to pick up an impounded car, and then hoping to make it to Bristol for the game at Rovers the next day. They had won eight of their first nine games, were still top of the table after 13 games, and clearly fancied their chances that season. I told him I was a Rovers fan and we chatted while his long-suffering girlfriend rolled her eyes. I wished him best of luck apart from against Rovers. We won that home game 1-0 and temporarily knocked Stoke off top spot. Later that season, in April, they put another run together and were hoping to return to the play-off places, but Rovers stuffed them 4-1 at the Britannia Stadium in front of almost 18,000, and widdled on their fireworks for the second time that season. It was amazingly our first away win since the infamous 6-0 mauling of Reading in January. Stoke finished eighth that season.

Man City - I took a train to Manchester, and thought I could easily walk to Maine Road. I got hopelessly lost in a pretty rough area (I think it was the notorious Moss Side but maybe I was just scared) and ended up stopping a taxi, who promptly took me about two hundred yards and around two corners to the away end entrance. The seated stand was all ticket and about 100 of us had to use a temporary corner stand with no roof but plenty of scaffolding. Shaun Goater was up front for City so the usual poohead chants accompanied him whenever he was on the ball. Rovers stifled them and got a 0-0 draw. Ten minutes from the end their fans in the Kippax started leaving accompanied by us singing 'you're going home..' to the Three Lions tune. I have a big respect for Man City fans though who turned up in huge numbers even when they were in the Third division playing minnows like us *[Editor's Note - 25,000 that day]*. Two weeks later I was in my local in Sheffield. I met a Man City fan and the first thing he asked me was 'what the hell is a sheeeeedheeeeed?'

Rotherham United - I took a local train just over the M1 to the Third Round F.A. Cup match, where Stephan Leoni scored the only goal for Rovers just before half-time. I had a very good time with other Gasheads in a pub near the ground before the match, and in the bar at Sheffield station after. Rotherham fans were in a jolly mood despite losing because it was the first time in about two years that their team hadn't been a total shambles, and they went on to get back-to-back promotions while Rovers went the other way in 2001. I tried to get to the Fourth Round in Bristol against Leyton Orient but British Rail wanted about £80 for a day return ticket! I said to the woman on the phone "I want to go to Bristol, not buy the ****ing place" and then had to apologise as it wasn't her fault. In the Fifth Round we got Barnsley but none of our 4,000 tickets even made it past the Season Ticket holders and Supporters Club members. I put a stupid bet on Rovers winning and Roberts getting a hat trick. The woman in the bookies looked at me like I was a two-year old. I heard the result in the pub with my mate Kev from Barnsley who had a jolly good laugh at me.

[Editor's geeky note - we lost 4-1, with a late consolation goal from Jason Roberts. This 'meaningless' goal later proved vital as it was the goal that ensured Jason surprisingly won the Golden Boot as the leading scorer in the F.A. Cup that season with seven goals in the competition]

Preston North End - In February I drove on a Motorway called the M62 or suchlike. I stopped halfway for a coffee at a service station high up in the freezing Pennines. When I got back in the car the battery had just died of the cold. I found I could bump start it quite easily with one foot out of the door pushing it along so I heroically decided to carry on to the match. David Moyes was Preston manager and Deepdale was halfway through re-building. Our stand and the side to the right were new, but the other end and the side to our left were Victorian! This came complete with three modern floodlights and one which looked like a wooden pole with some candles on the top. The game ended 2-2.

The car park was a bit of semi-solid waste ground and I belatedly realized that my one-man bump-start method, which worked fine on a smooth surface, was a very different matter on a lumpy mix of dirt and gravel. Some kindly PNE fans took pity on me and gave me a push. I thanked them and they walked off. The second they were out of sight I managed the stall the car. There was no one else around and it was now getting dark, and it took me an hour of getting in and out and shoving the car around until I finally managed to bump it again. I got home about 10pm having spent hours sweating on a now empty and dark cross-Pennine Motorway, praying that it didn't break down again.

Lincoln City - A month or so before this game I had been 'round a mates one Saturday and saw on Teletext an obvious mistake - Reading vs. Rovers, which had been 0-0 at half-time, was now 6-0 to Rovers. My mates were saying "top result for your lot" and I would insist it was a mistake - "I know Rovers and they DO NOT score six goals in 45 minutes. Ever. It just doesn't happen". It was only later that evening I found out this had actually happened.

I left for Lincoln at 9am so I could take it easy and stop for lunch some-where. As it was it took me six hours to get there anyway. It should not be possible for anywhere in England to be as far away from Sheffield as Lincoln apparently was. As far as I can remember I didn't get lost or stuck in any traffic. Most of the route was A Roads and yet I drove and drove eventually getting there just in time. On the way I was on a trunk route and there was one of those privately owned toll bridges that you usually get on back roads in Wales. The owner was a right git. He wanted 20p and I only had notes. He insisted he had no change and that was my problem. I was about to have to pay him a fiver to cross his little bridge when I found a 20p on the floor of the car, which clearly ruined his day.

Our heroic thrashers of Reading were all over Lincoln from the start but just couldn't find the net. Some nutter in their stand had an old hand-cranked air raid siren which he fired up whenever they had a free kick or corner, and it worked because they scored the only goal of the game from a corner. For some reason a few of the Lincoln fans wore Celtic type green & white hooped tops but I never found out why. Driving back was just as bad. I think there must be a time warp on the Lincolnshire border but at least I was ready with my 20p for the troll this time.

Walsall - I was driving down to Bristol to visit my Mum and Dad, and took in the match on my way. I got to the Bescott just as the game was starting. I had a blue and white quartered flag that I had made and hung it over a fire exit sign in the stand but their stewards made me take it down. Colin Cramb was upfront for Walsall so sheeeedheeeed & 'Colin Cramb is a horse's ****' was sung, to which he responded by scoring a penalty in the first half and ran past us holding his hand to his ear. In the second half Cureton got two back, including a penalty of our own, but Cramb scored again a few minutes later and when there was about five minutes left Walsall fans started leaving.

One of their players back passed to their keeper and Cureton kept a crafty watch on the goalie and the ball. The keeper hoofed it... straight into Jamie's face. It bounced off him, over the keepers head and in to the net. This is still my favourite Rovers goal ever; Cureton punching the air with one hand and holding his nose on his face with the other. Rovers almost got a fourth when one of our guys headed against the bar at point blank range. Every service station on the M6 and M5 back to Bristol was filled with Rovers fans laughing about it.

[Editor's Note - see photos by Glen Young on page 157 for that EXACT goal!]

Chesterfield. This is about 15 miles south of Sheffield and it was a Tuesday evening game. I drove there and found the ground easily. There were about 200 Gas (in a crowd of 2,621), housed in the end of an old wooden stand that shook ominously as we stamped our feet and kept up a continuous chant of 'Ian Holloway's Barmy Army' and 'You'll never get rid of the Gas'. There were home fans in the same stand and at half-time they were using the same food kiosk in the back of the stand. They just looked at us like we were loonies. I heard a guy tell his son "there must be summat wrong with the water down where they come from". At that time Rovers were near the bottom four and the dreadful 0-0 draw was a welcome point. It was raining and I was just glad we weren't on the usual uncovered away end. Saltergate was the old heap that stood in for Derby County's 1970's era Baseball Ground in the film of 'The Damned United'.

I worked with a few Blades fans that year as I lived in South West Sheffield near Bramall Lane. They were always trying to convert me to a 'proper team', but I was on good money at the factory and there was always Saturday overtime on offer which paid nearly £130 for an eight hour shift, so I only ever turned it down for Rovers.

Living on Abbeydale Road my blue and white scarf occasionally attracted 'attention' from tattooed types who I quickly had to show what team it was. This would immediately down grade me from 'Wednesday scum for the battering thereof' to 'funny bloke who sounds like the Wurzels'.

This was the season of Benny Hill at City, and their last away game was at the Blades. City were bottom of the table but had a slim chance of staying up if they won their last two games and other results went their way. I almost went to the game but ended up taking a locum shift at a job just up the road from the ground, and contented myself with a little chuckle as I heard the home crowd roar for the third time.

MARVELLOUS MILLER MAGIC MOTIVATES MILLERS MUTINY

BY MARTIN BULL

I spent a wonderful year at the University of Manchester in 1993/94. The academic year mirrors the football season quite well so I got to six Northern away games in that season, and as I was staying until September for my dissertation, I also got to visit Rotherham United at the start of the 1994/95 season before I moved back down to the West Country.

Although I didn't have that much time or money, or a car, or footy friends [is that the world smallest violin I can hear playing in the background?], I knew that this year may be my only chance to see the gorgeous Gas at some Northern matches, so I made a special effort to get to matches. I managed Huddersfield Town, Stockport County, Blackpool, Bradford City, Port Vale and Burnley in 1993/94, plus Man City's old Maine Road ground and Oldham Athletic with my Norwich City mate (it was the Latics' third and final season in the top flight).

To people who religiously go to every away match this may seem like nothing, but to an exile with a lot of other priorities and not owning a car until 1999 this is still the most away matches I have ever managed in 25 seasons following the Gas.

My abiding memory of **Huddersfield Town**, in their final season at the vast Leeds Road ground, was merely of a huge disintegrating terrace with not many Gasheads on it.

Stockport County also holds no memory to me at all, which probably just about sums up the Hatters. Nice fans, but not much personality. We won 2-0, and apparently Jim Gannon (who later on as their manager became a figure of intense amusement to Rovers fans for throwing a hissy fit over a postponed game) missed a penalty, and then missed the retake as well. It couldn't have happened to a nicer chap.

Blackpool was simply rain, rain and more rain (see my story in the 'England, Sweet England' section on pages 124-127). Pat Stokes also writes about that match and a resulting marriage (yikes!) on page 112.

Bradford City went down in notoriety for my brother and me as the only time we've ever been attacked by so-called footy fans. And it was a cowardly attack from behind, as we peacefully walked back to the train station.

My memory of **Port Vale** is exclusively the long dreary walk from Stoke train station and a barren atmosphere in a rather cavernous stadium for their support. I imagine everyone is saying that about the UWE though!

My final away game of the season goes down as my day of shame as I vaguely remember winning some money on correctly betting that Rovers would lose 3-1 at **Burnley**! I went through a short lived betting phase that season (only a quid or so) because Rovers and Norwich both had great away form and could never be written off in a game. I actually won a few correct score / away win bets, but that day I had a feeling the big boys would win out as my wonderful housemate Ben was a Burnley fan and could have crowed for England about how Turf Moor was a place that didn't suffer away teams taking any points home with them.

I learnt three things that day. One, that Ben was right - actually Ben was nearly always right anyway. Two, that even in March Turf Moor is cold. And to complete the trio I also learnt all the local pronunciations of the Lancashire towns as we drove the back routes from Manchester; Rawtenstall is Rottenstall, Bacup is an almost explosive Back-up, and so on. The secret is to imagine pronouncing it as it is spelt and then throw that out the window, drink six pints of Old Tom, put on a flat cap, smother luke warm gravy all over your chips, and then try again.

I saw three wins and three losses in that season 'up North', which was pretty much par for the course, as we only drew two away games that campaign, whilst winning 10 matches and losing 11.

My brother relays the sights and sounds of the Rotherham United game in September 1994 better than me (see his article at the start of this section, on page 204) but as I'm a history / stat monkey I'm keen to have a bash at putting the game into historical and cultural perspective.

The Millers were already in the relegation zone and we gave their fans the excuse they were looking for to have a pop at their own Board. An own goal by Chris Wilder (later the Oxford United and Northampton Town manager) started the rout off and a brace from Paul 'Caravan' Miller, all in the first half, meant we could just sit back and relax for the rest of the game. This was already their fifth loss of the season, conceding 14 goals in the process, although those losses were bizarrely punctuated by a thumping 4-0 home win over Bournemouth.

I don't know if the famous Templeborough steelworks closing down in 1993 had a massive effect on the whole town, but Millers fans certainly seemed down in the dumps en masse. As the game ended they came on the pitch from the opposite end and swarmed over to the dug out area, singing 'Sack the Board' etc. It certainly seemed like a lot of them, although as the history book reports that only 2,596 turned up, time must have amplified their numbers in my memory. At first we were calmly gawking at this car crash spectacle as it was undeniably a more attractive prospect than leaving for a tourist trip around Rotherham, the ex-steel capital of ...er... Rotherham. It was quite funny until they started coming over towards us. As they got closer and closer it rapidly looked like we could be in for one hell of a battle.

The prehistoric away end was still furnished with big old fences, but they only made things worse as it encouraged overindulgent shows of bravado from a few testosterone fuelled Gasheads. Suddenly the tense atmosphere turned though as we sang 'Sack The Board' back to them, and instead of shaking their fists at us, the Millers fans were now climbing the fences to shake our hands and 'congratulate' us for the humiliating first half display that gave them their justification for a good old fashioned demonstration.

Funnily enough the Millers had a mini rally after this game and by the end of the season had survived relatively comfortably. They were never so charitable to us again and this was our last ever win at Millmoor before they moved onto the ghastly Don Valley Stadium in 2008.

History counts for squat though. Whilst we've bumbled around they are currently (summer 2014) three Leagues above us, and in a nice new stadium. But then again so is everyone else it seems!

THINGS MAY NEVER BE THE SAME AGAIN

I did not intend to have a chapter to myself, but that is what has happened.

When I started this book project I wrote up various memories and ideas that had been floating around in my cavernous head for a while. I then tried to 'fit' the stories into chapters, hopefully without having to ram them home too hard.

These three pieces stood apart as quite different though, about defining moments in our recent history, so I decided to invent a final chapter for them. I realise that hindsight is an easy thing, but I certainly never deliberately wrote them as if I was trying to be clever, or trying to write something to end the book on. They just happened, organically (which in my opinion is the best way to write), as genuine stories about my adventures as a Gashead, woven with patterns that emerged when I looked into moments or matches that when viewed as if a bird were flying above them meant more than just the result that day.

THE DAY THE ROVERS DIED
BY MARTIN BULL

'My my, the Pirates died,
Drove my tractor to the levee but the levee was dry,
them good old Tote End boys drinking scrumpy and rye,
Singing this'll be the day the Rovers died,
Oh this'll be the day the Rovers died'

It may sound like an overly dramatic heading (and a dreadful alteration of Don McLean's 'American Pie' of course), but I seriously think we can put an exact date to the day that the Rovers we knew and loved died.

As I sit here writing these, predominantly upbeat, memories, I am partly using it to try to take my mind off our relegation into non-league after 94 proud years as a League club. Yes we had a few bad years before the Third Millennium Anno Domini started, but nothing could have honestly prepared us for just how scandalous most of the era from 2000 onwards could have been. If asked for your worst case scenario for those 14 seasons, I doubt most Gasheads would have come up with nine seasons in the bottom tier, and three relegations, the last of which took us into non-league.

The day the Rovers died was Wednesday 22nd March 2000.

I'll let you chew that over and I'll return to it later.

Reading still holds a special place in my life story. I was at Uni there and it was the place that I met a Rovers fan, Mark Drew, billeted along the corridor from me in ~~army~~, cough, I mean student accommodation. These were happy days as I got deeper and deeper into the greatest footy team in the world, prodded along by Mark.

My first ever away game was at Reading F.C.'s Elm Park, on 28th November 1989. It was a drab F.A. Cup First Round replay which was slightly enlivened by a David Mehew goal in extra time, after it had been 0-0 at 90 minutes. To this day Mehew is one of my favourite ever Gas players. His goal didn't settle the tie though and at 1-1 it had to go back to Twerton for a third game.

My second ever away game was also at Elm Park, later that season, and I saw my inaugural Gas away win courtesy of that free scoring blonde bombshell.

I don't remember much about these two games, although the record books show that this March game was just before the famous run of six consecutive 2-1 victories (see pages 83-84 for some memories of that phenomenon...)

My only real memories are of how pitiable their ground was, although to be fair most grounds were really shoddy around this time. The Hillsborough disaster had only just taken place and the improvements it helped bring about hadn't yet got through the pipeline. There were also very few rich owners around, and certainly no foreign money, or huge TV revenues flooding into the game.

Elm Park was even worse than most grounds as most stadia at least had some seats on both sides. At Reading only the Norfolk Road (Main Stand) had seats. The rest had huge terraces, rotting away with age. The home fans on the opposite side, the Tilehurst Terrace (a.k.a.South Bank), had the luxury of a roof and a great view, but us away fans in the Reading end (a.k.a. Town End) had nothing but crumbling concrete, huge fences, and a nasty trough to wee in.

This decrepit away end made no difference at these relatively low key matches, but it came home to roost at the high energy fixture a few years later, in April 1994, which I think safely goes down in my memory as the worst atmosphere I've been in at an away game.

I had left Uni by then and purloined my mum's old dogmobile to drive to this Easter Saturday match, after picking up three mates from Banjo Island. We got there nice and early and stopped at Prospect Park, to the west of the ground, for a little game of footy and some grub. It was an idyllic setting, with the sun beating down, a light wind filtering through the swaying trees, and acres of lush green space.

After picking one of my brothers up from the train station we drove back towards the ground, still nice and chilled. You could have easily forgotten that this was a crunch game, as we were sixth and (realistically) were fighting for a play-off place, while Reading were top and looking to keep a gaggle of teams below them, several of whom had games in hand. We had the second best away record in the League, but the Royals had the second best home record in the League.

Something had to give.

The agreeable atmosphere didn't last though as there were pockets of trouble in the streets behind the away end, and as we got towards the away entrance we found a vast swathe of Gasheads trying to get in, whilst the disorganised Thames Valley Police were being typically heavy handed. They always were.

I know Rovers fans aren't always angels but in my experience the worse you treat them the more chance there is that they will repay your malice. My bro had had a few drinks on the train and the cops were trying to indicate he shouldn't be allowed in. He wasn't at all drunk or annoying though, and the rozzers really were just trying to start a fight in an empty room. I had just got through the turnstile when I turned to see them still talking to him. I remember reaching back over and physically dragging him through before they could do anything. Once inside there was no more discussion that could be had, and we made our way up to the rotten terrace above.

It was on days like these that you wonder how more incidents and accidents didn't happen in these decomposing old grounds. Although I miss the character of the older grounds I don't miss their barefaced health and safety failures. Sterile new identikit grounds can be boring, but they are still better than what we used to have. It almost goes without saying that no-one should ever go to a football match and never make it home. #justiceforthe92   I remember sitting in my little room trying to revise for my first year Uni exams when the news about Hillsborough unravelled over my radio. It was hard to comprehend, especially via a radio, and it didn't fully hit me until I saw the TV pictures and the still photos later. Nothing in football, nay almost nothing in life, was ever quite the same again after that day. It sticks in my mind like a forever weeping sore.

We were towards the end of the now traditional fixture pile-up before and around Easter, with nine games in four weeks, and the bumper 8,000 crowd was a third bigger than the size of my previous visits to Elm Park. The atmosphere throughout was tense, almost ugly, not helped by Reading being the better team on the pitch. Home fans baited us caged up away fans from the safety of their large South Bank.

The flash point finally came when someone on that terrace was giving it all large style with his arms outstretched and doing the old 'come on then' motion, before slowly unzipping his jacket to reveal a bright red City top underneath. This 'incident' might sound pathetic when written down 20 years later on something as inorganic as paper, but at the time, with living breathing human beings in that pressure cooker environment it became a 'light the blue touch paper and stand well back' moment! Gasheads flipped and ran over the terrace to the corner, climbing the enormous fence and almost getting over it. This may merely sound like caged men bravado, but of all the times I've seen trouble inside a stadium that day is the one that sticks in the memory most. It really felt like people were serious about getting over that fence, and/or battling someone. Chaos ensued for a while, a lot of arrests were made, and later rumours went around that a Gashead had broke his arm in the midst of it all.

I remember nothing of the game and even had to look into the history books to find out that we lost it, 2-0. It was the first of four defeats in five games that pretty much scuppered our play-off chances. We finished eighth, only three points behind Burnley who grabbed the last play-off slot and were promoted a few weeks later after defeating Stockport County at Wembley, a team who had finished 12 points above them in the League.

That could have been us going up! Yet another occasion that we snatched defeat from the jaws of victory.

Ok, now the part you've all been waiting for. I can now finally reveal the exact date that the Rovers died.

What do you mean I did it earlier?

Oh yeah, so I did.

Ok, I'll explain my reasoning then.

By the time of my next visit to Reading F.C. in March 2000, they were now in their posh new stadium on the outside of town, and were heavily bankrolled by a multi-millionaire backer with a bad comb-over.

They had been struggling, but by the time we met they were pulling away from trouble and had won three out of the previous four games. We were having our best season since promotion 10 years previous. We'd been in the top four virtually all season and had been continuously in the automatic promotion places ever since beating Gillingham in mid January.

But the wheels fell off our entire history that Wednesday night.

A win would have put us top of the League above Preston North End, but we lost 2-0 and it proved to be the start of a shocking run where we managed to earn only six points from the last 10 games of the season, culminating in dropping out of the play-off places on the last game of the season, an anaemic 1-0 loss at Cardiff. That was the first time since August 1999 that we hadn't been in a play-off spot.

I was originally planning to relay the whole story of the repugnant behaviour of Martin 'Mad Dog' Allen (Reading's new Assistant Manager) that fateful night, which explains why some Gasheads have therefore loathed him ever since, but then I realised that he personally is just a tiny mosquito bite in our long history, whereas the defeat, and the almost fatal dose of F.C. Malaria that followed it, has shaped us and defined us for a much long time after. It's now 14 years since that night and we are still afflicted with gasmodium falciparum.

Reading finished the season in a very healthy 10th position, so looking back they had no real need to entice the Mad Dog to metaphorically cock his leg and be so chopsy to the officials and our bench.

We finished the season seventh, with an astonishing 80 points. That would have got us into the Third Tier play-off places every other season since the play-offs started in 1987, right up to the present day (2014). Indeed in one of those seasons 80 points would have even gained us automatic promotion! I don't believe at all in 'luck', as it's usually a lazy excuse to blame something, or someone, else for your failure, but I can just about accept that we have had some awfully unfortunate times in our history.

That night, and what followed as the season took a colossal nose dive, ripped the guts out of our club, our supporters and our team (Jason Roberts and Jamie Cureton both left soon after, feeling they weren't going to get much further in their careers with Rovers). 'Ollie admits that it shook him to the core. The next season was a tangled mess and we were relegated to the Fourth Tier for the first time since it was created in 1958.

My my, that was the day the Rovers died.

A LOCAL CLUB FOR LOCAL PEOPLE

BY MARTIN BULL

My brother and I enjoyed a couple of local trips to Oldham Athletic a few years ago. I used to work in Royton, and drove past Boundary Park everyday. Oldham fans were generally nice people and very local. As Oldham are surrounded by other teams, and the area cherishes a potent inertia which results in people tending not to move further than the next street down [whoa, steady on boy... don't move too far], it means that if you live even a few miles away you are more likely to be a supporter of someone else. Rochdale and Bury are both a metaphorical stone's throw away, and of course the two Manchester behemoths hold a magnetic allure to people who prefer their success to be of the more instant variety.

I never heard an Oldham fan refer to their team as 'Oldham' or 'Oldham Athletic'; it was ALWAYS 'Latics', usually without a 'the' in front of it. Plain, sharp speak for plain local people. I liked that. It was rather romantic and intimate, as though their local club really belonged to them.

By the time the February 2009 game came we were a pretty decent team who had found a scoring habit, and as my brother and I had a relaxed fag outside Boundary Park a young-ish lad asked if we had already bought our tickets. As we answered 'No' he gave us two tickets, for free, even though we offered to give him something for his magnanimous gesture. I hate to suggest that smoking is good for you (it isn't kids, it really isn't!) but if we hadn't stopped for a fag we would have already been inside and each £20 lighter. A comfortable 2-0 win ensued, a six match unbeaten run was underway, and the world was a happy place.

Fast forward a year to our next encounter and the Gas world was not so happy. After being in third place throughout most of September 2009 and winning seven of our first 10 games, we erroneously concluded that we had been coping well upfront without the departed Sir Rickie of Lambert, and thus never properly replaced him. Our April 2010 meeting with the Latics suggested we were now coasting in neutral to a lazy mid-table finish, and cracks in the team were beginning to show. Those crevices widened as the season petered out with only one point from the last six games, and they became chasms in the 2010/11 season which saw sacked managers, 'player power' to the fore, and ultimately a feeble relegation (another season with no wins in the last six games) amidst recriminations of a second relegation to the bottom tier in 10 years.

As we got to Boundary Park we were peckish and I was slightly surprised that we couldn't find much nearby. The best we could do was a newsagent. It was one of those ageless rundown ones where you can't even tell if it's open or closed until you tentatively try the door. As we walked in a bell sounds, we wipe the cobwebs off our heads, and after a short pause a stout lady shuffles out from a back room.

We had walked into a shop co-run by the League of Gentlemen.

A small glass case on the counter housed hand made food, wrapped in thick layers of weapons grade cling film, although it was all heavily meat based and useless for a veggie like me; in fact I would wager that if they had recognised that I was not a heavy consumer of suspect meat products, they would have taken me out the back and fired up the Wicker Man. Although the shop was in a time warp, the lady was pleasant enough and my brother came out with the thickest, cheapest sausage sarnie known to man. Hand made and heated up as well. And it hasn't killed him.

Yet.

The game went less well, losing 2-1 to a Latics team in considerable danger, just two points off the drop, and who clearly wanted the points more than us. The weak willed Rovers players gratefully offered them the win on a plate. We were eighth before this game and still harboured a play-off hope. Several heavy defeats saw us finish 11th that season, and a growing anxiety about the following August. In fact I'd go as far as to say that this Latics game was the start of our relegation march back to the dreaded League Two a year later.

And who knows if it was also this game when the Rovers Board of Directors spotted the grit and determination that Dave Penney, the Oldham manager, had instilled in his strugglers. Penney briefly became our manager the following season, and was going to shake the club up after the gluttonous conclusion of Paul Trollope's reign, but the Board lost their bottle and sacked him before he could rearrange our comfy sofas.

As we trudged out of Boundary Park, Nathan, a well known Gas character, walked out on his tod and shouted solely the single word that is widely considered the most offensive word known to humanity as his one word observation on the game.

Looking back at it now, with two relegation's and five 'permanent' managers sacked in the four following seasons, his analysis was more prescient than any of us realised at the time!

THE DAY WE PARTED COMPANY
BY MARTIN BULL

My best friend, Mike, is a Norwich City fan. For over 23 years now we have gone to each others games, like we were in an unofficial carrot crunchers club. As I'm trying to [slowly] visit all 92 League clubs this comradeship helps me with the 'bigger' clubs and mercifully he never reminds me of the inequality of the football we get to watch when he comes to some of our matches. Nor does he carp about the god forsaken places I drag him to; Dagenham & Redbridge in 2013 being yet another low-light in our 'Odd Couple' relationship.

Although our teams did meet in the League Cup in 2004, we had never met in the League in all the time I'd know him. Our clubs used to meet regularly though; we met most seasons between 1920 (when both entered League 3 [South]) and 1953, and thereafter we actually stayed above them for the rest of the 1950's. Sadly our paths then separated and we consistently remained in a League or three below them from 1962 to 2009, except for a solitary season in 1974/75 when we temporarily occupied the Second Tier together.

It was no surprise then that when Norwich were surprisingly relegated from the Championship in 2009 the League One fixture at Carrow Road the following season was going to be a match that would attract a lot of away day Gasheads. I had been there back in 1991 with Mike to see a Norwich match, but most Gasheads wouldn't have ever had a chance to visit there unless they were rather old, or had managed the aforementioned League Cup match in 2004 on a Tuesday evening.

A truly unexpected stat is that over the 48 previous League encounters we could have been split by a Canaries tail feather. Rovers had won 17, Norwich had won 17, and there had been 14 draws. We had bagged 77 goals, whilst they had netted only 73. And in cup competitions we were clear leaders though, with three wins to their one.

I was finally going to be 'equal' with my glory hunting friend [that phrase is inserted here just to wind Mike up when he reads this], even if it was mainly due to Norwich's fall, rather than anything progressive that we did, and that it had taken a mere 18 years since we started going to games together in 1991.

The fixture list allocated us 3rd October 2009. As the formative games of the season went by the results were making our forthcoming crunch meeting even more tasty. After a stunning unbeaten September we found ourselves consistently third in the table averaging over two points a game, whereas Norwich were ninth and were already nine points behind us. Their infamous 7-1 opening day mauling at home to Colchester United (a local-ish rival who were usually far beneath them; imagine us losing by six goals at home to Cheltenham Town...) was fresh in the memory, although they had already done two brilliant pieces of business to swiftly arrest the decline and placate the fans, one of whom had heroically (or foolishly?) thrown his brand spanking new season ticket at the hapless manager Bryan Gunn during that inauspicious first game.

I can just imagine the Boardroom meetings that had followed. After hours of earnest analysis of the disastrous early season form, and a myriad of conservative proposals to paper over the cracks, one bright spark pipes up and says, 'Let's cut the twaddle and go and nick the mastermind behind that scandalous defeat!'. And so it was that Paul Lambert became their most successful manager for many moons.

I'll come to the second eureka moment [a.k.a.theft] in a minute.

I drove to the match from Manchester, via Leeds to pick one brother up. My other brother came on the train from Kettering, and Mike came from Oxfordshire. A combined total of about 1,250 miles, round trips! Unfortunately they gave us a grievous 5-1 thumping and the well stocked away end had the wind well and truly sucked out of our sails. They were good but we helped by backing off. We even made one of their slowest (but most dangerous) players, Grant Holt, look like Billy Whizz as we gave him a golden key to waltz through our midfield and crack a goal from far out.

Knowing all about their goalie sadly didn't seem to help us either.

Their second eureka moment, after stealing Paul Lambert, had been to purloin our exciting young keeper after we'd only had him on loan from Newcastle United for a month. We saw his potential and gave him a stage to shine on. Norwich then dumped a bag of cash on that stage, shined the footlights in our eyes, and nabbed him whilst we were blinded. That man was Fraser Forster, who rapidly went on to be a Champions League player with Celtic and an England international.

Jomo Kenyatta, the great inaugural leader of an independent Kenya, is reputed to have said, "When the missionaries arrived, the Africans had the land and the missionaries had the Bible. They taught us how to pray with our eyes closed. When we opened them, they had the land and we had the Bible." Well, I think Norwich did the same to us and when we opened our eyes, they had our goalie, and we had Rhys Evans. AGAIN!

Let's be honest, our slide after the Norwich game was partly our fault. We had got drunk on our early season success, especially the late win at Southampton, the other big boys of the division. Thinking of Soton, we had rather swept the timid loss of Rickie Lambert to them under the carpet and never replaced him. As if this wasn't enough, the day before the Canaries match Paul Trollope had been given the poison chalice that no fan wants to hold; the dreaded Manager of the Month award, which always seems to be a hot potato in the hands of a smaller club.

The wheels fell off our wagon at Norwich, and it set in motion a run of five losses on the trot (all our League games in October), where we leaked 15 goals in the process. By the 24th October Norwich were already above us and the 'natural' order of the world seemed to be restored. It looked like the butterfly who had flapped his wings in Papua New Guinea and caused this chaotic series of events had just been eaten by a lizard. Or a Canary maybe?

My glee at our little club being better than Mike's jolly (yellow &) green giant had lasted about two months, and after our meeting Norwich went on to plunder an astonishing 47 points from the next 54 available. We are now (Summer 2104) three divisions apart again.

That truly was the day we parted company.

Acknowledgements & Thanks

Firstly, this book would not have been much without my fellow writers & photo takers, who were - Alex Auchterlonie, 'BishopstonBRFC', the Bluedeemer, bluegloss54, Paul Bradbury, 'BRFC 1883', Chris Bull, Rich Clark, David Colley, Wayne Collins, John Coles, Phil Cook, Mark Cousins, Colin Emmitt, FabGas, Matthew Foster, Mike Fry, 'german pirate', Glen (Gas4life!!!), 'gregsgas', Nick Hodgson, Andy Holmes, 'hung drawn and quartered', Jon Hunt, Mike Hutchins, Mike Jay, Jozer, Russ King, Shane Leonard, 'LPGas', David Maddy, 'miagsygas', 'mjhgas', Ade Monnery, 'quartermaster', Craig R. Rex, Nick Rippington, David Roberts, Josh Searle, Southmead Gas, Pat Stokes, Lucas Swain, Tilly's Thighs, David Titchener, Glen Young, Pete Webb, Rick Weston, 'wreckless', & WSMjohn.

At times it has proved hard to contact some of the kind people who wrote away memories on forums, in order to thank them and properly credit them. If anyone has contributed but could not be properly credited with the name of their choice, please feel free to make yourselves known to me. Email = hello@awaythegas.org.uk

Thanks to Sam Martin, who has handled all the print brokerage on my books.

Plus a general thanks to all the Gas forums, and their administrators / moderators (a truly thankless task if there ever was one!), who played a part in this book just by their very existence. It would have been hard for me to get in touch with so many interested Gasheads without such outlets for publicity and messages.

STILL AVAILABLE: BANKSY LOCATIONS & TOURS

Volume 1

Following the runaway success of his original self-published book, Martin Bull has now totally updated, re-written, and re-designed his best seller for this new 5th edition. This unique, unofficial, book was the first independent book to be published about Banksy's art & is based on the ground breaking free tours & location information that Martin researched & offered to the public in 2006. Those free street tours were also a first, although many imitators now offer paid for tours.

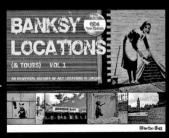

A few of the 65 locations are still holding out (& worth visiting), but the practical walking tours of the past are now the street art archaeology of tomorrow.

★   180 pages, with over 125 colour photos / RRP = £9.50

★   5th Edition (Oct 2013) / ISBN: 978-0955471254

Volume 2

This unique, unofficial, and unashamedly DIY book follows on from BLT1 by rounding up the rest of Banksy's UK graffiti from 2006 to 2010, as well as older survivors. It includes over 135 different locations of Banksy's street pieces, past and present (almost a third of which are still worth visiting); information, random facts & idle chit-chat on each location; a full walking tour of his remaining work in Bristol; and also snippets of art/graffiti by Eine, Faile, Inkie, Kato, Mode 2, BA / DBZ, and Rowdy.

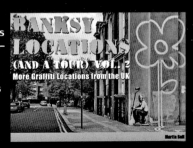

★   382 pages, with over 230 colour photos / RRP = £12.50

★   1st Edition (Dec 2010) / ISBN: 978-0955471230

"...an eminently likeable book, full of down-to-earth humour and unexpected trivia."
📖 Venue Magazine - February 2011

"...a reminder of how far the nation's favourite tagger has come [and] an exhaustive guide to those subversive stencils and where to find them, with more than 200 photos and even a walking tour of Banksy pieces in his native Bristol."
📖 Telegraph - January 2011

"This prosaic approach is refreshing in a book about street-art ... So, keen Banksy fan or merely mildly curious, this book delivers exactly what it promises: "...at the end of the day it's just a grown man doing what he enjoys in life" "
✒ Eye Magazine - January 2011

ABOUT THE EDITOR

MARTIN BULL BECAME A GASHEAD IN 1989 AND IMMEDIATELY FELL IN LOVE WITH TWERTON PARK, STANDING NEAR G PILLAR. HAVING BEEN EXILED FOR MUCH OF HIS PAST, AWAY GAMES HAVE ALWAYS BEEN SPECIAL FOR HIM. BACK NOW IN THE WILTSHIRE BADLANDS, REGULAR HOME GAMES ARE A REALITY ONCE AGAIN.

HE CURRENTLY ENJOYS WRITING A WEEKLY ONLINE BLOG COLUMN FOR THE BRISTOL POST NEWSPAPER, ENTITLED 'G IS FOR GAS'.

IN 2006 HE WROTE, PHOTOGRAPHED AND PUBLISHED THE FIRST INDEPENDENT BOOK ABOUT THE ARTIST BANKSY, AND WAS THE FIRST TO OFFER (FREE) TOURS AROUND LONDON'S MOST ARTY STREETS.

HE'S BEEN INVOLVED IN PUBLICATIONS ON AND OFF FOR OVER 20 YEARS BUT THAT BOOK WAS HIS FIRST FULLY PUBLISHED WORK. IT BECAME A DIY FAVOURITE ALL OVER THE WORLD AND IS ON ITS 5TH EDITION IN THE UK AND 2ND EDITION IN THE USA. A KOREAN VERSION APPARENTLY EXISTS BUT HE HAS NEVER SEEN IT; RATHER LIKE A GOAL BY STEVE YATES. A MAJESTIC VOLUME 2 WAS RELEASED IN 2010 BUT PEOPLE BOUGHT VOLUME 1 INSTEAD.

MARTIN HAS DONATED £34,723 TO CHARITIES THROUGH SALES OF HIS BANKSY BOOKS AND RELATED FUNDRAISING INITIATIVES, AND WILL DONATE 10% OF ANY PROFITS FROM THIS BOOK TO THE BRAIN TUMOUR CHARITY (REG. CHARITY # 1150054) IN HONOUR OF NATHANAEL HORNBY, A 25 YEAR OLD GASHEAD WHO PASSED AWAY FAR TOO EARLY IN LIFE.

PLEASE FEEL FREE TO CONTACT HIM VIA TWITTER (@AWAYTHEGAS) OR EMAIL - HELLO@AWAYTHEGAS.ORG.UK

Cover photo of Colin Clark at Blackpool in April 1999 courtesy of Rich Clark

Inside cover photo of the Leyland DAF Cup Final at Wembley in May 1990 courtesy of Rick Weston